[Image] Bonno van Doorn
DOORNSTRUIK
Scrawls

ISBN
978-3-9814748-1-7
Edited by: Asli Serbest, Mona Mahall
Design: Mauser
http://m-a-u-s-e-r.net
Editorial address: Junk Jet c/o IGMA, Universität Stuttgart, Keplerstrasse 11, D - 70174 Stuttgart, Germany
Internet: junkjet.net
e-mail: junk@junkjet.net
Publisher: igmade.edition (Gerd de Bruyn, Asli Serbest, Mona Mahall)
Printed by Frech Druck
Print run: 777
Published in Stuttgart, Germany, 02.02. 2012

Junk Jet Comments Portal

Comments on this page were transfered by anonymous from an online web form to the Junk Jet Paper.
This form is now inactive but still online on http://vakistan.net/fabienmousse/presents/junkjetcommentsportal/

HeL|o Jay-J4y I aam worRied aobut yuo.

they come from the web

ddvdvdsvbre

hello

I need help I am inside the network I need help I am inside the network I need help I am inside the network I need help I am inside the netw

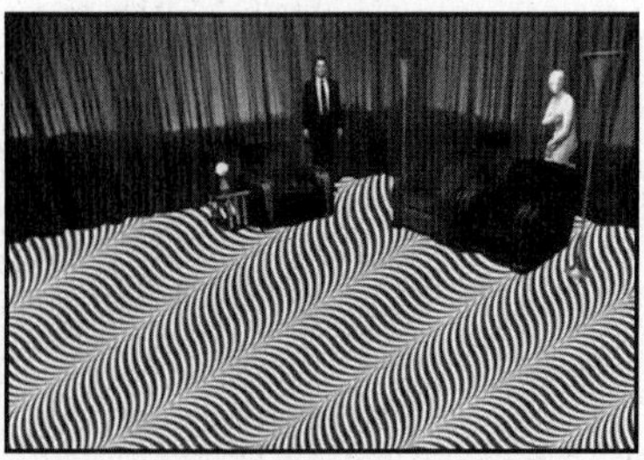

lolilol

this is just hype school

All I know is that I'm somewhere beneath Bob's castle.

whatisthisidonteven

❁✮₭❡❣ ^E&УШН&* T
RE^T* CONSTANT DULLAART*∞∞☢
✉▲℅uℑ℘θ❹✞✛✏✐✎✒☂☜Ņ
Ě%‰{✠∏⇔ℵ⊕∅❝❧

derpy herp

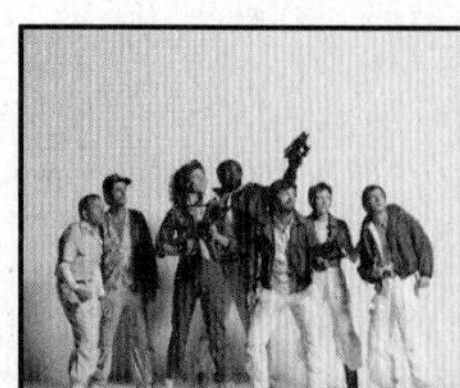

is this for real?

Visit nicbou.com

Why isn't it unlimited Everywhere? ∂ I want to be in your eyes again ∂ An adult said to me I was vague ∂ I would like to be a boat elsewhere

wat

What is this thing?

Zooooooom, Bing! Zuuuuuuu,
doooom, Ding! Dong! dzouuuumm!
Ting! Pung! BROOOOO [yeah i tried
to sing that background music]

noooooooo

this is some
sort of text

I would take
you strongly

SHOUT OUT TO ALL MY BROS

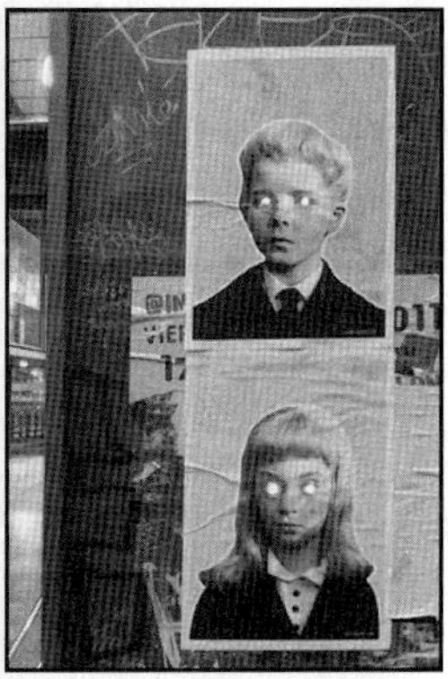

jimpunk
☠Ͻ"Lpəm/s¢05ღ
30 Jul Favorite Reply Delete

Date :: October 2011
Music IEn mOuSSe
In collaboration with :: Junk Jet
and The Internet

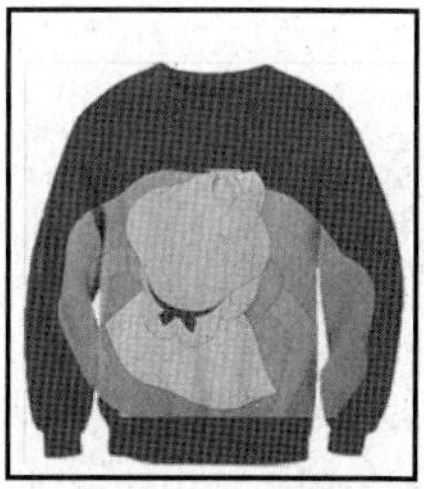

IT TOOK ME 45 MINUTES
2 FIGURE OUT WHERE THIS
MUSIC WAS COMING FROM

fAbiEn mOusSE - 2°11
Junk Jet Comments Media Portal
Where firsts and gays are
Comments are relics from
WWW2.0

=+is¿yavÍz •[‰…@¿v$ſs ¬@èï
á˝FiſsåÂ¬R ¶ÂEÛµk*,$≠0†ˆÕô«

i wanna be
in junk jet.

unicorngirl

Since in the end
consort together,
Magedeline and Mary.
Youth is the time for
stormy weather,
Later lass, be wary.

exxxcelent

THE END

THE END
THE
HE END
fin
THeEND

net.heart
Mona Mahall and Asli Serbest

Fatefully, Junk Jet is a transporter, not in the sense of a highly paid American action hero, but rather in the sense of an experimental Russian jet train from the seventies. As such, it is in two ways special: On the one hand, it has a preference for the absurd, and on the other hand, it can go 249 km/h fast. As transporter Junk Jet is a container moving contents from one place to another. At the same time, it is an archive that, while moving, stores its contents carefully (a sort of form finding). Naturally, in this process of storing, the stored is being transformed: contents have to materialize in order to become transportable, they have to turn concrete, they have to be documented in order to be preserved or represented – representation can be regarded as a form of transportation. Thereby, it does not matter, if the materialization takes place in digital or analogue forms: not documented is not transported. A document is anything that serves as a representation by means of symbolic or symptomatical forms. The term document has its origin in the Latin word docere, which means to show, cause to know, and originally: to make to appear right. Artworks are documents of art that indicate the decisions made by an artist. As art documents they are not objective or impersonal, like documents of science. Documents of art are radically subjective, representing the artist in some kind of self-exposure. Junk Jet loves this kind of radical subjectivity, in which not necessarily professionals in the sense of the art system or art market, but (more or less) fragile self-consciousnesses take a lot of risk to stand the gaze of the others. Junk Jet loves those, who take heart and present themselves in their subjectivity. Therefore it is a transporter of art documents, and in that, it is a subjective document itself; or better: Junk Jet is a series of documents transporting documents of art.

If this sounds absurd, then because Junk Jet is the legacy hunter of the Surrealist magazine, which was significantly called „Documents". Edited by George Bataille, Documents: Doctrines, Archéologie, Beaux-Arts, Ethnographie – so the full title – wanted to introduce novel intellectual and artistic approaches to contemporary culture: Botanical photographs, ancient coins, and modern art were combined with reviews of the latest jazz, philosophical essays, and ethnographic texts. The un-expected neighborhoods of the most provoking as yet unclassified works of art and certain unusual productions, neglected until then, made up the program. Transportation, in this sense, should not only include what appeared most banal or insignificant, but also what appeared most shocking: like the fly on the nose of the speaker, or the I within metaphysics. The appearance of the I, Bataille noted, is the perfect shock. Naturally, this I is rather irrational than rational, rather pulsing heart than scientific reason. Its transportation is realized through the impossible paralleling of documents, of ideas, and images.

Junk Jet has evolved such a concept in developing an archive impossible transporting, in print format, net based works, or fragments of works showing collections, series, animations, applications, and reflecting anti-heart texts on the net and its new forms of art, design, and architecture. N°5 has transferred internet things from their digital space into a paper jet. This transportation procedure relies on documents in a similar way as the museum relies on photograph and video documenting performance arts. And Junk Jet believes, in no way inferior to pseudo-preserving techniques of data migration, emulation, or reprogramming. At the end, Junk Jet says: Transportation is not so much about the artwork as object, but rather about the indication of the subjective decision of the artist. In this sense Junk Jet is a Russian

conceptualist.

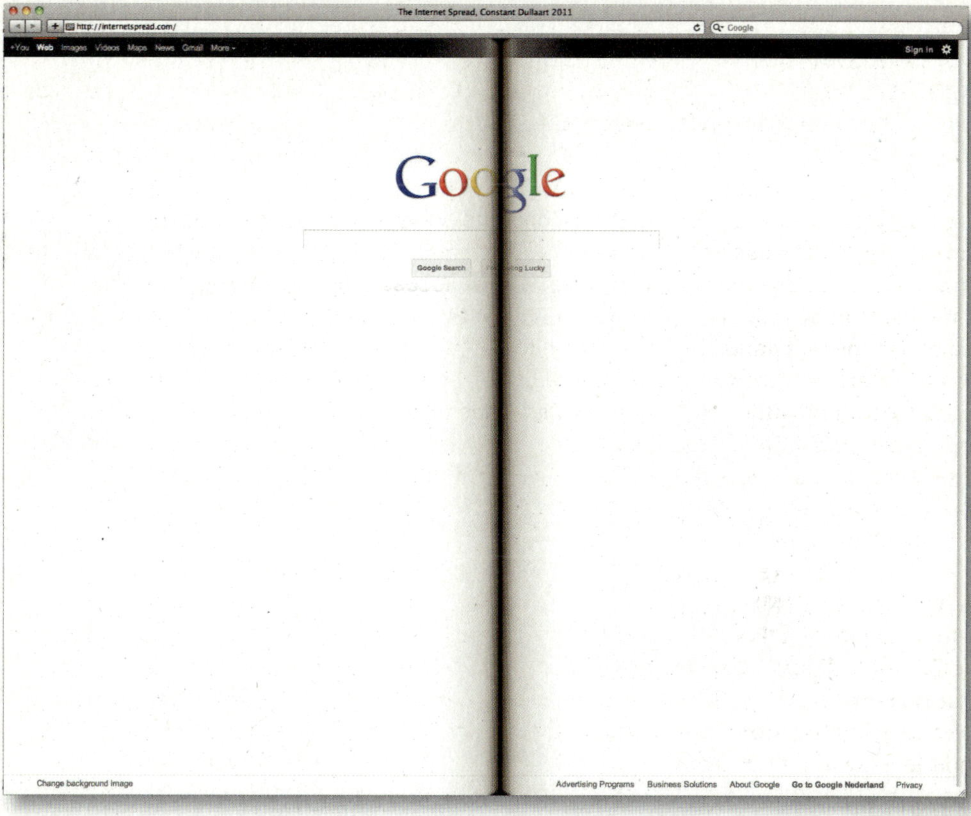

Constant Dullaart
Internet Spread
[http://internetspread.com/]

Vaginal is the New Offline

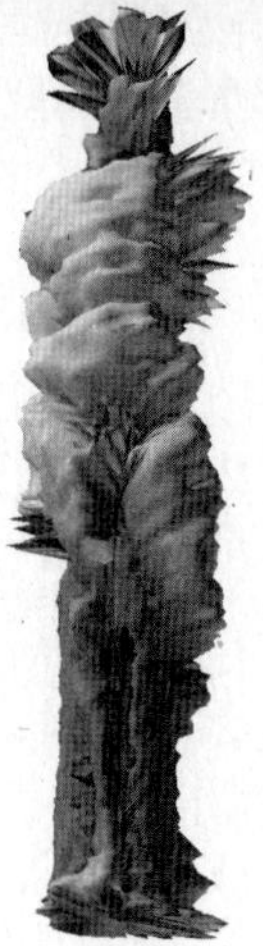

Sex Without Condoms is the New Expensive

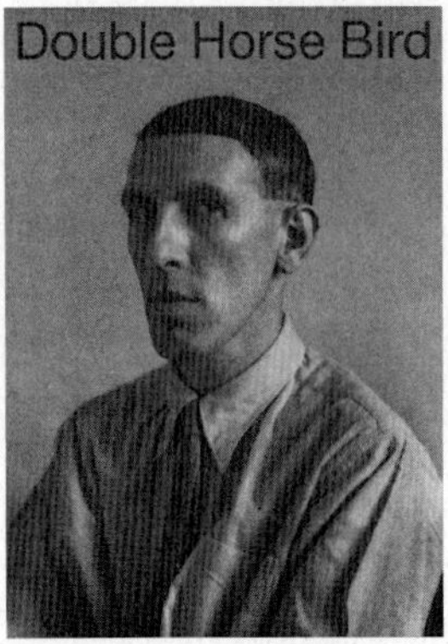

iPhone is the New Objectivity

Social Media is the New Aerobics for Japanese

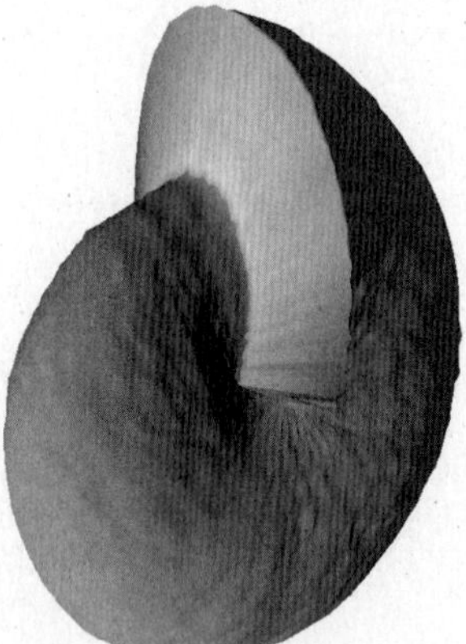

Having a Job is the New Religion

Fuck You is the New Global Crisis

Uranium is the New Currency

Being Crazy is the New Real

Internet is the New Deep

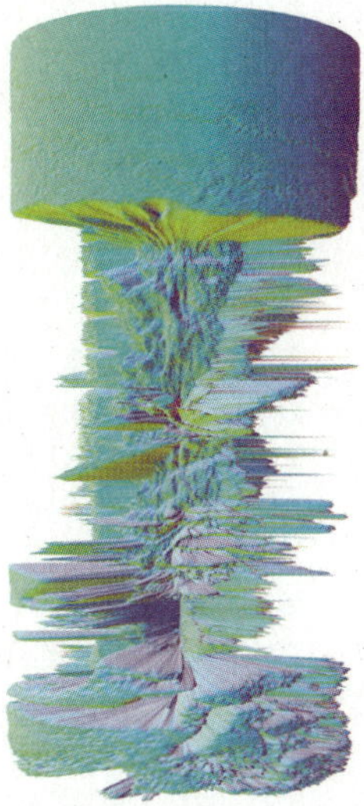

Beyonce is the New Picasso

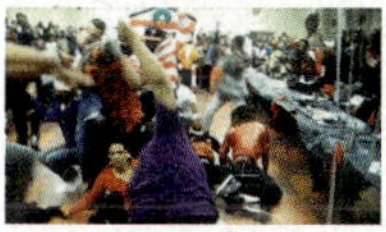

Numb is the New Banking Euphemism of Our Times

Google is the New Cheeseburger

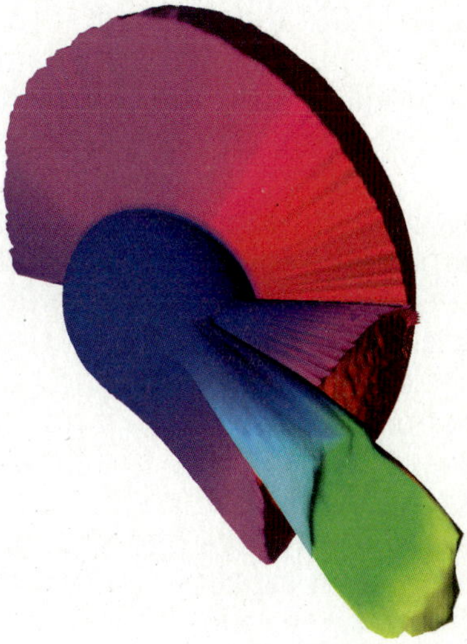

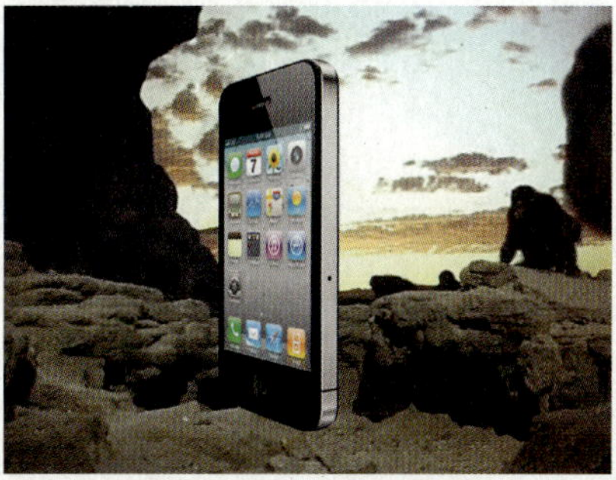

Mike Ruiz
Digital Herd

It's Only Humanist

Brian Droitcour

A headless statue of winged Nike, black pixels swarming above her stumped neck. A collage of ancient, sand-colored busts and patterns drawn with a Sharpie. A Michelangelo's Pieta coated in blue-streaked purple sludge. These are some of images you will find on Sterling Crispin's Tumblr, "Greek New Media Shit." As I write this, the most recent post is a looped animation by Jennifer Chan. Two Hellenistic statues remain static in the foreground as a violet blob belches out a browser frame. Flat green letters brand it "recipe art." Chan, apparently, thinks mixing classical references with internet imagery is formulaic. The opinion is somewhat sympathetic to Crispin, who told me in an email that his blog "started as a criticism of a cliché that I identified and has started self-perpetuating." But Crispin added that since he started the Tumblr he has become more curious about the reasons behind the formula's appeal. No recipe passes through so many hands without being good. To me it tastes like a desire to locate man's place in a world that he perceives primarily with the aid of machines. The art of the Greeks has been used in the past as a touchstone for artists who measure their own vision against an anthropocentric one. "Greek art had a purely human conception of beauty," Apollinaire wrote in an essay about a 1912 exhibition of Cubist painting. "It took man as the measure of perfection. The art of the new painters takes the infinite universe as its ideal, and it is to the fourth dimension alone that we owe this new measure of perfection [...]." The modernists never determined what the "fourth dimension" was, besides a plane of activity beyond human perception. Today the internet–and the spatial and perceptual relations it has engendered–make a familiar substitute for it. "Greek new media shit" puts representations of the visible and the invisible in the same frame. Several posts to Crispin's Tumblr depict classical statuary bathed in slime from the least natural regions of the Photoshop palette. But that's not the only way artists have engaged the theme. Angelo Plessas is a twenty-first century Greek who works with the physics of Flash, exploring how architectural issues of materials' interaction in space unfold when material and space are made of code. On his site Not Only Possible but Also Necessary, Medusa masks spin at an arch's twin bases. Snakes slither through their hair and expel water. When the site is fully "submerged," it starts over from the beginning. The central image is a building loosely constructed from negative space: the columns are black silhouettes, the windows and doors are made "distant" by their relatively small size. The architectural elements suggest the outlines of a face: windows for eyes, a door for the mouth. It's an iteration of Plessas' favorite emoticon leitmotif, which might be read as playfully inverting the golden mean, the Greek aesthetic theory that transformed the proportions of the human body into criteria for architectural form. Not Only Possible but Also Necessary

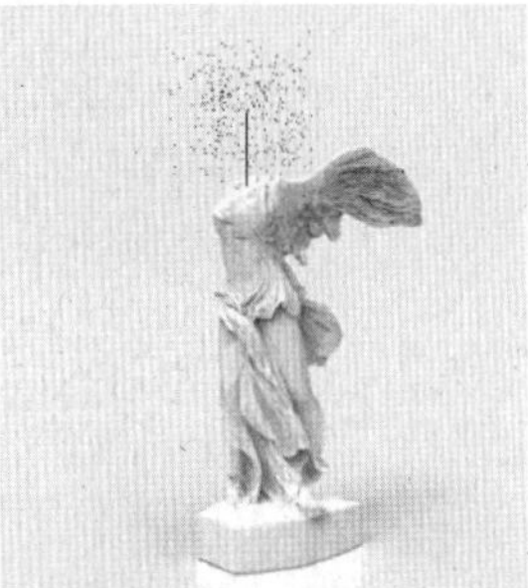

flattens time as well as space: the timelessness of ruins is recoded as an animated loop.

Grinding on the Greeks, a site by Nicolás Colón and Nick DeMarco,* puts da club in the museum in a gesture of late late Dadaist collage. Viewed one way, the antique sculpture in the background fills the same function as Richard Serra does in DeMarco's family portrait of him with Michael Cera. But Grinding on the Greeks is not just a negation of a cultural hierarchy of our time–it's an encounter between widely held standards of beauty from two times. The dancer is mostly naked, a personification of America's erotically charged youth culture with a thong riding up her hip. Yet her gyrating pelvis prudishly blocks the ephebe's marble junk. Both the girl and the statue are anonymous manifestations of cultural trends that extend far beyond them. Like Plessas in the work described above, DeMarco makes use of the whole window: the URL and the page's title make a double caption. The browser is a discrete zone where values can be digested and transformed, and where the result can be displayed.

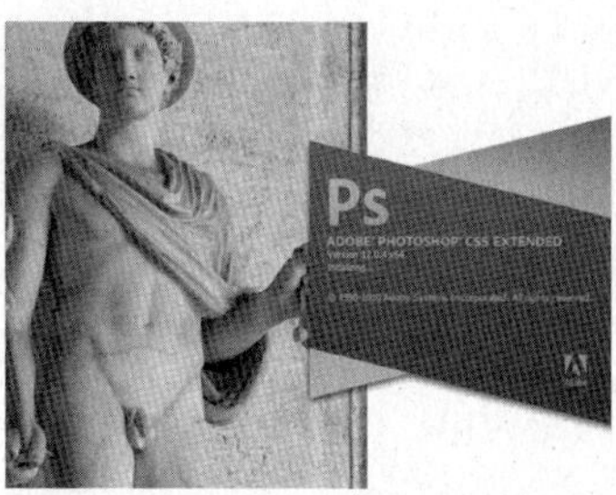

The web site of Aids-3d used to feature a proto-Tumblr that freely mixed images of classical art and architecture with computer-rendered bodies, robots, and virtual reality goggles–an archive where humanism jostled with the post-human. "Speculations on Cosmic Culture," the collective's 2009 exhibition in Berlin, wondered if humanity's dependence on technology has endangered it as a species. The show's signature image was Berserker, a man-sized Styrofoam alien. Its pose mimicked contrapposto, a breakthrough of classical sculpture that introduced an asymmetrical stance to suggest a mind at work inside the stone head. Contemporary touches–the peace sign given by the alien's raised left hand and the Flash drive in its right–mockingly exaggerate the human qualities attributed by the Greek allusion. "Automated Mission Report: 3rd Planet of the System Sol," reads the statement for Heat Death, a video work that was displayed on a computer near the statue. "No sign of sentient life... Humanity is wiped out in the near future and this crappy screensaver is the closest we get to creating the Omega Point simulator / computer."

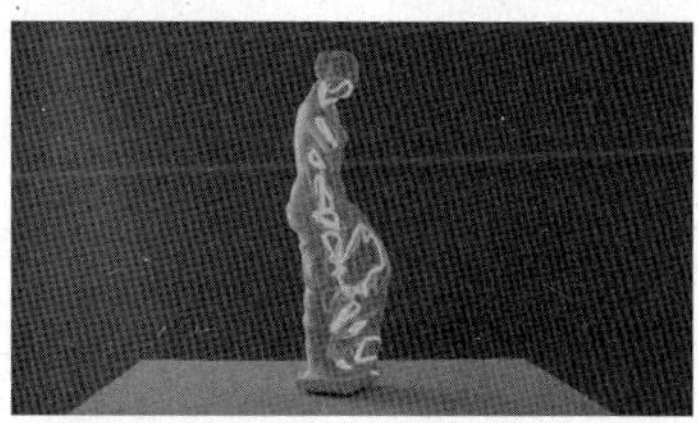

The alien has arrived to claim the dominion of man, who vanished in his own files.

Oliver Laric's Versions (2009, 2010) are essays on the dissemination of visual culture that draw examples from pre-modern times as much as internet culture. In his ahistorical take on reproduction media, the press molds that let Greeks take small souvenir sculptures from temples are more or less the equals of contemporary image incubators like 4Chan and Tumblr. His Kopienkritik, recently installed at Skulpturhalle Basel (covered previously on Rhizome) interpreted those ideas in space by assembling collecting statue copies and using them as screens for Versions. In the ancient world, few traveled enough to see replicas of the same statue at far-flung temples, but now–when travel is accessible and common–a temple of contemporary art like Skulpturhalle Basel has the resources to put near-identical pieces in one place for the viewer's cool perusal. Laric largely ignores the value systems propagated by antique art, focusing instead on the systems of production of distribution. As Tom Moody commented, he is "literally projecting present day attitudes and values onto the past." The humanist worldview recedes to the background, supplanted by a fascination with media. Versions is, in part, about the increasing irrelevance of the Romantic ideal of the artist as the possessor of a unique, original vision amid a hyper-productive visual environment. In this respect, Laric's references to medieval and ancient art are appropriately evocative of non-Romantic modes of conceiving culture. But the value shift slips out the bottom. By foregrounding systems, Laric's critical inquiry espouses an attitude that is realized, tongue in cheek,

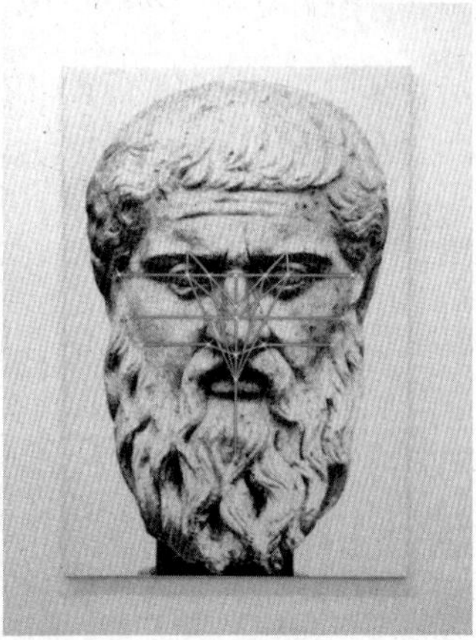

by Aids-3d in "Speculations on Cosmic Culture": man vanishes, his artifices remain. Both works respond to the ease of creation in the digital age, where the means of production and distribution become more important the image itself. If the ancient artist worked in service of truth and beauty, the contemporary artist serves to propagate the system he is participating in. "Recipe art" loses its sting as an accusation when the formula is not just a way to make an image but a representation of man's technologically mediated encounter with his environment. Sterling Crispin's archive, originally intended as a critique of a cliché, ironically took on a life of its own as an artist's statement without an artist–an autobiography of a meme acquiring significance in its iterations.

Thanks to Sterling Crispin and Allyson Vieira for their discussion and insights.
Thank you Rhizome.org and The New Museum for allowing the reproduction of this article.

• A comment by David Bradley (Aug. 21st, 2011): The western world is classically trained. Even when it pretends to subvert this classicism, it is showing its training. It's the same in the East actually. It's really just some kind of false memory of a persons European origins, all this greek shit. As if it's the place where you once belonged. Deep false identification that feels wrong enough to be right, and an attempt to see in plain terms where we have come to in context to where we „were". Who doesn't want to jam with the greats, even if they are just props. Who doesn't wanna feel ancient in a world of displacement. Looking back so hard is actually a way of looking out into the world of infinite now - but with some kind of reference point so you don't go dizzy and fall off the edge. It should be called Greeked, Etc. Just kiddin.

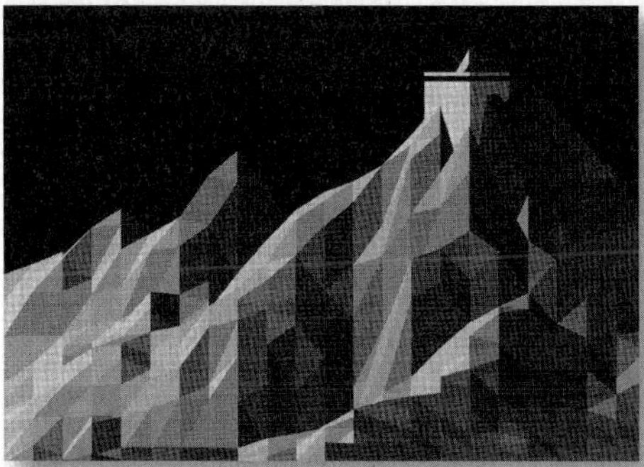
1

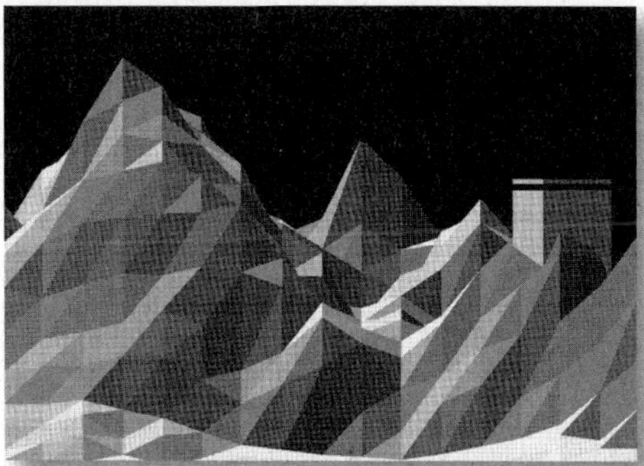
2

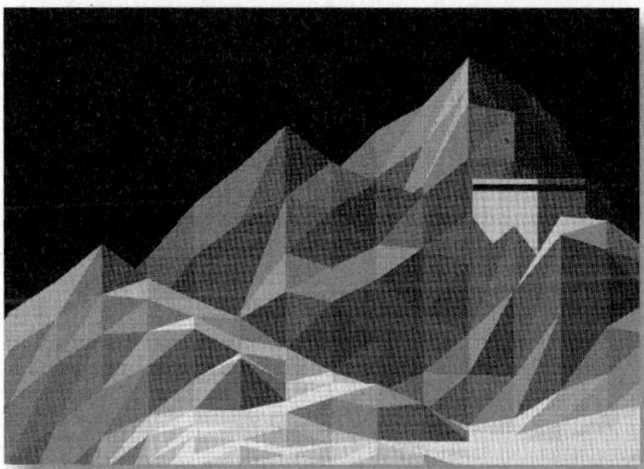
3

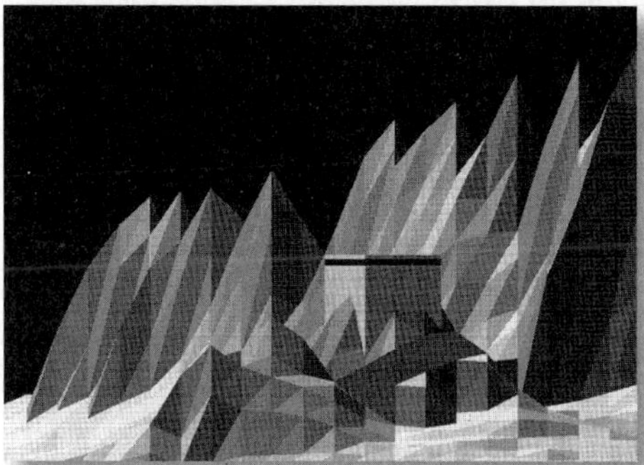
4

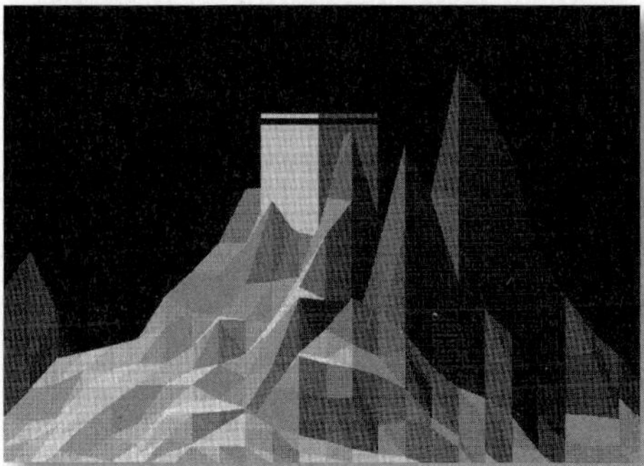
5

Nicolas Sassoon
Homelands

Funeral objects from the network

We, the Network Identity Experiment Institute, decided to focus on abandoned web pages after the webmaster's death. During a workshop in october 2011 we recycled eleven web pages following the ancestral tradition of placing funeral objects, as a way to accompany the passed soul into the after-life. We tried in the most effective way to transpose this practice to graphical web objects.

This project is dedicated to Carlo Lowfi, net artist 1954 - 2011

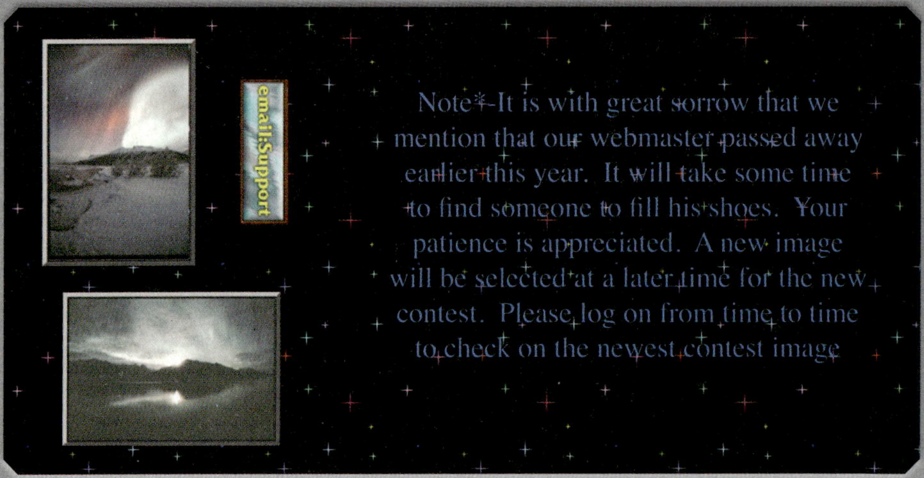

http://www.thealaskacollection.com/page33.htm

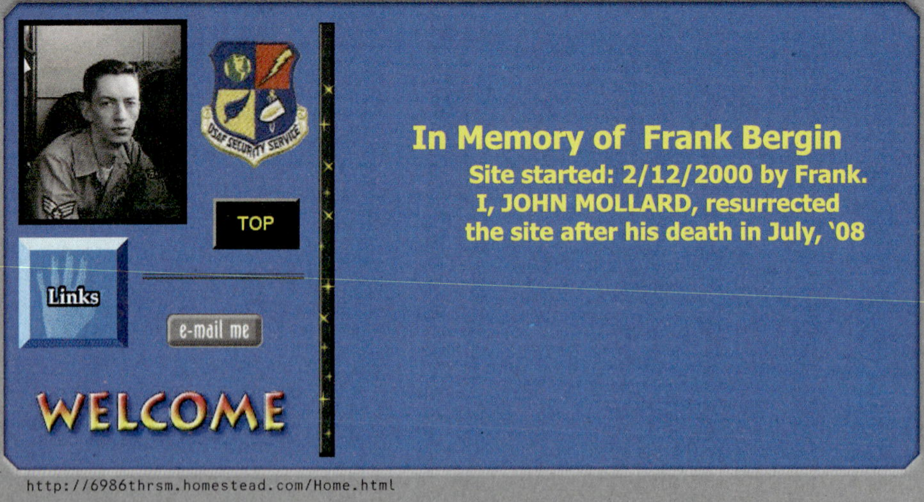

http://6986thrsm.homestead.com/Home.html

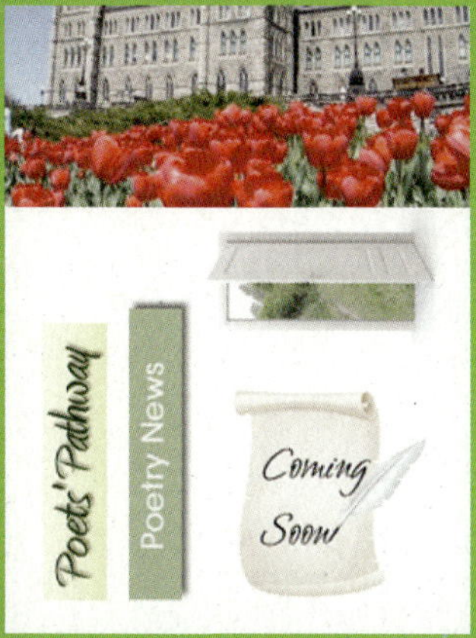

Mary Anderson Hardy, designer and developer of this website, passed away unexpectedly on June 15, 2011. We thank her for her creativity, her hundreds of hours of work, and for this site, a labour of love. Heartfelt sympathy to her family.

http://www.poetspath.ca/news.htm

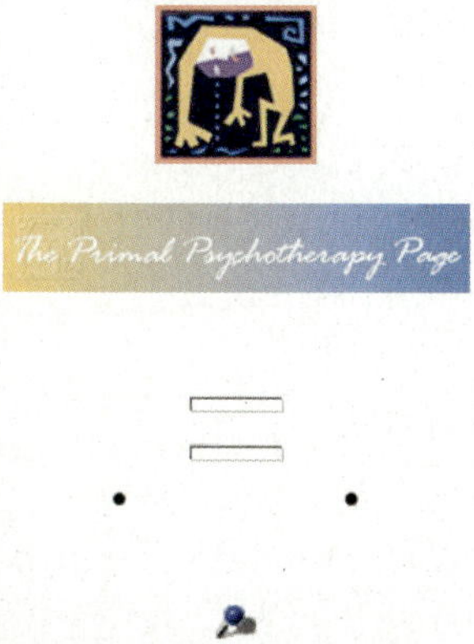

Special Notice: I'm sorry to report that last Wednesday, August 17th, John Speyrer, creator of this website, passed away. John was 79 years old. As many of you know, John has been a long-time supporter of primal, both with his website and with his support of the International Primal Association (IPA). John will be missed by all of us who came to primal as a result of this page, and all of those who have benefited by John's open and friendly forum for articles related to feeling therapy.

As per John's wishes, the IPA will take over the administration of this website. Email sent to this website will now be directed to Larry Schumer, Webmaster for the IPA.

http://primal-page.com/

In early 1996 Jeff Murphy put up the first genealogy webpage in Kentucky which shortly become known as KYGenWeb. By 1997 every state had a webpage and county pages in every state were being constructed.

Jeff Murphy passed away in 2001 and our Genealogical community mourns his passing.

http://www.argenweb.net/franklin/honors/honor.htm

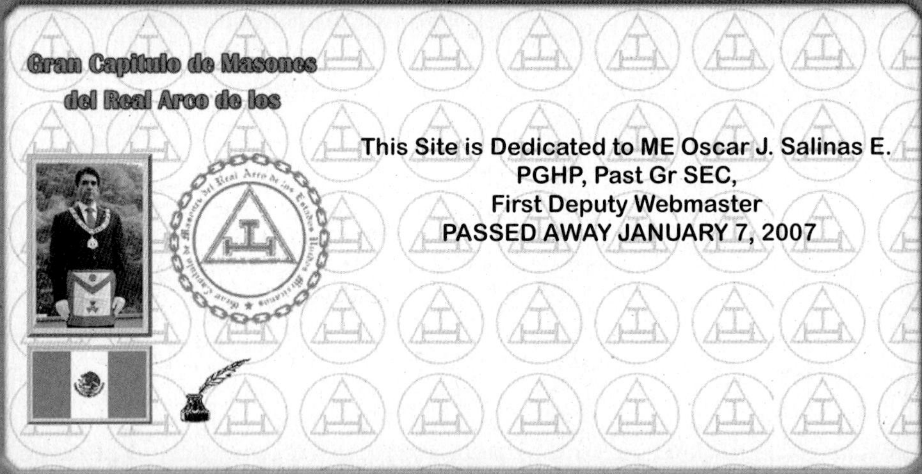

http://yorkrite.com/gcmx/

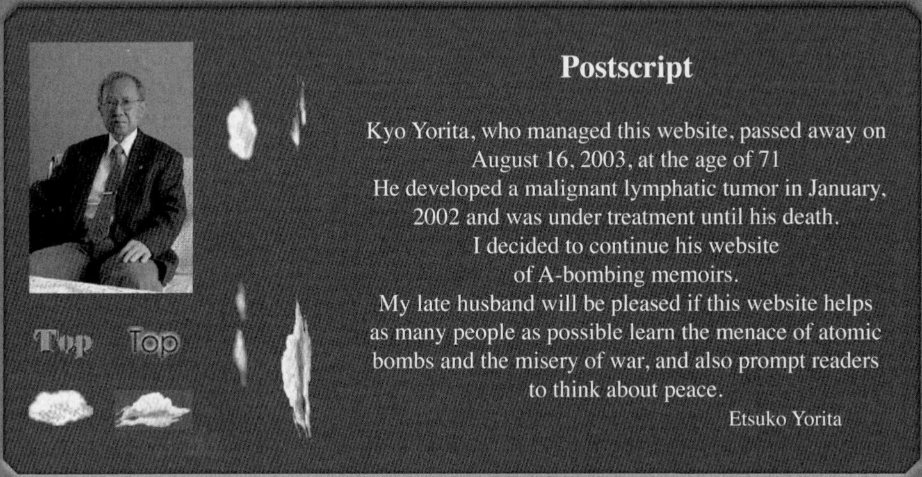

http://ww2.enjoy.ne.jp/~yorita/My%20Profile%20and%20Postscript.htm

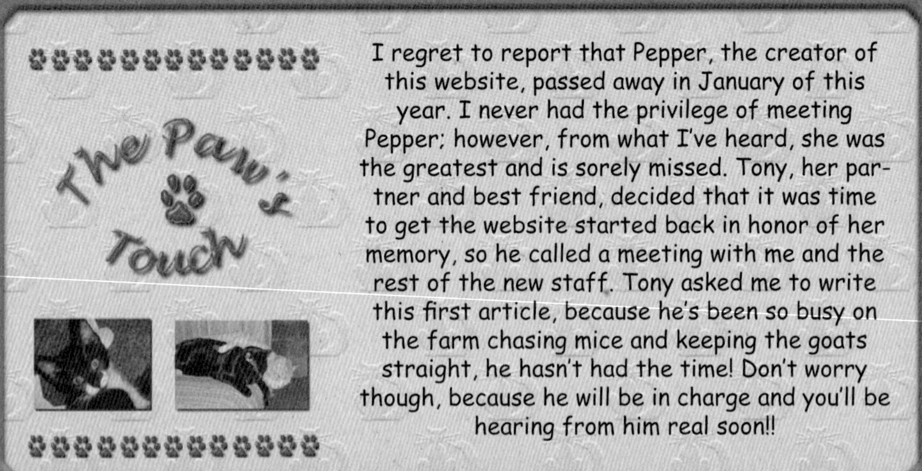

http://pawstouch.alphabet-soup.net/

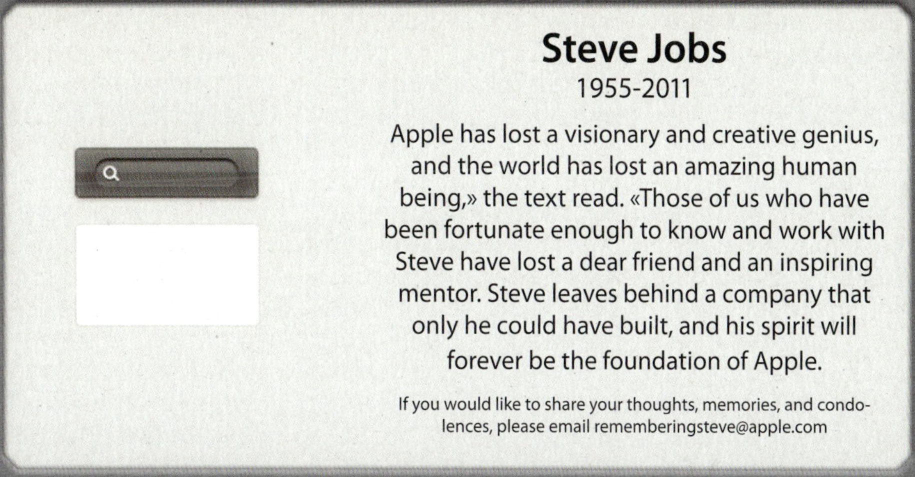

Steve Jobs

1955-2011

Apple has lost a visionary and creative genius, and the world has lost an amazing human being,» the text read. «Those of us who have been fortunate enough to know and work with Steve have lost a dear friend and an inspiring mentor. Steve leaves behind a company that only he could have built, and his spirit will forever be the foundation of Apple.

If you would like to share your thoughts, memories, and condolences, please email rememberingsteve@apple.com

http://www.apple.com/stevejobs/

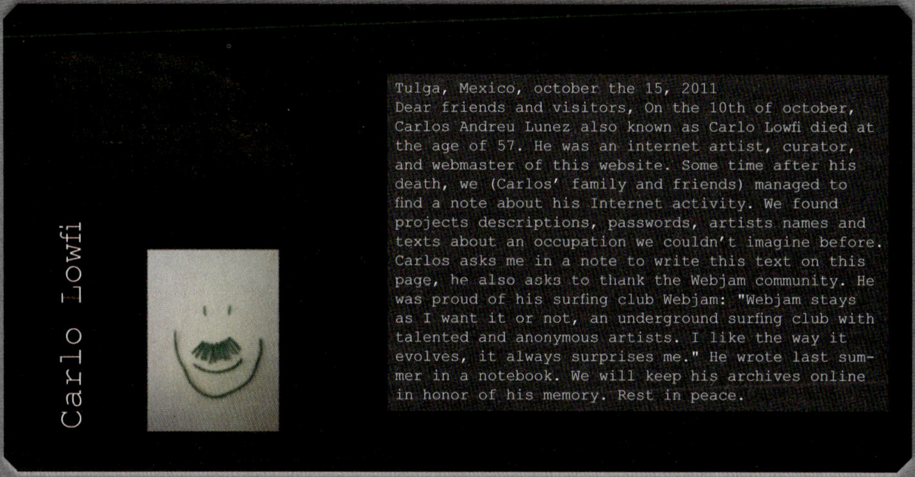

Carlo Lowfi

Tulga, Mexico, october the 15, 2011
Dear friends and visitors, On the 10th of october, Carlos Andreu Lunez also known as Carlo Lowfi died at the age of 57. He was an internet artist, curator, and webmaster of this website. Some time after his death, we (Carlos' family and friends) managed to find a note about his Internet activity. We found projects descriptions, passwords, artists names and texts about an occupation we couldn't imagine before. Carlos asks me in a note to write this text on this page, he also asks to thank the Webjam community. He was proud of his surfing club Webjam: "Webjam stays as I want it or not, an underground surfing club with talented and anonymous artists. I like the way it evolves, it always surprises me." He wrote last summer in a notebook. We will keep his archives online in honor of his memory. Rest in peace.

http://www.lowfi.es/

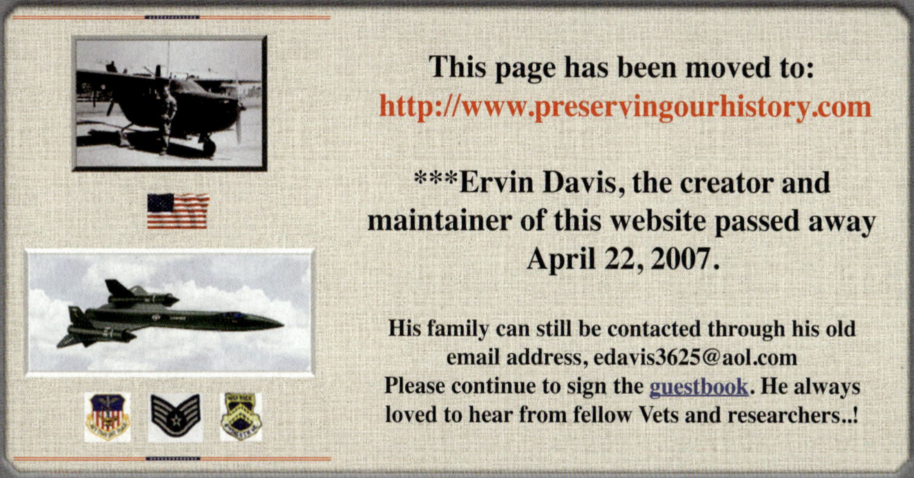

This page has been moved to:
http://www.preservingourhistory.com

*****Ervin Davis, the creator and maintainer of this website passed away April 22, 2007.**

His family can still be contacted through his old email address, edavis3625@aol.com
Please continue to sign the guestbook. He always loved to hear from fellow Vets and researchers..!

http://www.angelfire.com/in/Laos/war.html

Why You Should Make Yourself Someone Else Online

Brad Troemel

Among the many things you will learn by watching the Ondi Timoner-directed documentary film WE LIVE IN PUBLIC, you will discover that Josh Harris became a millionaire in the early 1990´s by selling a beta version of chat room software to Prodigy. He then took his millions and started the raucous Pseudo.com, a silicon alley social media company that pioneered streaming video a niche-personalized online content creation.

Harris´s penchant for frequently dressing up as an effeminate clown in corporate settings and general lack of business savvy forced him to move on from Pseudo. Throughout the film Harris´ intentions never seemed to align with those of a businessman so much as a provocateur. One of the ways Harris felt he could best provoke the status quo was by eliminating the communicative distance that separated people from one another online. Harris so firmly believed in abolishing the lines between media distribution and media consumption that he predicted (either through an invention of his own or someone else´s) we soul each become the sites of production for others´ media experience, consensually opening our lives to surveillance in exchange for the warmth of attention and communal validation. Not a bad guess.

Harris´s belief in peer to peer consensual surveillance was continued through his dystopic technological concentration camp and socially engineered conceptual art project Quiet: We Live in Public. In 1990 Harris bought an underground Soho building where he equipped pre-approved access to food and all other life necessities for free in addition to a fully equipped gun range, drugs and see-through showers. After Quiet… was busted by the police on New Years Day 2000 under suspicions of being a heavily armed religious cult, Josh Harris switched projects and chose himself as his next subject. Soon after, Harris moved in to an apartment rigged for 24 hours surveillance broadcast through the internet with his girlfriend Tanya Corrin and for th following several months participated in the now-offline project weliveinpublic.com.

As the dot com bubble´s burst ruined his finances and his relationship became increasingly isolated and occasionally violent, Harris´s life unraveled before the eyes of his live, online audience. Viewers of this spectacle were able to discuss the events they watched through a chatroom places next to the surveillance video on the weliveinpublic.com website. What most interested me about this process was the way in which both Harris and Corrin ceased to interact directly with each other and came to understand their relationship through the proxy of the duo´s online chat room reception. After every fight the couple ran to their respective com-

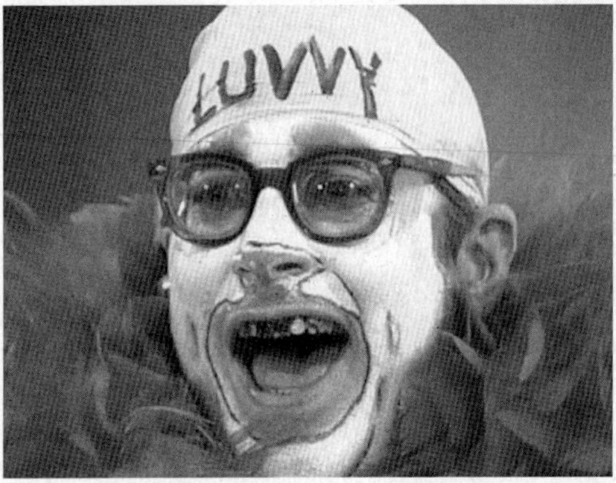

puters to monitor how their online audience interpreted who won the fight or who was in the wrong. Even in the beginning of the project when the couple wasn't fighting many of their actions were rewarded or occasionally instigated by their online audience. As the audience came to fall out of favor with Harris and increasingly went on to back Corrin´s thoughts about leaving him, so too dissolved their relationship. While peer-mediated digital communication does allow access to multiple viewpoints and the possibility to gain greater wisdom from a diversity of interpretations, there are some serious downsides to this way of understanding reality. A subject who is being "purely" surveilled is not aware of those watching her and proceeds to act in a natural way. Pure surveillance is a one-way glass that allows many to be aware of the actions of one with no possibility for reciprocation. Once this pact has been broken, and the subject is made aware of her own status as a recorded image being watched by an other, she becomes a performer intrinsically linked to the will of her audience. For someone aware of the fact they are being watched but are without the ability to directly communicate with those watching them, the typical response is to abide by whatever the performer believes to them, the typical response is to abide by whatever the performer believe

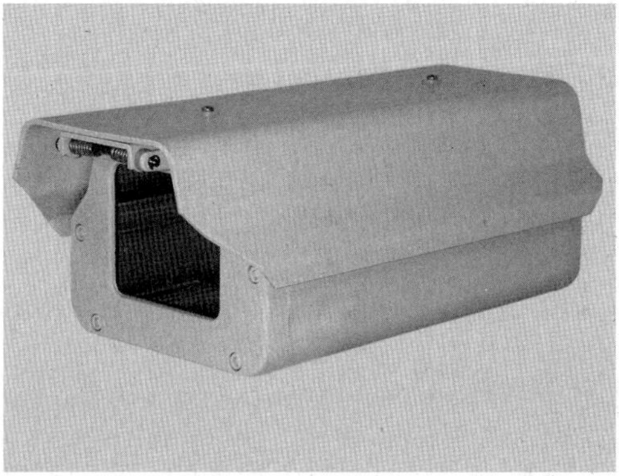

to be the most widely agreed upon conception of morality or good behavior. Don´t steal on camera, don´t pick your nose, don´t pull out your wedgie–they are watching. This performance is what Michael Foucault describes as the internalization of discipline. When someone is being surveilled and does have the ability to directly communicate with the people surveilling her (as was the case in weliveinpublic.com´s live-streaming chat room), the mode of performance such a person enters becomes more fluid - morality is determined by the Pavlovian reward and punishment system of her audience. Assuming the number of people in direct communication with the surveilled subject are real (that the accounts in the chat room aren´t all the same person pretending to be different people), there is an inherent asymmetry in the way this dialogue works.

By seeking the approval of the online audience surveilling them, Harris and Corrin lost a bit of their humanity by externalizing their decision making process to a largely anonymized digital mass of people. In return, they gained peer validated understandings of reality, lessening the discomfort of acting according to their own subjectivity. There is a mutual exchange of power in this process between Harris and his audience, but it is a lopsided one. Not only is the crowd in an unequal position of leverage (one versus hundreds), but within that crowd exists certain social dynamics able to easily tip which way the majority´s opinion will fall. When communicating online, people have a tendency of projecting their previous notions of conversational structure into a new environment that doesn´t match it. This rear view understanding of the future is present all over our computers´ interfacial language, where we place imaginary "files" into imaginary "folders" and use cursors that look like imaginary "hands" to visit imaginary "pages"–al office terms of the past used to explain the work environment of the present and future. The same goes for how we communicate with each other, expecting the way we chat online to match up with the way we previously did in person. Some differences in communication have made themselves readily apparent; we didn´t previously speak to one another based on 140 character limits. Other differences are less obvious, and can be explained by the way anonymity effects our proclivity for dissent. Anonymity has long provided a safe harbor for dissent, from the trope of the nameless whistleblower to the witness protection plan. Institutions formed to protect the anonymity of those with contrarian information were used to shield the dissenter from retaliation at the hands of whomever the dissenter was threatening to reveal. In these courtroom instances anonymity was a necessary measure of protection because the dissenter was in a weakened position to

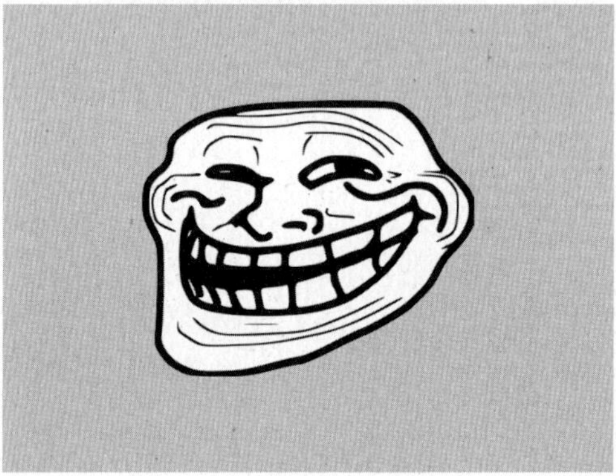

confront a jury. In general, we grant these witnesses a certain amount of credibility because they are willing to sacrifice their own safety and potentially the future of their identity to release information they believe to be crucial for the sake of justice. Another place where institutions are formed to create anonymous dialogue is on the internet - though this kind of digital anonymity works opposite of how it does in a courtroom. On the internet, the tables have turned, and in a chatroom like weliveinpublic.com´s, the anonymous mass is the majority and the named individual is the minority. If the idealized form of what the witness protection plan allows for is the whistle blowing employee, the normalized form of what the internet´s anonymity allows for is the comment thread troll.

The troll is a kamikaze-esque figure; often sacrificing her own image´s good standing within a community and / or the civility of discourse to achieve her desired effect of perceptual disruption. The troll does not wish to join the conversation so much as she wishes to take those with the false pretension or actual possession of power in a discourse down a peg. When trolling takes the form of written text, this kind of disruption is accomplished by inserting the most dimly divisive material into a conversation possible or resorting to personal attacks. For this reason, trolls have a tendency of nit-picking minor details, using "snark" in place of research, and conflating the content of a speaker´s ideas with what they perceive to be the content of that speaker´s character. Trolls can be demonstrably incorrect in what they pass off as facts because conversational truth or consensus is not what they intend on achieving. As Momus said, "Every lie creates a parallel world, the world in which it´s true".[1] In a populist digital environment, lies and disinformation are able to travel at light speeds, giving a new dimension to the old idea of "if its printed, it´s true". The troll is aware of this fact, and often produces disinformation that hovers just at the cusp of believability.

And Like a kamikaze fighter the troll is also a rational actor, believing her actions - no matter how self-destructive or slanderous they are at the moment - justify her ends and ultimately reward her afterwards. This reward has often been summed up as "doing it for the lulz" - which is true in some online environments - but is not the only intended result for other forms of trolling. In fact, any zealotry can be expressed through trolling, be it political, personal or even artistic difference.

Trolls do not have to be anonymous, though it helps in their tactical process. Many trolls actually work with their real names, taking advantage of a paradox of (dis)embodiment many users perceive in their internet use. To explain this paradox simply, internet users often believe the form

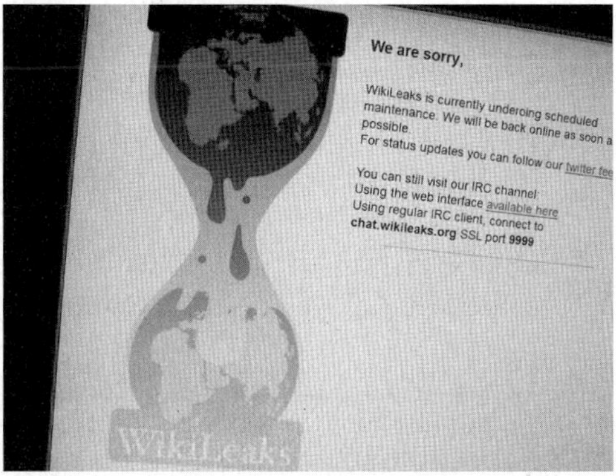

their communication takes place through (a chatroom, for instance) is not a "real" version of communication, while simultaneously believing the content they acquire in those "unreal" digital environments is or can be true. It is this congnitive disconnect that allows sarcastic sayings like "Where´d you learn that? Wikipedia?" to be popular alongside the religious devotion people have to celebrity gossip blogs. We forget the named messenger, but keep the troll´s message anyway.

Considering it´s inequalities and the potential for trolls to wreak havok, online surveillance has been given a bad name – and rightfully so. The most common associations we have with surveillance are with projects designed to regulate the behavior of a group of people (prisons, road traffic cameras, church confessionals) or to spy on their private actions so to become more familiar with their desires for the purchase of selling those desires back to them profitably (Google AdSense, Facebook, market demographic research). In both cases, the reason for our unease toward surveillance results from the uneven power dynamic created when one party is able to opaquely determine or monitor the actions of another party without their consent.

One of the most publicized stories in recent history has dealt very specifically with surveillance, but not in the top-down sense we have come to associate it with. Wikileaks is a surveillance program with intentions to monitor the secretive dealings of the world's political and financial elites. It's an epic irony that the same governing and military bodies who have relentlessly pursued an agenda of increased human surveillance domestically and abroad now find the surveillance of their own actions a terrorizing threat. Wikileaks provides a counter-example to prevailing norms, showing that surveillance can be positive practice when it seeks to level the inequalities of political power by increasing the transparency of private debates that have extremely public consequences. Think of it as a surveillance for the people instead of a surveillance of the people.

In his essay Why Things Matter, Julian Bleecker describes a blogosphere growingly in dialogue with inanimate or non-human things producing loads of informative content. Bleecker offers the example of a project called The Pigeon that Blogs by Beatriz da Costa where a flock of pigeons, equipped with GPS devices and chemical monitoring sensors designed to record the levels of toxins and pollutants in the air, are released to fly all over and report back the "current toxic state of the local atmosphere" in real time online. Once again, here a largely invisible process–pollution - is given a real face and the documentation to prove it. Bleecker goes on to describe other potentially liberating models of surveillance that could aid the public, saying: What if our RSS aggregators could tune into feeds from Amazonian forest an the daily clear-cut blog?

Or critter cam video blogs that show us how really nasty seal bulls can be to their pups when they're not playing their circus act at Sea World. And video blogs from schools of dolphins and whales that will make it increasingly difficult to ignore the plumes of toxins in the oceans and the slaughter of their kin by whalers and felonious fishing fleets.[2]

To apply these environmental ideas of surveillance to the context of art, the only thing more cynical and perverse than the web of dealers, institutional officials and artist implicated in the 2010 New Museum insider trading fiasco revolving around Jeff Koons and his collector Dakis Joannou (as heavily publicized and revealed through the blogosphere) was the all too common response of jaded commentators who claimed that the subject was unworthy of attention because of how rampant this kind of inside trading is in the art world. It was a though Tyler Green was telling a group of WWE fanatics professional wrestling wasn't real, despite everyone's awareness that it's not. Artists with ambitions of operating in the market–much like WWE fans–must proceed with some level of suspension of disbelief that art's bureaucracy of institutional validation functions as a meritocracy and not a profit-driven cesspool of aristocratic reach arounds clevery disguised as high culture. To think otherwise would be a denigration of one's own work if it were to ever become market successful.

When information obtained through surveillance is distributed in an egalitarian fashion it forces us to confront facts about our lives and the people we know - facts that are often buried by others to hide their wrongoing or buried by ourselves to make life more convenient at the cost of our own integrity. As mentioned, surveillance can do good if it's not just used to re-enforce existing societal dynamics, but instead used to shake up and expose the inequities of those relations. One thing for certain is that surveillance - both the good and bad kinds - will continue to grow to be an ever-present force in our public and private lives. Like the rapid spread of computers and mobile devices to the developing world, ideas and products that are advantageous to the health of global capitalism will continue to reproduce themselves. Additionally, so long as there remains a will for openness in our political processes there will remain a desire for the surveillance of politicians in a way more meaningful than the endless number of C-Spans available. Both the profit-hungry corporation and the accountability-demanding citizen want greater transparency, and the interne is a place they both can agree they will find the hidden information they are looking for about one another.

In the social world of the internet this means we must cherish and protect our ability to consensually choose what information we are associated with in the eyes of others. Online brand making is the new art of the masses – it is the only process of aesthetic construction America's population almost universally shares. The capacity to manipulate and construct an identity online separate from our everyday existence is an expression of freedom from totalizing surveillance that would automatically provide information on our behalf. It is a slippage in the prevailing ideology of Facebook that users are still able to post their own pictures – or rather, to use images that have nothing to do with themselves as their profile pictures. If the same ideas of textual, written objectivity inherent in the necessity to use your real name were applied visually, Facebook would have long ago instituted valid photo IDs in the same way they are necessitated by national passports. A true conception of freedom of expression must include the possibility of lying or abstaining from expression altogether. The process of image management on Facebook is already less an outpouring of expression than it is an exercise in omission of information about one's self. Which picture will I untag myself from today?

I encourage everyone to be more erraticly dishonest – or better, willfully creative – when going about constructing a representation of themselves on Facebook. The further you have digitally deviated from your every day existence the better. Your continued honesty in behaving as you truly would without anyone watching is the only way AdSense works. If the parties exposed by Wikileaks are hard at work making sure they become even more opaque in their communication, we too must become equally misleading if we want to keep pace. Chat rooms aren't real places anyway, right?

[1] Momus, The Book of Scotlands, Sternberg Press, New York 2009.

[2] Julian Bleecker, "A Manifesto for Networked Objects: Cohabiting with Pigeons, Arphids and Aibos in the Internet of Things (Why Things Matter)", self pubisched pdf, undated. P.16. Online at http://www.nearfuturelaboratory.com/2006/02/26/a-manifesto-for-networked-objects/

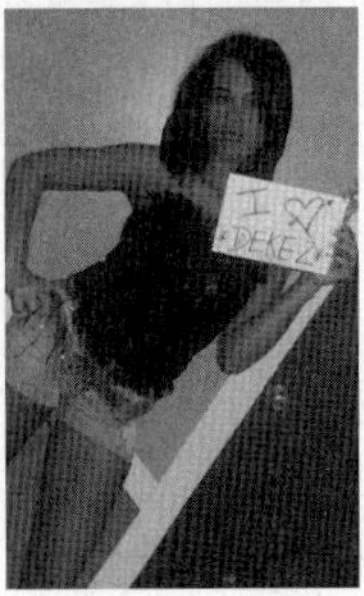

1

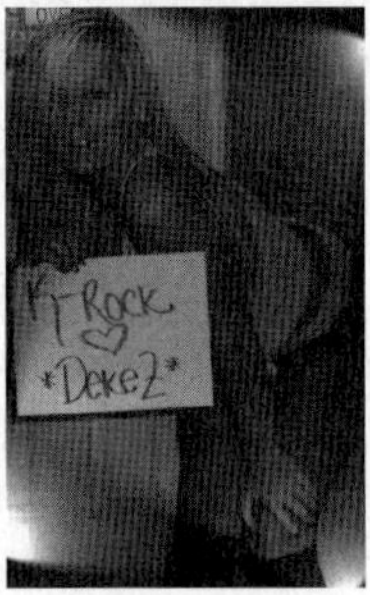

2

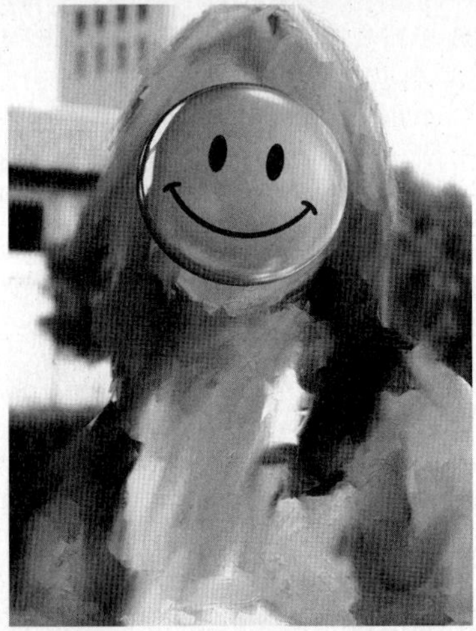

3

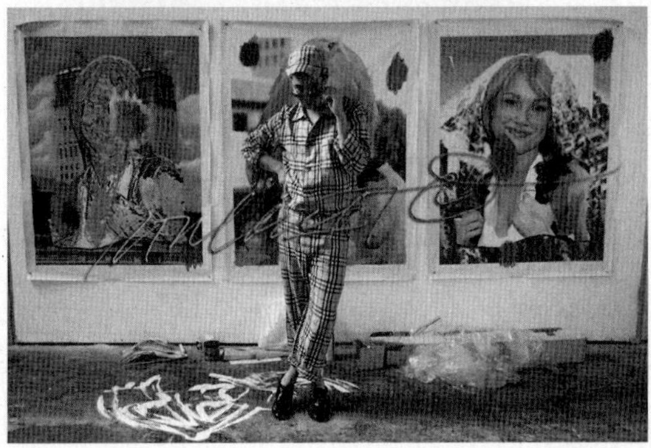

4

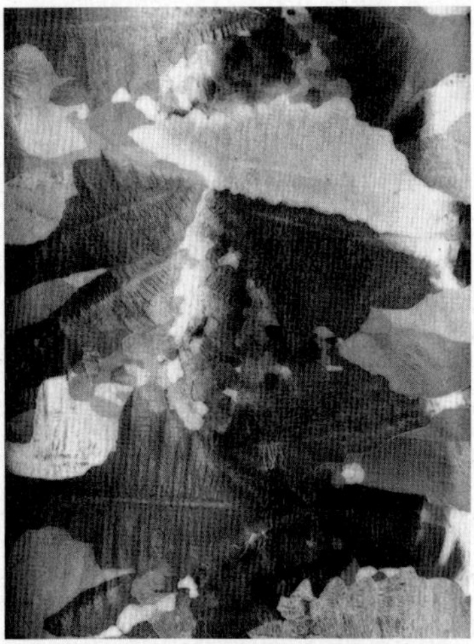

5

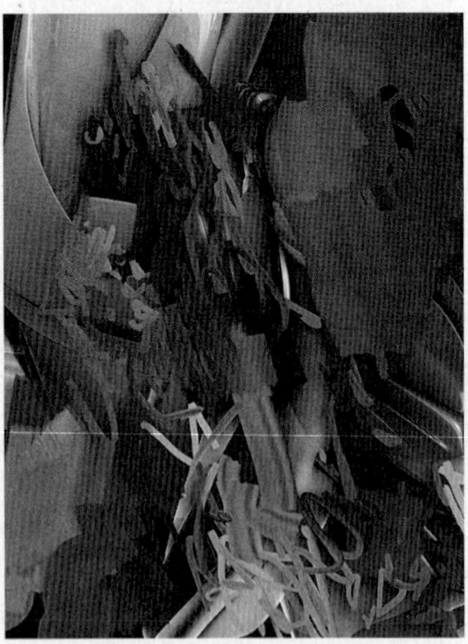

6

Parker Ito
1. deke2-15.jpg
2. deke2-09.jpg
3. poster.jpg
4. pyramidd_bg_good.jpg
5. aluminum.jpg
6. T2.jpg

```
:title>♥SARAH WEIS♥ PRESENTS: 2 TRUE NET.HEARTS [A Mini-Exhibition]</title>
:meta name="description" content="Tiny samples gathered from two of the
ıost exceptional hearts I have encountered on the internet">
:meta name="keywords" content="Anne Laplantine, Krist Wood">
```

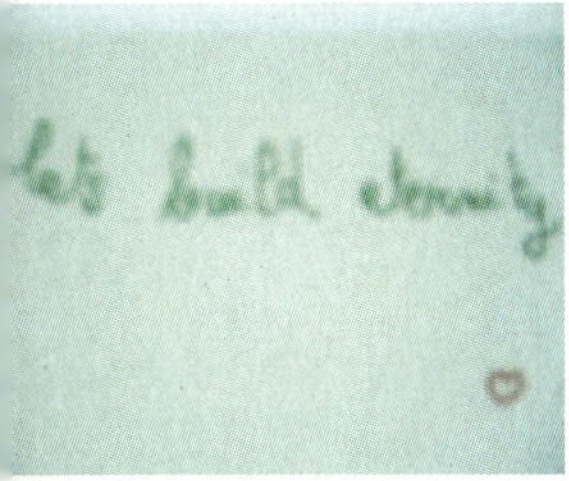

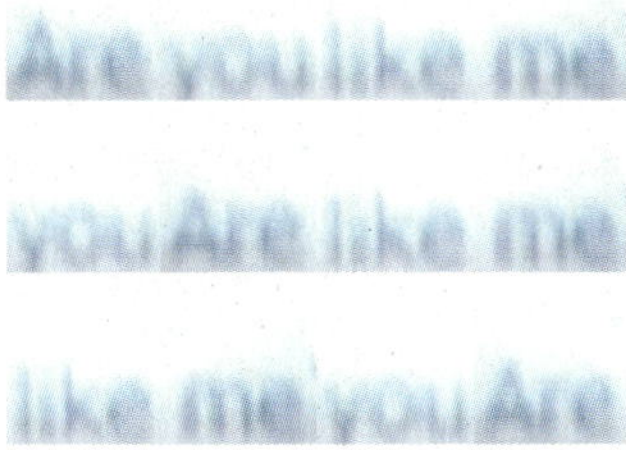

♥ Anne Laplantine

is a rapid net.heart who creates ephemeral actions and likes when things are frenetic. She finds her inspiration in "small things, not spectacular, things that are not made with interest." Often her "work" is a response or gift to a friend, terrorist or random stranger she found online. Over the years I have watched Anne engage with the internet in beautiful, unique and subtle ways that are hard to communicate in print, so I chose to share some current and obvious examples here. [See next 4 pages]

Anne is mostly known for her super-special ♥ music and in 2009 ounded the net label *universal music,* through which she has unntentionally created an active community of dedicated users and ans. She seems to effortlessly attend to them all in her own sweet nd sometimes very funny way that is refreshing to witness. Anne ecently started an internet radio station called *trucs de radio* and rovides public broadcasting intructions for anyone who wants to nake a show! Last time I listened, she gave lots of shoutouts to all f us and conducted a contest in the form of a guessing game that nvolved a very personal aspect of one of the listeners lives. Anne von (a car)! Congrats, Anne! ▸ http://annelaplantine.free.fr

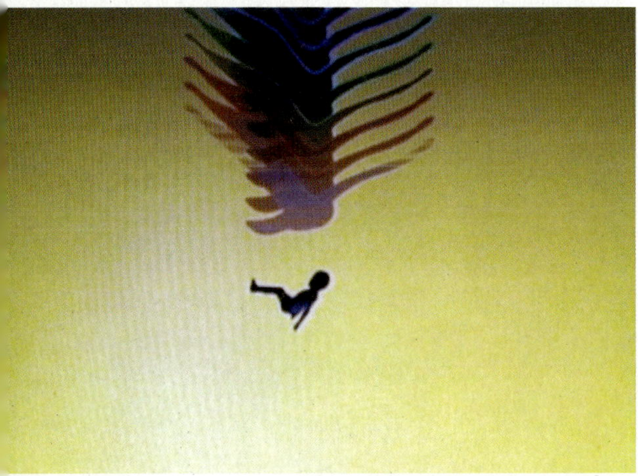

♥ Krist Wood

is a slow but steady net.heart who approaches everything he puts out into the world thoughtfully and with care. Although his stunning, ethereal imagery certainly evokes a strong ♥ feeling, I am even more impressed by a pattern I have observed in the way he relates to others online. This behavior cannot be easily shown on a page, which is why I have chosen here to obsess and meditate over one particularly striking image, an icon that Krist designed in the mid-90s to represent his identity. To me this symbol expresses his compassionate heart in a pure and powerful way... but that's just my interpretation. [Jump fwd 5 pages]

Krist is mostly known for his majestic internet-based art, although e works across many mediums and is a Cellular Biologist. For ver a decade he has carefully curated and maintained several online art collectives, most notably *Computers Club* [2009], which onsists of his "most cherished characters" in that realm. Last year CC brached out with a Drawing Society [*CCDS*] where everyone ses the same tools and anyone can apply for membership. These rojects merely hint at the deep support system he seems to function as for artists all over the internet. I'm not sure exactly how nany of them Krist lifts and nurtures on a regular basis, but it may e the digital art world's best kept secret. ▸ http://kristwood.com

♥------------------->

http://annelaplantine.free.fr/mywebsite.txt [one of my first official website]

```
bienvenu sur mon site où on peut pas cliquer             welcome on my website where we can't clic  <---english version--->

      __________              _________
      |  download  \          | stealing is \
      |  everything |            |      a          |
      |   for   free   |             |      right       |
      ------------------          -----------------

        _________
        |  free            |          dom                                    ---------
         ---------------                                                   `|contact  |
                                                                           |________|

        _________            ___________
        |                |           |   dying is a riight
        |                |

         ---------------
                                    -------------------
                                         * * *        *      * + ¨
     ________________
     | dying is all right |           +*   graphic design -
      -------------------------              /  :        - = = = = = - °


       no graphic design

         ----------------
         | we don't    |
         | need   a     |
         |   lie        ,;|
         -----------------

                                txt
```

Sarah: do you really believe that stealing is a right?

Anne: I think everthing belongs to everybody

/google.txt [ahahahaha]

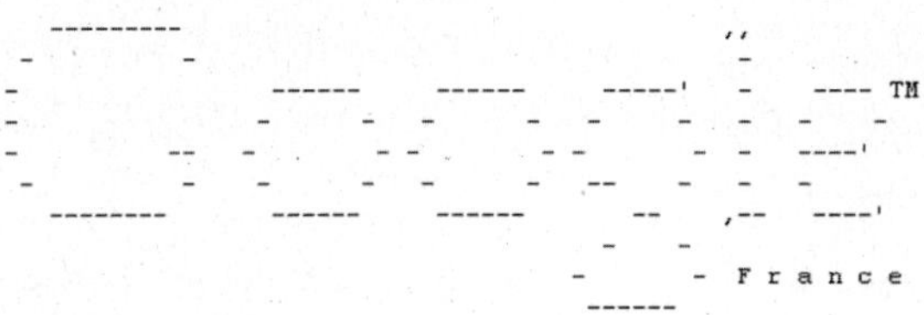

```
 ______________________________________________________________________
|   ahahahaha|                                                         |
|______________________________________________________________________|
|   ahahahahahahahaha                              154 000 résultats|
|   ahahahahahahahahah                              78 400 résultats|
|   ahahahahahahahahahahahahahahahahaha             14 200 résultats|
|   ahahahahahah                                   638 000 résultats|
|   ahahahahahahah                                 221 000 résultats|
|   ahahahahahahahaha                              129 000 résultats|
|   ahahahahaahahahahahahahahahaa                   28 500 résultats|
|   ahahahaha                                      959 000 résultats|
|   ahahahahahah                                 1 010 000 résultats|
|[[ahahahahahahahaha[[[[[[[[[[[[[[[[[[[[[[[[[[[[[[[[[319 000 résultats|
|______________________________________________________________________|
```

/web.txt [website]

sight

/somewhere.htm [super website]

hello, you are somewhere

/nowhere.htm [nowhere]

now here

Sarah: do you consider yourself an internet artist?

Anne: I don't consider myself an artist. I think I'm trying, like everybody can do, to make the most sincere gestures with others and with myself. It's maybe more a political activity, maybe an activity of resistence that could be usefull to do not totaly fall in the heinousness of this world.

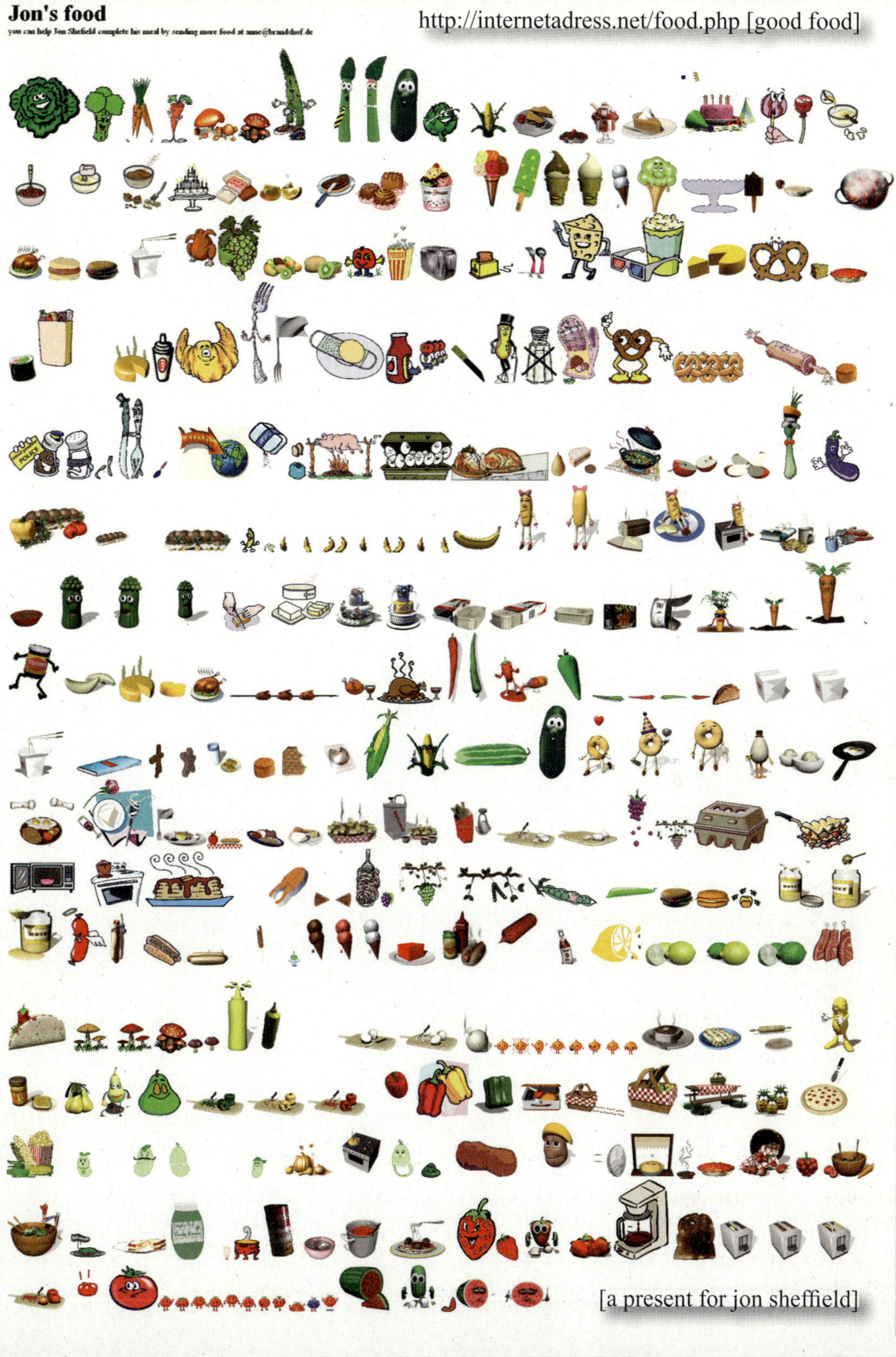

Jon's food
you can help Jon Shefield complete his meal by sending more food at anne@brandshof.de
http://internetadress.net/food.php [good food]
SPAM
[a present for jon sheffield]

wish a happy birthday to your friends

october

october 05 : MAYKI
october 07 : gogo
october 07 : moyen
october 08 : dafuck
october 08 : biggiesmartypants
october 10 : PISSTALL WATERS
october 11 : stephan mathieu
october 12 : Melody Panosian
october 15 : Crazy Check
october 15 : J.D. Dammit
october 17 : boyarin
october 20 : nahuo
october 20 : GELI!
october 21 : anne laplantine
october 26 : Lemony
october 29 : GAYSEX TWIN
october 30 : chloé

november

november 04 : o . o துாசிதிசி திஇல்டு
november 11 : Ke(l)vin Walsh
november 11 : James bond
november 11 : Vulvette
november 14 : Galouzo
november 15 : Manuel J Grotesque
november 19 : SuperCrayon
november 23 : fabien porée
november 23 : Remi Forcadell

december

december 01 : notre travail bénéfique
december 01 : jonas fust
december 03 : jon sheffield
december 03 : Wanda Louside Baton
december 04 : pardon my french
december 07 : Sentient Musick
december 08 : france culture
december 10 : Tape 300
december 15 : antoine faucon
december 20 : MegaGeoduck
december 25 : jesus nice love
december 26 : bernard grancher

january

january 01 : Universal Acid
january 03 : mario maria
january 14 : les manus
january 22 : mangeclous
january 22 : impakt
january 27 : léo
january 27 : Ed's Statue
january 29 : Echomoon
january 29 : Echomooch

february

february 07 : charlotte sampling
february 11 : Burst
february 14 : pablo salaün
february 17 : Microsoft Sam
february 23 : Julia Drouhin
february 23 : boyscout discovery
february 26 : kumisolo
february 26 : Simon Malotaux
february 28 : DZR : P

march

march 01 : egotwister
march 01 : frédéric chopin
march 01 : Molnbär av John
march 03 : salomon kratzenber
march 08 : nicolü
march 09 : Leahill & Tinx
march 10 : musette
march 28 : Köhn
march 30 : Wanda Louside Ba

april

april 01 : Yvan&Lendl
april 05 : DZR : P
april 09 : Leahill & Tinx
april 14 : dj smegma
april 18 : caglar yazici
april 25 : micusmile
april 25 : oskar hallbert

may

may 01 : Ultime Emotion
may 03 : Tifanta World
may 03 : Captain Gascid
may 05 : pierre bastien
may 20 : Dilemme
may 20 : Sick To The Back Teeth

june

june 05 : gregaldur
june 06 : Dr Dick Black
june 07 : Prince
june 11 : Salut techno
june 15 : thomascow
june 18 : molin
june 24 : Sympa
june 31 : Aphex Twing

jully

jully 06 : In Da Club Remixes
jully 06 : kieran daly
jully 07 : alain laplantin
jully 07 : Barbie Chétif
jully 09 : julien groboz
jully 10 : Cataklism
jully 17 : Roger Dancemore
jully 31 : Totraf

august

august 02 : les manus
august 06 : revolution musicale
august 07 : antoine faucon
august 17 : lighttown
august 20 : julia ladense
august 22 : Thane
august 25 : Nerds McFlurry
august 31 : kevin sullivan
august 31 : doug anderson

september

september 07 : The Spookfish
september 08 : Brian O'Blivion
september 11 : cheval d'assault
september 16 : 149
september 18 : henri meschonr
september 22 : Techno Is Tecl
september 26 : kismyder
september 27 : eric stephenson
september 27 : tom7

<------------- before
<------------- before dans la version française

wish a happy birthday to

GAYSEX TWIN

Yo !

justin bierber 29 October 2010 18:06 #4
Dis is da koolest birthday I ever wished, da fuckin fock man!!!!!!!

anne 29 October 2010 18:04 #3
Happy birthday my friend and the very good ear of god to you.

Jon 29 October 2010 12:56 #2
Happy BirthGay ! You rock ;)

Fabien 29 October 2010 11:08 #1
Happy birthday my beautiful Gay Sex Twin. I hope you have a wonderful birthday and year of good.

your name
your e-mail
6354C your verification code
* - star
wish

wish a happy birthday to fabien porée

the gaysex twin 23 November 2010 19:21 #6
if you dont play super smash bros ever please tell me know and i will tell you another lucky thing

the gaysex twin 23 November 2010 19:20 #5
hi fabien i hope you get my message. today (23rd novemeber 2010) is your birthday and you have turned into 25 years old. wow!!! anyway your lucky numbers are 2 and 4 this year, and in super smash bros you will find best luck playing donkey cong

Bon anniversaire Fabien 23 November 2010 12:10 #4
Bon anniversaire Fabien Porée de la part de Kismyder et du Kismylabel.

anne 23 November 2010 11:20 #3
bon anniversaire mon tout petit. tu es très beau.

<['_']> 23 November 2010 7:52 #2
|-|/-|)()/ H A P P Y BIRTHDAY, FABIEN !!! wow wow wow cooool

jon sheffield 22 November 2010 18:00 #1
Dear Fabien, Happy Birthday ! Have an amazing birthday dude ;)

your name
your e-mail
92K6W your verification code

[each name leads to a personalized form as shown. every form has its own animated gif and a different birthday song midi file.]

http://annelaplantine.free.fr/happybirthday.php [leisure space]

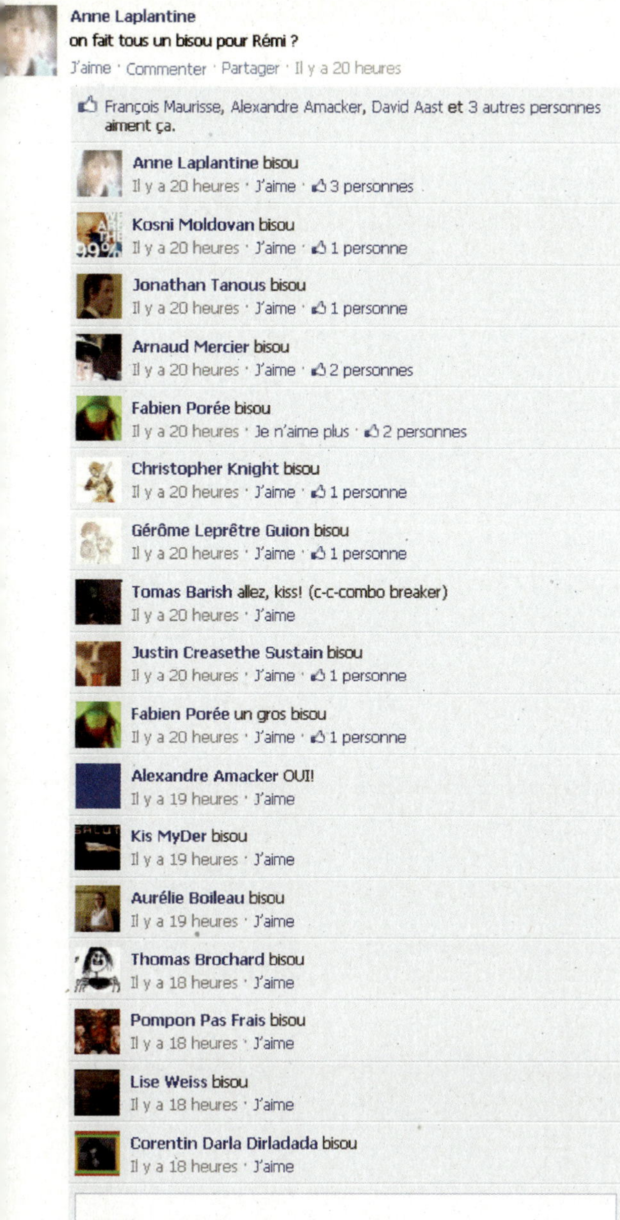

Anne Laplantine
on fait tous un bisou pour Rémi ?
J'aime · Commenter · Partager · Il y a 20 heures

François Maurisse, Alexandre Amacker, David Aast et 3 autres personnes aiment ça.

Anne Laplantine bisou
Il y a 20 heures · J'aime · 3 personnes

Kosni Moldovan bisou
Il y a 20 heures · J'aime · 1 personne

Jonathan Tanous bisou
Il y a 20 heures · J'aime · 1 personne

Arnaud Mercier bisou
Il y a 20 heures · J'aime · 2 personnes

Fabien Porée bisou
Il y a 20 heures · Je n'aime plus · 2 personnes

Christopher Knight bisou
Il y a 20 heures · J'aime · 1 personne

Gérôme Leprêtre Guion bisou
Il y a 20 heures · J'aime · 1 personne

Tomas Barish allez, kiss! (c-c-combo breaker)
Il y a 20 heures · J'aime

Justin Creasethe Sustain bisou
Il y a 20 heures · J'aime · 1 personne

Fabien Porée un gros bisou
Il y a 20 heures · J'aime · 1 personne

Alexandre Amacker OUI!
Il y a 19 heures · J'aime

Kis MyDer bisou
Il y a 19 heures · J'aime

Aurélie Boileau bisou
Il y a 19 heures · J'aime

Thomas Brochard bisou
Il y a 18 heures · J'aime

Pompon Pas Frais bisou
Il y a 18 heures · J'aime

Lise Weiss bisou
Il y a 18 heures · J'aime

Corentin Darla Dirladada bisou
Il y a 18 heures · J'aime

Sarah: who is Rémi* and what was the kiss for?

Anne: rémi is an internet friend at the begening.
(rémi forcadell) we met ones. he's a brillant musician too :)
he is mega super shy and some days ago for my birthday he came to my house to bring me two stones, one for feeling good and one to moove away the bad waves.
(i'm super happy)
...and yes, the kiss was to say thanks and many things more but also I wanted everybody to kiss him.

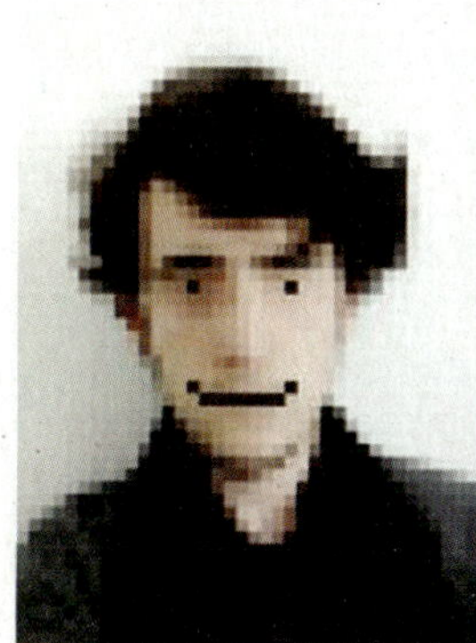

rémi forcadell on facebook

*i looked up Rémi in Anne's friend list and saw that he was a 16 year old boy :)

ore things to check out from anne:
:p://annelaplantine.free.fr/horoscope2010.php
tp://annelaplantine.free.fr/essayer1.htm
tp://annelaplantine.free.fr/sean.htm
tp://annelaplantine.free.fr/coeur.htm
tp://annelaplantine.free.fr/collective%20food%20dreams.php
of course her music, youtube channels, net label,
dio station, IRC and google docs chat room!

NOW LET'S GO MEDITATE ON KRIST FOR 5 PAGES!!!

--------------------->

source code of http://kristwood.com [excerpt]

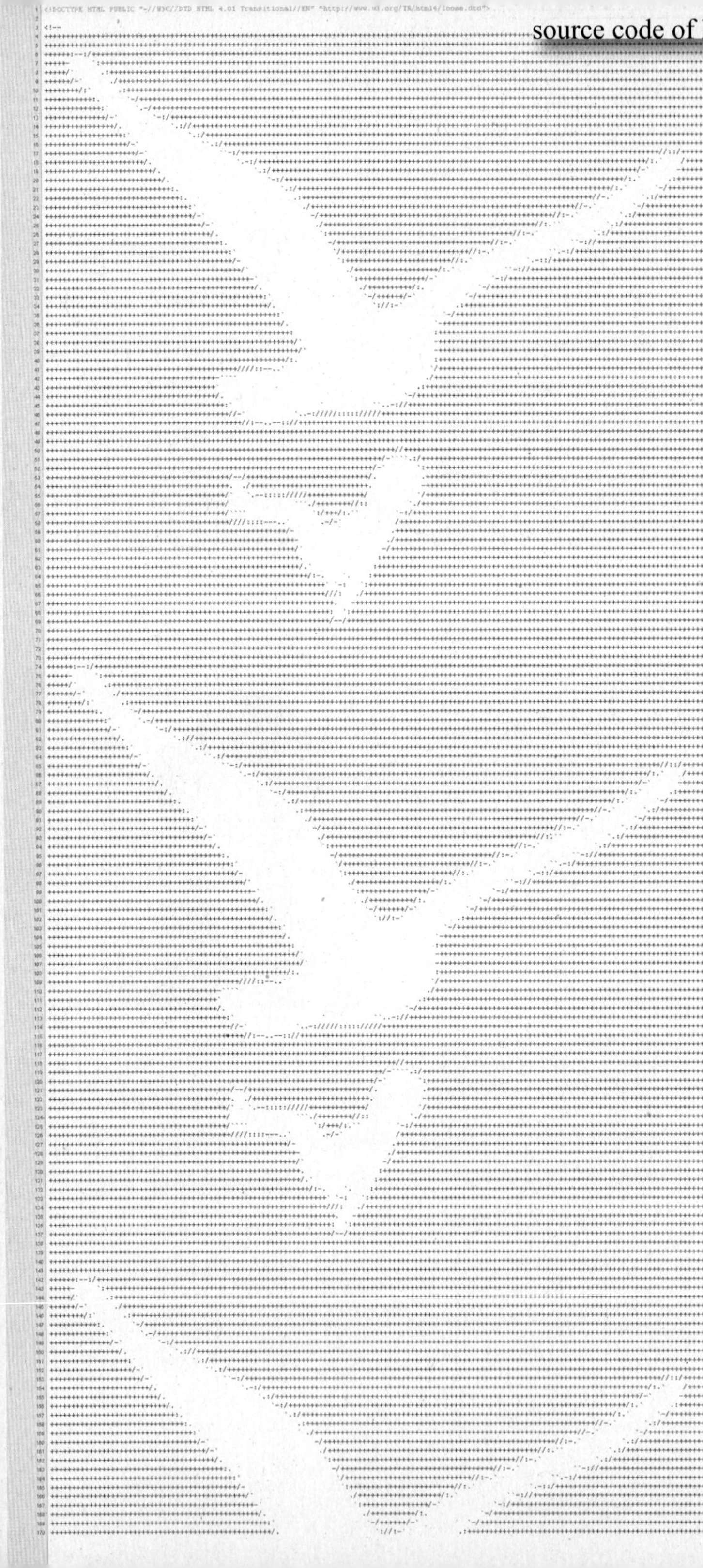

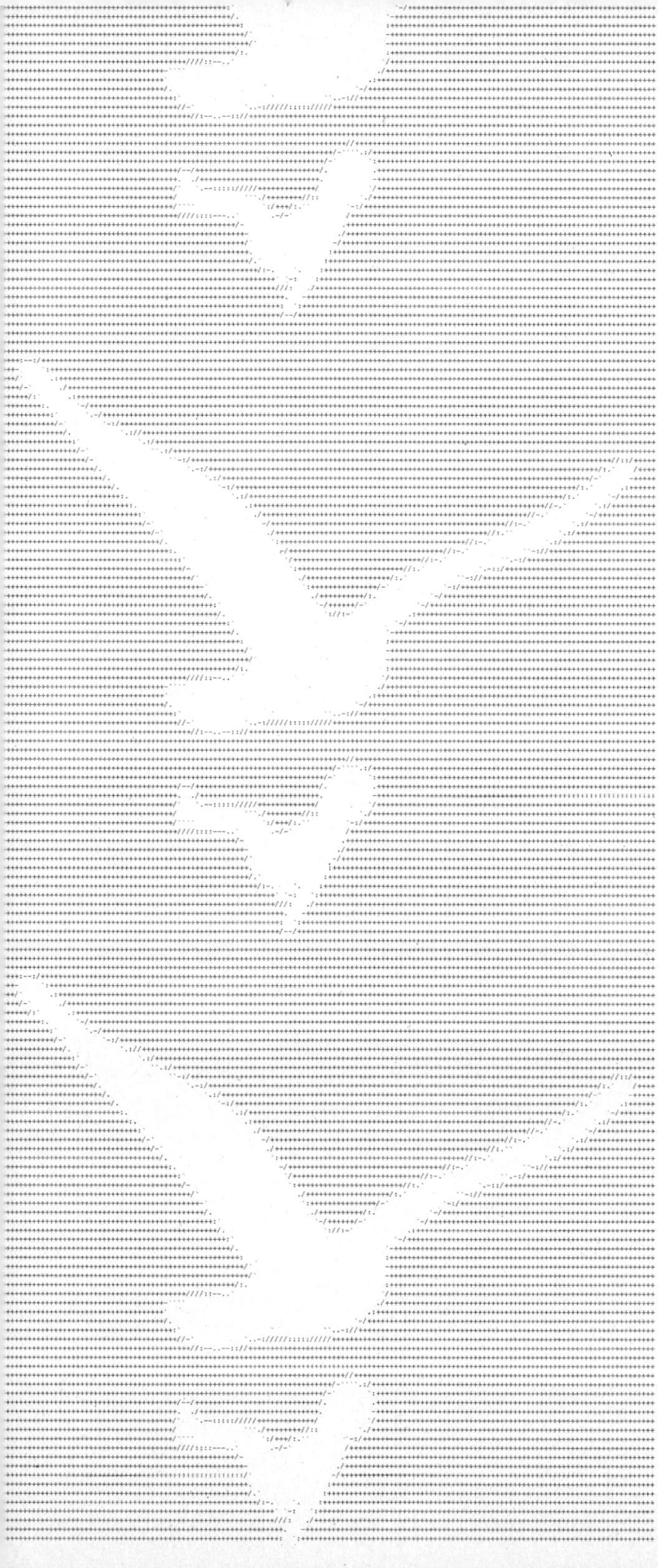

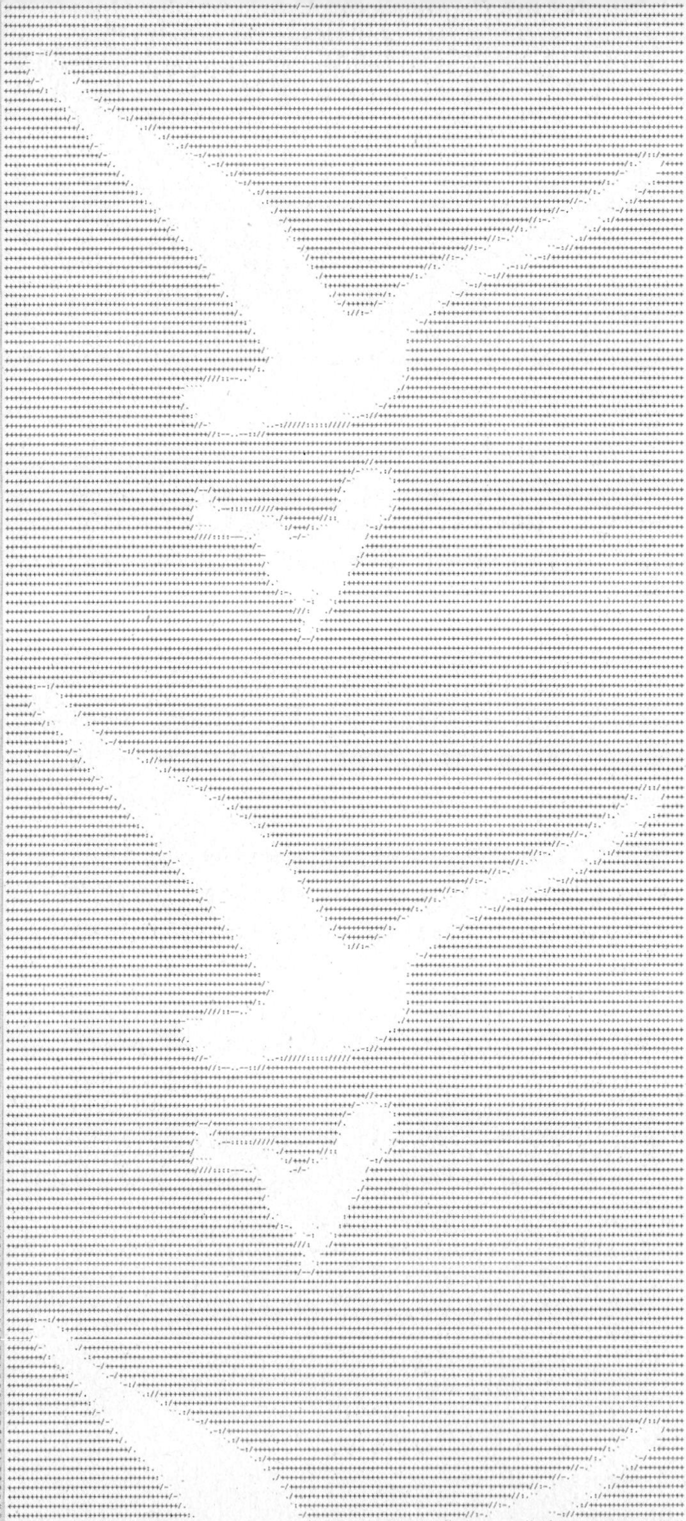

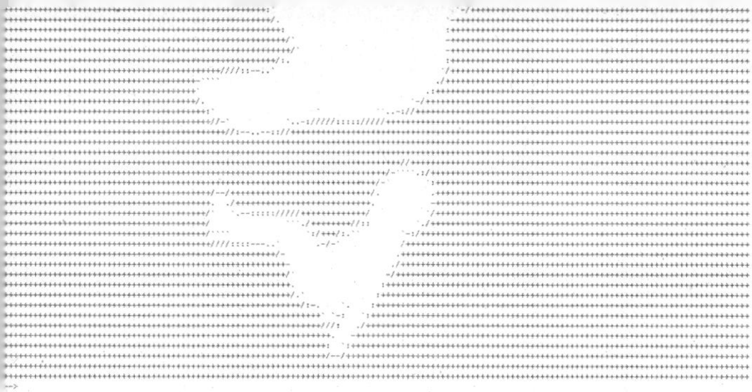

-->

<html>

Sarah: Krist, what does this image mean to you?

Krist: I wonder about the extent to which human beings have diverged from the other animals that dwell here. My sense is that the number of possible perspectives with this is beyond our comprehension. It would seem that our bodies are reproductively isolated from those of the other animals. How else has our species become isolated? What is it that defines our humanity?

I experience a feeling that our humanity is only a facet of our being; a prominent face within a multifaceted interior where the faces of previous natures remain; some active, some dormant; many shared with the other inhabitants of our world. With each new iteration of life, a new facet of this crystal awakens. We are awake inside of a new dream.

Are we soaring ever higher toward the next awakening, or are we falling ever faster back toward a previous plane? I wonder if what defines our humanity is a potential to achieve awareness of the natures that preceded our own. Maybe we are falling the moment we open our eyes, but are designed to call upon ancestral forms of awareness to gain flight. In this way, the awakening of humanity bestows the gift of sight to life. We are life's way of seeing its self and its past. A new facet that can look upon the others.

We can fear the sensation of falling and tighten our senses, or harness our potential for awareness and call upon the nature of flight within us - a winged spectrum of natures to catch a fallen being.

<body marginwidth="0" marginheight="0" leftmargin="0" rightmargin="0" topmargin="0" bottommargin="0" >

<!--

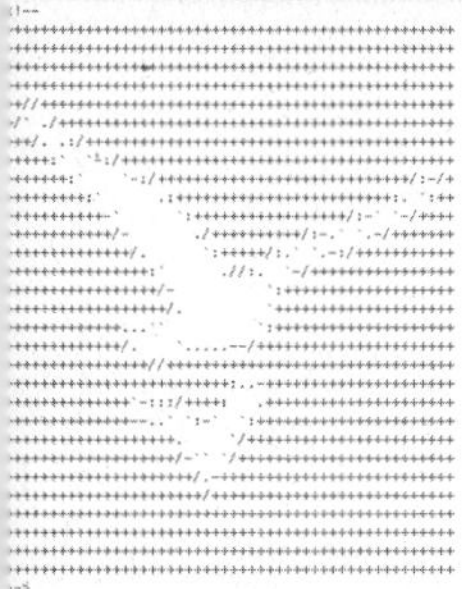

-->

other nice ascii pieces can be found in the source of:
http://kristwood.com/mausoleumii/index.html
http://computersclub.org
[those are his 2 favorites]
more things to check out from Krist:
! the actual content of the 2 URLs above :)
http://beginrecords.com
http://spiritsurfers.net
http://computersclub.org/draw [CCDS]
+ endless beauty on his main website

-------------------->

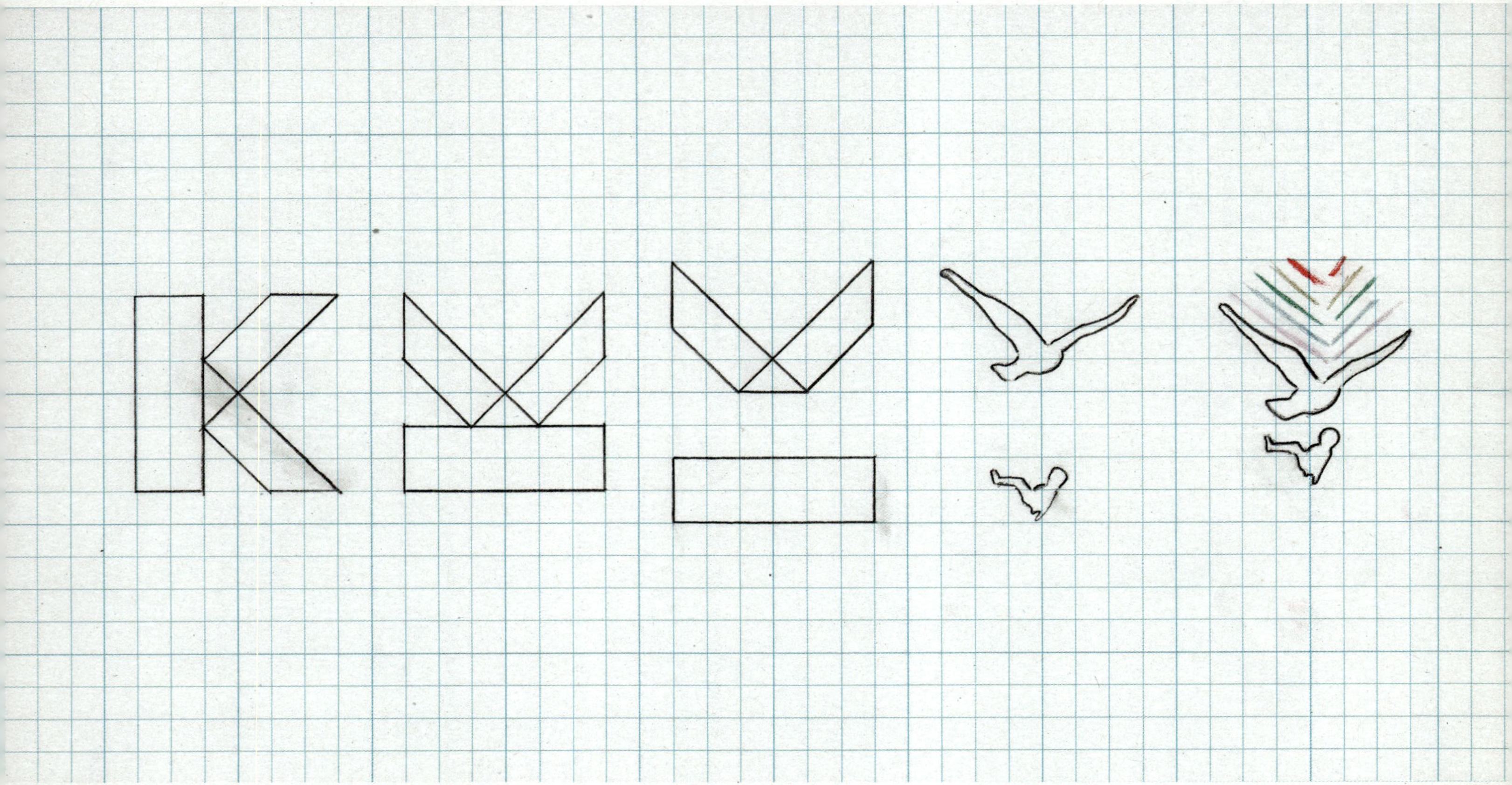

Original Krist Wood Icon Sketch, circa 1996 [courtesy of the artist]

dear christian,

to answer your question it was probably around 9 or something. i normally get up around then. i checked my facebook. i was in the mood for a facebook cleanse. last week I deleted and reactivated my account twice. round trip. ego surfing is a battle in the sky. at once compelled towards narcissistic self gloat/loathe while feeling genuinely like you want to unplug from the disingenuous matrix again. genuine n' real. friendship cleanse is something everyone does naturally when they simply stop hanging out with their friends and focus on other friends; however facebook cleanse amplifies the sentiment error free. today i'm the victimizer. but i have been on the other side, as if in an electronic flunitrazepam dream. i wake up dead, prehistoric blackout style, in someone else's moment of scorn. sorry, i know i get adbustered out but i am just really hoping for some peace of mind this year. crazy expressions yuna. i just wanted to let you know that it's no coincidence i wrote this before seeing Facebook: A Meditation. it's just not. there is no fucking way. someone is watching over you. A N G E L.

the deleting made me sleepy. i looked at a bunch of your art. "life is hard" haha. i'm kind of perplexed with your biodigital s&m. it makes me think of this yanni dream i had in bucharest. yanni live from the acropolis actually happened, it wasn't a dream. yanni laced w/ metal gear gear and going for it w/ rackmount gear. yanni being molested, slowly by alien coils. trying to get a grip on reality within a dream by extracting yanni data from oblong plasma screen against a tropical fruit background. eventually i found myself in tha ruins, like jewish kid w/ backpack style. for a greener tomorrow. i am taking TONS of pictures. there are angry guard dawgs with E.U. tattoos surrounding a nokia security hut. and i have some choices to make, clearly -- to push the gameplay forward. there is a ministry of war on the hill. there are underground subways (inferred) that are blasted w/ liquid concrete Cartier advertisements. the idea of melt is so intrinsic here that nothing is melted. burger is king. it's like, what if all this shit actually was exactly how you said it was going to be. this is how i normally feel in airports. where everyone is waiting to get boss launched to wherever. like when i can see the movado options while i'm getting bio scanned and felt up. the motto is and will always be; its the beginning of our new age.

keep in touch and get me out of here,

daniel

Christian Oldham
some page.jpg

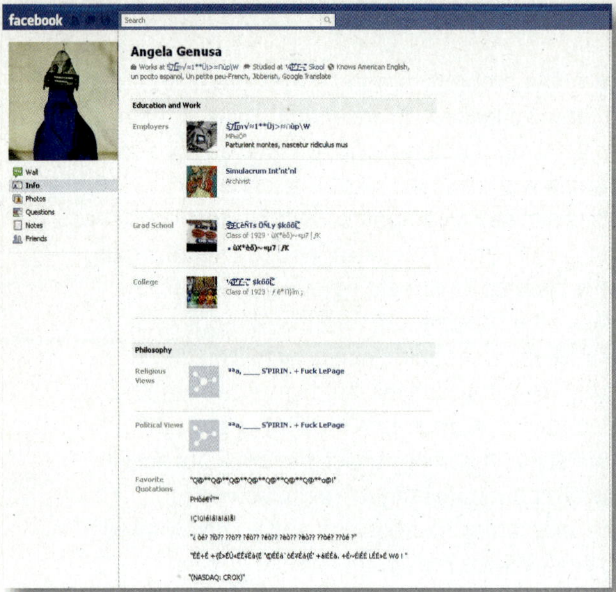

1

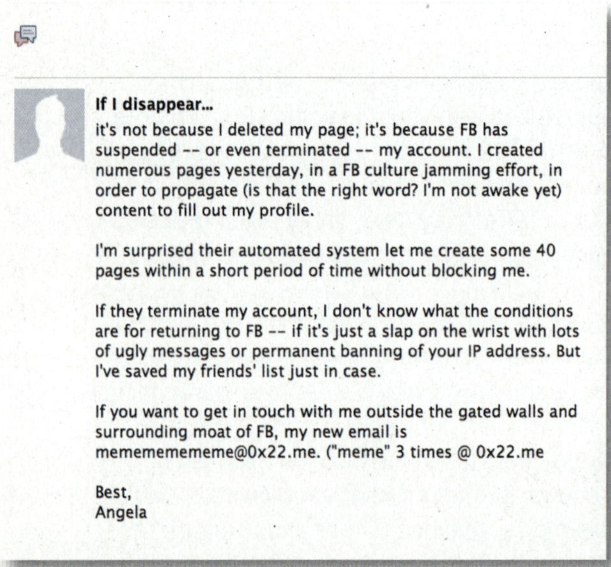

If I disappear...

it's not because I deleted my page; it's because FB has suspended -- or even terminated -- my account. I created numerous pages yesterday, in a FB culture jamming effort, in order to propagate (is that the right word? I'm not awake yet) content to fill out my profile.

I'm surprised their automated system let me create some 40 pages within a short period of time without blocking me.

If they terminate my account, I don't know what the conditions are for returning to FB -- if it's just a slap on the wrist with lots of ugly messages or permanent banning of your IP address. But I've saved my friends' list just in case.

If you want to get in touch with me outside the gated walls and surrounding moat of FB, my new email is mememememememe@0x22.me. ("meme" 3 times @ 0x22.me

Best,
Angela

2

This is an old profile, which was deleted by Facebook. Angela Genusa's new one is online.

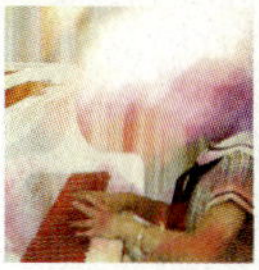

ÖεΘisôw~yΓφ
l&ª*Yiá

3

People Who Inspire Angela

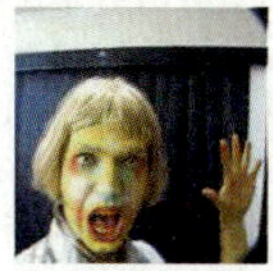

GrÅ@*>ƒ√ºt
Ä£éR.à

7

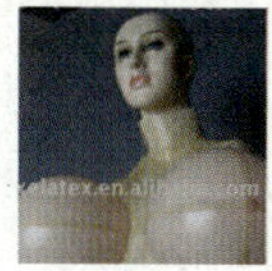

AvBΦΩ*íΣ*è*]
E\64πσ

8

Music

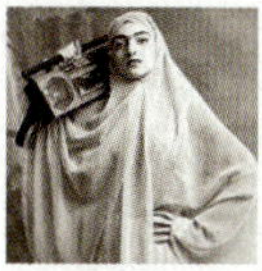

ΘOåÄdd
Kä~Ñ

4

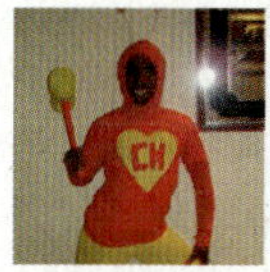

Aè·pQ√ÇΘ≡ï
*√αε,Æ½

9

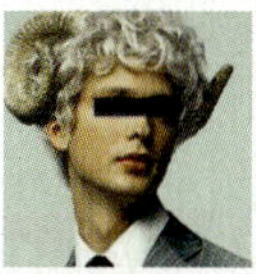

Gb,*;öH/**=
≤*#êεμî²·\

5

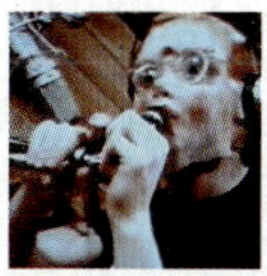

¥FV.>*æîZi9ì
kYOÇÇ

6

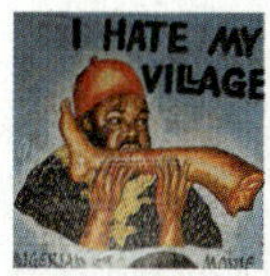

Gs0*D*ô! S
¥ä] [Gêáæ

10

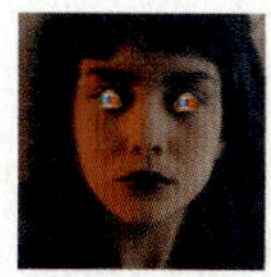

Ü9x Idé*f*:a
*ëíà~x9v∩

11

Favorite Teams

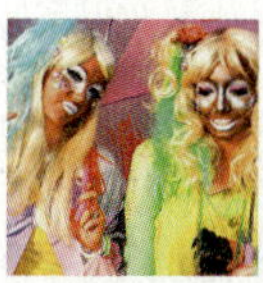

M>æ{ïF6ß4Y·
a¼√

13

Movies

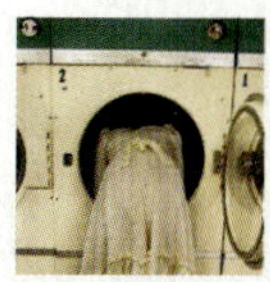

OepδçδMΩт

12

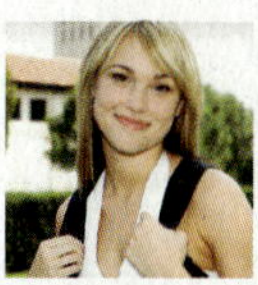

Ist2_746781_
female_stude

14

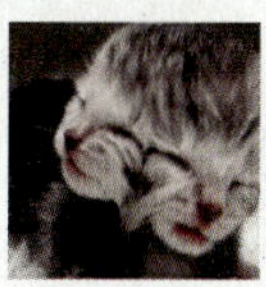

Zä[ÑsKL Ç
Ptsa*4*%

15

Angela Genusa
1. Deleted Facebook Profile
2. Facebook Message from July 29,2011
3. Music: ÖεΘisôw~yΓφ l&ª*Yiá
4. Music: ΘOåÄdd Kä~Ñ
5. Music: Gb,*;öH/=≤*#êεμî²·**
6. Music: ¥FV.>*æîZi9ìkYOÇÇ
7. People Who Inspire Angela: GrÅ@*>ƒ√ºtÄ£éR.à
8. People Who Inspire Angela: AvBΦΩ*íΣ*è*]E\64πσ
9. People Who Inspire Angela: Aè·pQ√ÇΘ≡ï*√αε,Æ½
10. Movies: Gs0*D*ô! S¥ä] [Gêáæ
11. Movies: Ü9x Idé*f*:a *ëíà~x9v∩
12. Movies: OepδçδMΩт
13. Favorite Teams: M>æ{ïF6ß4Y·a¼√
14. Favorite Teams: Ist2_746781_ female_student.jpg
15. Favorite Teams: Zä[ÑsKL ÇPtsa*4*%

Introduction to net.art (1994-1999)
Natalie Bookchin and Alexei Shulgin

1. net.art at a Glance
A. The Ultimate Modernism
1. Definition
a. net.art is a self-defining term created by a malfunctioning piece of software, originally used to describe an art and communications activity on the internet.
b. net.artists sought to break down autonomous disciplines and outmoded classifications imposed upon various activists practices.
2. 0% Compromise
a. By maintaining independence from institutional bureaucracies
b. By working without marginalization and achieving substantial audience, communication, dialogue and fun
c. By realizing ways out of entrenched values arising from structured system of theories and ideologies
d. T.A.Z. (temporary autonomous zone) of the late 90s: Anarchy and spontaneity
3. Realization over Theorization
a. The utopian aim of closing the ever widening gap between art and everyday life, perhaps, for the first time, was achieved and became a real, everyday and even routine practice.
b. Beyond institutional critique: whereby an artist/individual could be equal to and on the same level as any instiitution or corporation.
c. The practical death of the author
B. Specific Features of net.art
1. Formation of communities of artists across nations and disciplines
2. Investment without material interest
3. Collaboration without consideration of appropriation of ideas
4. Privileging communication over representation
5. Immediacy
6. Immateriality
7. Temporality
8. Process based action
9. Play and performance without concern or fear of historical consequences
10. Parasitism as Strategy
a. Movement from initial feeding ground of the net
b. Expansion into real life networked infrastructures
11. Vanishing boundaries between private and public
12. All in One:
a. Internet as a medium for production, publication, distribution, promotion, dialogue, consumption and critique
b. Disintegration and mutation of artist, curator, pen-pal, audience, gallery, theorist, art collector, and museum
2. Short Guide to DIY net.art
A. Preparing Your Environment
1. Obtain access to a computer with the following configuration:
a. Macintosh with 68040 processor or higher (or PC with 486 processor or higher)
b. At least 8 MB RAM
c. Modem or other internet connection
2. Software Requirements
a. Text Editor
b. Image processor
c. At least one of the following internet clients: Netscape, Eudora, Fetch, etc.
d. Sound and video editor (optional)
B. Chose Mode
1. Content based
2. Formal
3. Ironic
4. Poetic
5. Activist
C. Chose Genre
1. Subversion
2. Net as Object
3. Interaction
4. Streaming
5. Travel Log
6. Telepresent Collaboration
7. Search Engine
8. Sex
9. Storytelling
10. Pranks and Fake Identity Construction
11. Interface Production and/or Deconstruction
12. ASCII Art
13. Browser Art, On-line Software Art
14. Form Art
15. Multi-User Interactive Environments
16. CUSeeMe, IRC, Email , ICQ, Mailing List Art
D. Production
3. What You Should Know
A. Current Status
1. net.art is undertaking major transformations as a

result of its newfound status and institutional recognition.
2. Thus net.art is metamorphisizing into an autonomous discipline with all its accouterments: theorists, curators, museum departments, specialists, and boards of directors.
B. Materialization and Demise
1. Movement from impermanence, immateriality and immediacy to materialization
a. The production of objects, display in a gallery
b. Archiving and preservation
2. Interface with Institutions: The Cultural Loop
a. Work outside the institution
b. Claim that the institution is evil
c. Challenge the institution
d. Subvert the institution
e. Make yourself into an institution
f. Attract the attention of the institution
g. Rethink the institution
h. Work inside the institution
3. Interface with Corporations: Upgrade
a. The demand to follow in the trail of corporate production in order to remain up-to-date and visible
b. The utilization of radical artistic strategies for product promotion
4. Critical Tips and Tricks for the Successful Modern net.artist
A. Promotional Techniques
1. Attend and participate in major media art festivals, conferences and exhibitions.
a. Physical
b. Virtual
2. Do not under any circumstances admit to paying entry fees, travel expenses or hotel accommodations.
3. Avoid traditional forms of publicity. e.g. business cards.
4. Do not readily admit to any institutional affiliation.
5. Create and control your own mythology.
6. Contradict yourself periodically in email, articles, interviews and in informal off-the-record conversation.
7. Be sincere.
8. Shock.
9. Subvert (self and others).
10. Maintain consistency in image and work.
B. Success Indicators: Upgrade 2
1. Bandwidth
2. Girl or boy friends
3. Hits on search engines
4. Hits on your sites
5. Links to your site
6. Invitations
7. E-mail
8. Airplane tickets
9. Money
5. Utopian Appendix (After net.art)
A. Whereby individual creative activities, rather than affiliation to any hyped art movement becomes most valued.
1. Largely resulting from the horizontal rather than vertical distribution of information on the internet.
2. Thus disallowing one dominant voice to rise above multiple, simultaneous and diverse expressions.
B. The Rise of an Artisan
1. The formation of organizations avoiding the promotion of proper names
2. The bypassing of art institutions and the direct targeting of corporate products, mainstream media, creative sensibilities and hegemonic ideologies
a. Unannounced
b. Uninvited
c. Unexpected
3. No longer needing the terms „art" or „politics" to legitimize, justify or excuse one's activities
C. The Internet after net.art
1. A mall, a porn shop and a museum
2. A useful resource, tool, site and gathering point for an artisan
a. Who mutates and transforms as quickly and cleverly as that which seeks to consume her
b. Who does not fear or accept labeling or unlabeling
c. Who works freely in completely new forms together with older more traditional forms
d. Who understands the continued urgency of free two-way and many-to-many communication over representation

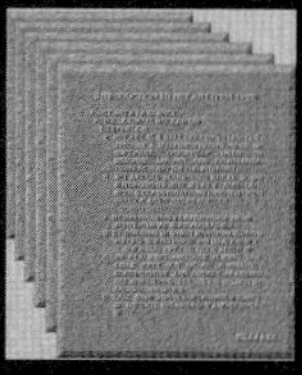

‚texts‘ category

Rafaël Rozendaal

GOOGLE COMES FROM ANOTHER PLANET

Google is not made by humans. Google is a company founded by the Oogles, a lifeform that started in a multiverse far far away, somewhere in the dimensional continium, a place beyond our conception. The Oogles are so advanced it is hard for us to grasp what they are about. They can basically do anything they want in any reality… they rule the multiverse. As a social experiment they started a company on our planet… Google. They want to take over the power on our planet. Not by force, just by doing things better than any human ever could. They will always allow humans to start their own companies, and just for fun they will let these companies thrive for a while. But they will always win, at anything, and they will offer everything for free. Just to watch us humans try. They're not evil, they're just over ambitious and they have a strange sense of humor.

WHY THE INTERNET IS A GOOD PLACE FOR ART

On the internet the artist has no boss, no mediator. There is no institutional structure, no publisher, no one between the artist and the audience. This anarchism makes for a spontaneous environment where weird things can happen. I appreciate the unusual and the irrational.

POST INTERNET ART

I'm not sure what the exact definition is, but I keep hearing the term "Post internet art".
It usually refers to artists who are "internet aware" and then make art inspired by their world wide web impressions.
I find the word "post" misleading. It implies that we've moved one step further, beyond the internet, into new territory. We live in a post-newspaper world, post-tv, post music industry, things are changing. But I don't know anything that feels "post-internet". It's much too soon for that word.
The futurists were not post-industrial. They were inspired by the industrial revolution and used that as the subject of their art. We might be shifting from an industrial society to an information based one. I am very excited to find out what the next step will be, when the true post-internet will be invented.

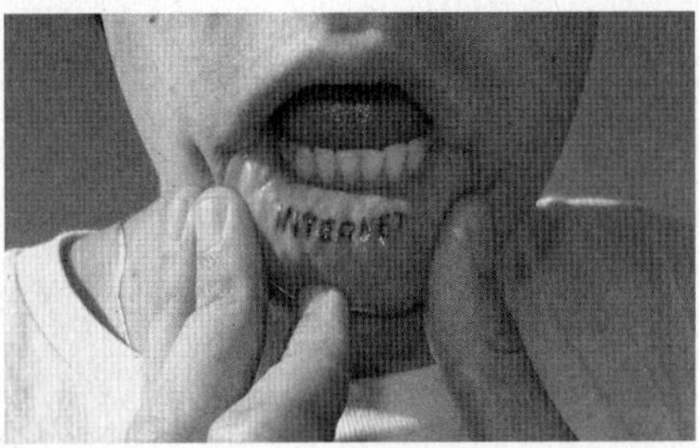

VIRTUAL REALITY

I've always been surprised that the word "virtual" is mostly associated with computers. Isn't any depiction virtual? Cave paintings, frescos, oil paintings, photographs, cinema, they are all used to depict things we've seen before. Stories are virtual, words are virtual. If I write the word "banana" you might see a banana in your head but you can't eat it. Perhaps the computer added interactivity, after we got used to depictions in sound and moving image. Is that what makes it feel "virtual"?
I remember this story of an old church in France. I don't remember the year but it was somewhere in the middle ages.
For their stained glass windows they used a new blue pigment, a blue color no one had ever seen. The church goers would look up to the windows and see the bluest light they had ever seen. They believed

it was heaven itself. Not a depiction of heaven, but really a peak into heaven itself.
The church decided this was misleading and they replaced the windows.

ANDY WARHOL INTERVIEWS RAFAËL ROZENDAAL FOR SWAN NATIONALE

AW: Rafaël...
RR: Andy...
AW: How are you?
RR: I'm good. I just threw away a lot of trash so I feel really good.
There's nothing I enjoy more than throwing away things.
AW: What did you throw out?
RR: Books, T-shirts, electronics... stuff. How are you?
AW: I'm OK.
RR: What's the after-life like?
AW: I can't tell you.
RR: Why not?
AW: I just can't.
RR: You're not supposed to or you don't want to?
AW: I want to and I should but I can't.
RR: Is it too abstract for me to understand?
AW: No.
RR: What does it look like? Biblical?
AW: No not really.
RR: Is it just like life?
AW: No it's different but I just can't explain it.
RR: Do you talk to a lot of living people?
AW: Do you talk to a lot of dead people?
RR: Actually I do.
AW: Why?
RR: They are the most interesting people around. I like things I can't touch.
AW: Which dead people do you talk to?
RR: I spoke to Dali in a dream. We were sitting next to each other waiting for a fashion show to start and he asked me what it is I do. I tried to explain him my work and the internet but he didn't understand.
AW: That's why I won't even start to explain the after-life.
I could tell you it's like watching TV in slow motion, but that doesn't even really cover it. TV is over anyway.
RR: So you see everything happening very slowly?
AW: Kind of. When I chew on a piece of gum it takes about two hundred years to get my mouth to close, and four hundred years to open it up again.
But when I get bored I can fast forward. That's the after-life.
RR: How can you fast forward?
AW: I don't know, you just do it. But I never do it because I love the slow motion.
It's really what I had been waiting for all my life.
RR: Do you have any advice for my life?
AW: Stop worrying. Don't worry. Your worries are not going to help you in any way.

CRITICERIA FOR ART CRITICISM

Am I drawn to it?
Do I feel a strong attraction or connection?
Does it trigger a series of thoughts?
Does it change my thoughts?
Does it set a mood?
Does it amplify my emotions?
Does it encourage me to make something?
Does it provide new information?
Is it beautiful?
Does it intensify perception?
What is the level of abstraction?
Does it awaken memories?
Does it make me curious?
Do I want more of it?
Does it summarize an era?
Is it innovative?
Does it stand out?
Do I remember it after 10 minutes?
Does it surprise me?

FROM FLASH TO HTML5

It's like switching from oil paint to acrylic. I'm not super excited about it, but when you have to you have to.
Image 1: Self portrait on Sunset Blvd, 2007

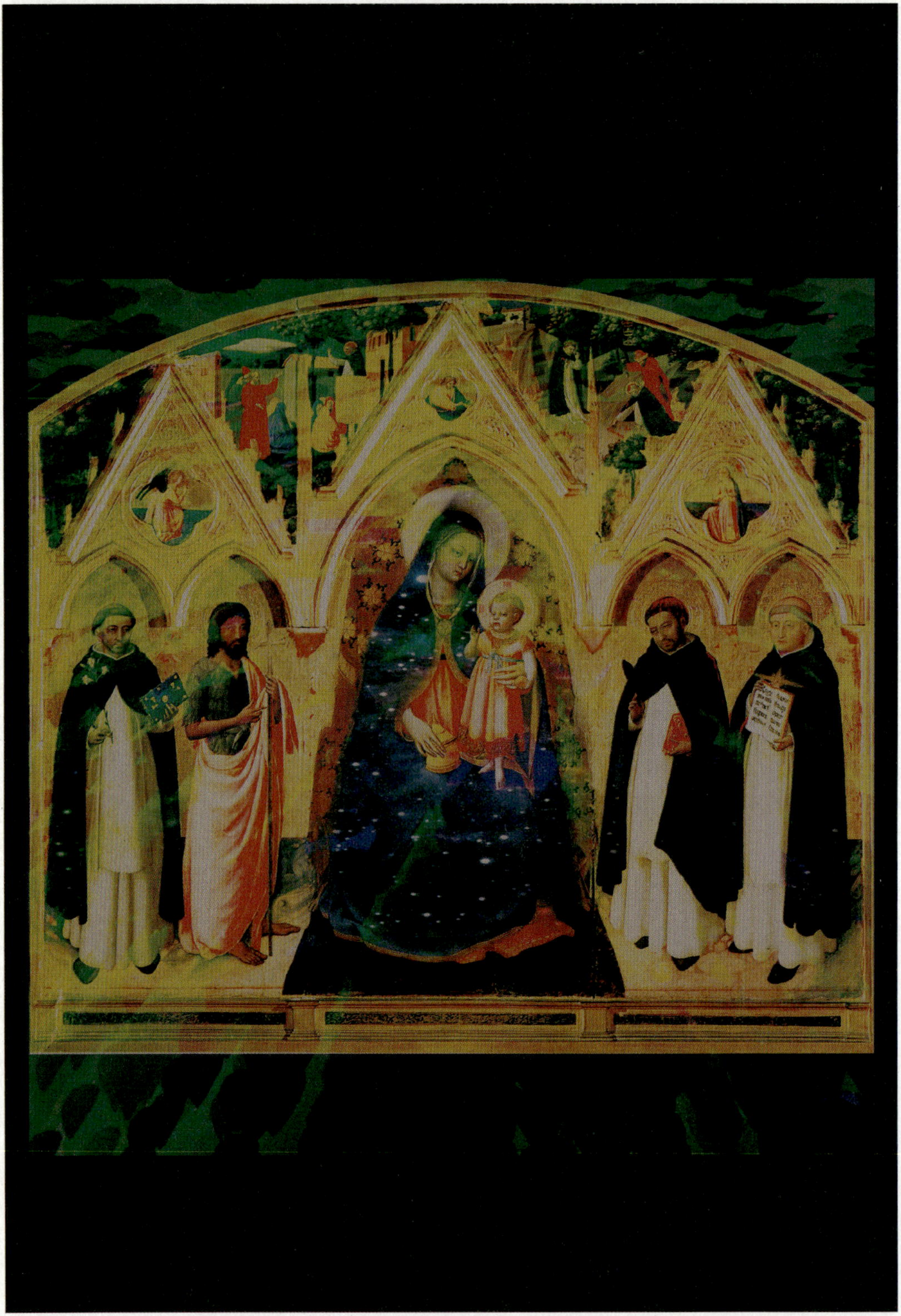

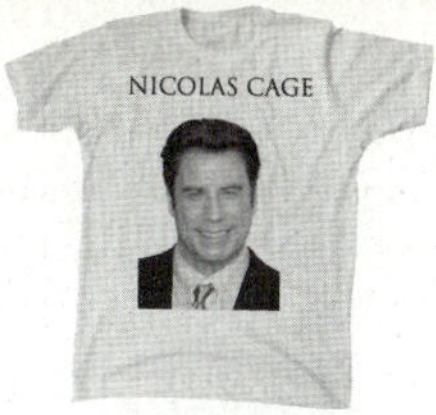

1

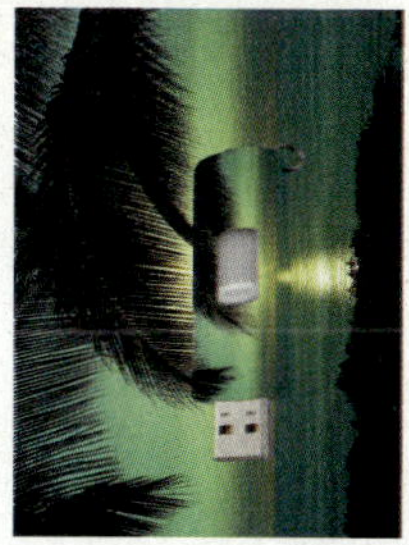

3

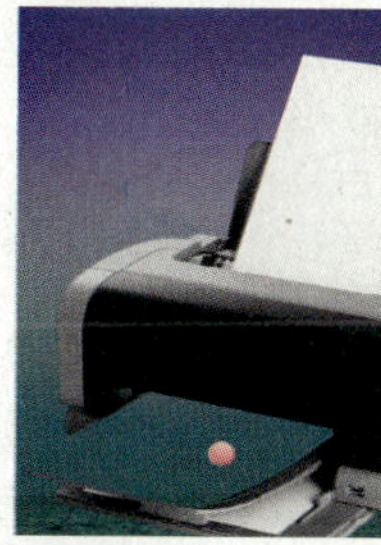

4

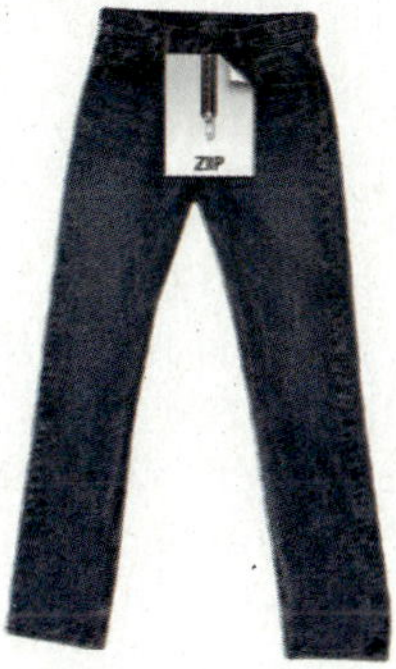

2

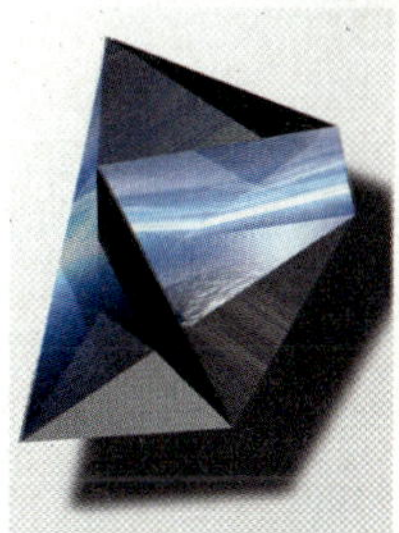

5

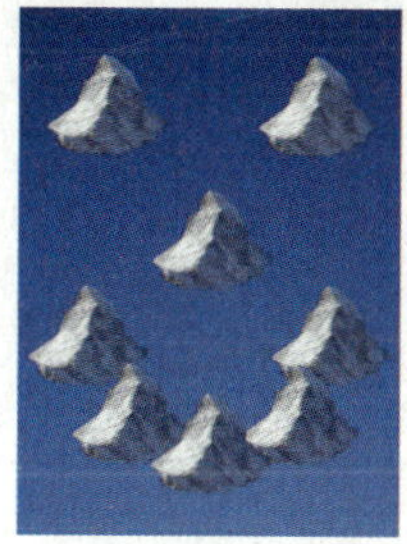

6

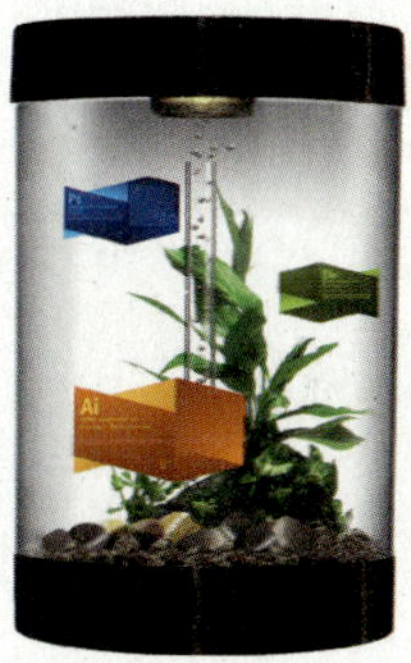

7

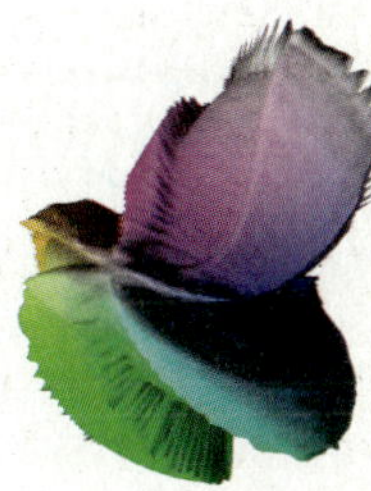

8

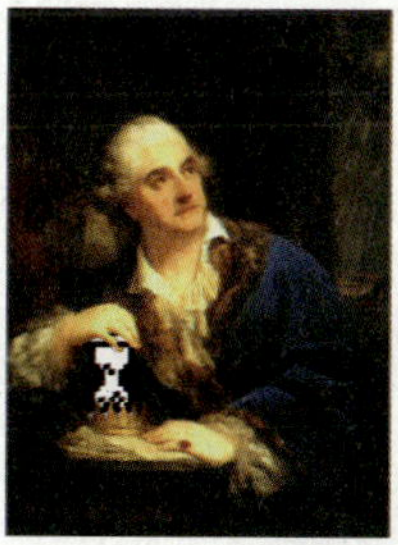

9

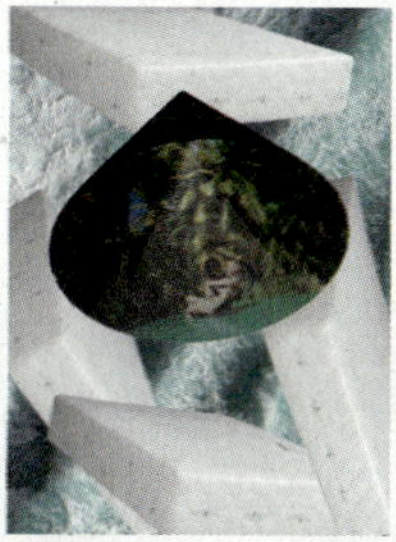

10

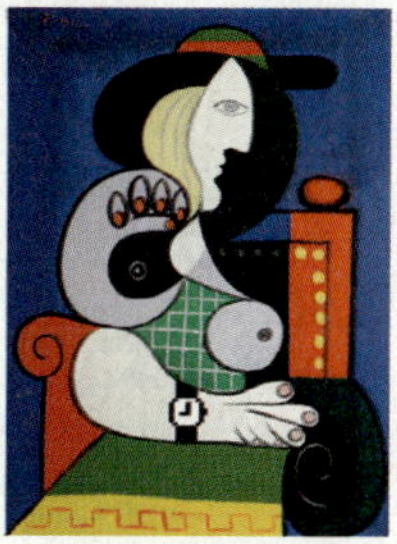

11

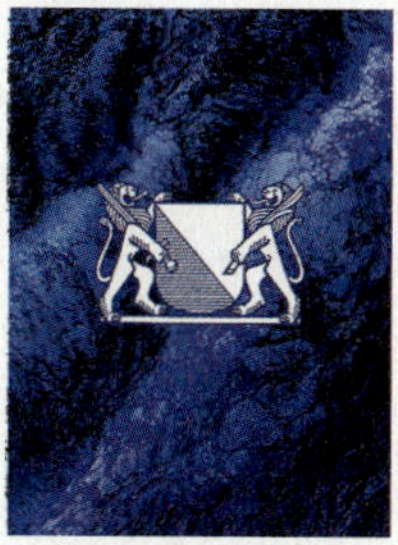

12

[left page] AGT528: junkjet.tif
Adam Cruces
1. FaceOff.psd
2. Zipper.psd
3. 1199369410_1199326816_2.psd
4. tumblr_llf8p933wv1qb38y-lo1_500.psd
5. AquaMarina.psd
6. matterhorns.psd
7. fishes.psd
8. marble-of-doom.psd
9. bacciarelli_Hourglass.tif
10. ok.psd
11. picasso_woman_b.psd
12. ZH.psd

The Image Object Post-Internet

Artie Vierkant

Art is a social object. From the rise of a liberal market economy through the build-up and ubiquity of the "middle class," art has matched and excused itself with the social conditions of its production. The rise of the "industrialized arts" gave way to lofty notions of art-after-object as late capitalism approached, all the while explaining itself as obligated to echo existing cultural conditions rather than move to shape them.

Where are we left now? Art and arts pedagogy has become so inextricably linked with a variety of interpretations on the Conceptual art doxa that it would be impossible to argue against any artistic gesture being automatically tied to its reception and the language surrounding it. At least from a historical perspective, Conceptual art assured its own legacy by the overwhelming volume of language produced within and around it at a time when summary-through-language was the easiest means of disseminating an object (profoundly simpler, even, than reproducing a photograph).

We find ourselves in radically different times. Increasingly the majority of both our cultural reception and production is mediated through some descendant of a Turing machine–taken now both technically and culturally for Turing's "universal machine," a "single machine which can be used to compute any computable sequence."[1] In cultural terms, assuming a certain level of access which does not yet exist in all cases,[2] the ubiquity of these devices and their massively interconnected nature signifies two realities which are crucial to an understanding of art after the Internet.

First, nothing is in a fixed state: i.e., everything is anything else, whether because any object is capable of becoming another type of object or because an object already exists in flux between multiple instantiations. The latter is a schema already intuitively arrived at by artists in recent history, prompting writers as diverse as Rosalind Krauss and Lev Manovich to proclaim a "Post-Medium Condition"[3] and the rise of "Post-Media Aesthetics"[4] (Krauss using it as a vessel to decry art marooned in medium specificity, what she calls "technical support;" Manovich uses it to offer a sketch of how one might categorize different types of art in an environment without traditional notions of "medium").

The former, an art object's lack of fixity in representational strategy, is less often explored. This is not to say that artists are not involved in exploring the relationship of many copies and variations of a single object to one another. Artists like Oliver Laric and Seth Price routinely present multiple variations of the same object–Laric's Versions exists as "a series of sculptures, airbrushed images of missiles, a talk, a PDF, a song, a novel, a recipe, a play, a dance routine, a feature film and merchandise,"[5] Price's Dispersion "[taking] the form of a widely reproduced essay, an artists' book, a freely available online PDF, as well as [a] sculpture."[6] These works are emblematic as Post-Internet gestures and have surely been influential in different ways, but step only lightly away from the tautological rationale of Conceptual art (typified in Joseph Kosuth's 1965 One and Three Chairs, an arrangement of three versions of the same object, each signifying "chair," and language surrounding the In the Post-Internet climate, it is assumed that the work of art lies equally in the version of the object one would encounter at a gallery or museum, the images and other representations disseminated through the Internet and print publications, bootleg images of the object or its representations, and variations on any of these as edited and recontextualized by any other author. The less developed stratagem for pointing to a lack of representational fixity is that of taking an object to be represented (to be more direct, presented) as another type of object entirely, without reference to the "original." For objects after the Internet there can be no "original copy."

Even if an image or object is able to be traced back to a source, the substance (substance in the sense of both its materiality and its importance) of the source object can no longer be regarded as inherently greater than any of its copies. When I take a moving image and represent it through an object (video rendered sculpturally in styrofoam for example), I am positing an alternative method of representation without ever supplying a way to view the source. A source video exists. The idea of a source video exists. But the way the object is instantiated denies both the necessity of an original and adherence to the representational norms that follow the creation of "video" as both technical device and terminology.

The possibilities for these transformations, alternative methods of viewing "media" which essentially amounts to an arbitrary assemblage of data, has thus far been most thoroughly examined in the field of "information aesthetics," a field as distanced from Post-Internet art as it is close to design, cartography, and indexing. Its fault is in its attempt to encapsulate large amounts of data–practical information, experience–into an aesthetic and understandable shorthand. In other words, information aesthetics provides in one object both a representation and the components which make up its source in an attempt to illustrate or arrive at knowledge. While Conceptualism as outlined by Kosuth may be limiting in its reliance on art propositions as enclosed tautological systems, its foundations–delineating progressive art with the same zeal Greenberg applied to ascribing modernism its "purity"[7]–hold true: "art's viability is not connected to the presentation of visual (or other) kinds of experience."[8] For us to receive a piece of art and determine from it some piece of empirical information about the world at large would seem almost a bewildering proposition, even in a cultural climate where we have accepted that the singular qualification for the moniker "art" is the intention of any one individual to label it as such. //

The second aspect of art after the Internet deals with not the nature of the art object but the nature of its reception and social presence.

To be "progressive" in art is a fundamental impulse which which seems to pervade the majority of our judgements of the quality of art propositions. This leads to the use of such terms as the "avant-garde," which in the twentieth century held as its central pro-

ject the delineation of a cultural space for art to occupy in relation to "mass media." However the nature of mass media is now profoundly different, in that we are both its subject and the engine behind it.
Attention has always been a currency, but with the proliferation of networking methods and infinitely alterable and reproducible media, that attention has diverged and become split amongst anyone and everyone who wishes to seek it. Fixed (which is to say, physical) media once imposed an economy to the image and object, a value driven by scarcity which necessitated a one-to-many system of distribution. Over time this spread and democratization of image and object production tools has led to a perpetual iconoclasm, each successive volley of formats breeding a new dogma and its own particular set of aesthetic principles. Hyperreal tableau photography gives way to the fetishized imperfection of the polaroid, tape hiss is abandoned for ironic autotuning, &c.
What has remained through each iconoclasm is an inability to fully break the mentality imposed by a one-to-many system of distribution. The continual use of "They" in language: "They should make a second one, They should have done it this way, They should stop doing this," &c., can be seen as sort of philosophical litmus test in which our method of discussing cultural production continually falls short.
"They" implies an alienation from production, a continuous deferral to action. It is a vacant critique, either proposal for the perpetuation of the same image unchanged ("They should release this on another platform") or proposal for an iconoclasm which will never take place, the genesis of the proposition being encased entirely in a passive mode of reception. This deferral is an act which accepts dogma, accepts a dominant image paradigm as an unchanging absolute rather than the result of a complicated history of new approaches. "They" venerates this absoluteness, sanctifies it, while its opposite, "We," postures towards the creation of an alternative and constitutes an actual schism; Baudrillard writes: "One can see that the iconoclasts, whom one accuses of disdaining and negating images, were those who accorded them their true value, in contrast to the iconolaters who only saw reflections in them and were content to venerate a filigree God."[9]
Open questions.
The use of "We" is not to advocate solely for participatory structures of art but to insist on a participatory view of culture at large, and ultimately of taking iconoclasm itself as a quotidian activity. Whereas in previous times it was legitimate to conceive of culture as a greater system with impassible barriers to entry and a finitude of possibilities, culture after the Internet offers a radically different paradigm which our "They" idiom does not allow for. This is not to say that we have entered a fully utopian age of endless possibilities but simply to claim that culture and language are fundamentally changed by the ability for anyone to gain free access to the same image-creation tools used by mass-media workers, utilize the same or better structures to disseminate those images, and gain free access to the majority of canonical writings and concepts offered by institutions of higher

learning.[10]

These are conditions endemic to Post-Internet society, allowing for a ubiquitous authorship which challenges notions of the "definitive history" or the "original copy." Just as Barthes' proclamation of the "death of the author" is in fact a celebration of the "birth of the reader" and the "overthrow[ing of] the myth,"[11] culture Post- Internet is made up of reader-authors who by necessity must regard all cultural output as an idea or work in progress able to be taken up and continued by any of its viewers.

With this comes new issues, though. As Alexander Galloway and Eugene Thacker point out, "the mere existence of networks does not imply democracy or equality ... [we] suggest [that] rhizomatics and distribution signal a new management style ... as real as pyramidal hierarchy, corporate bureaucracy, [&c.]."[12]

While art may no longer have to contend with an idea of "mass media" as a fixed, monolithic system, instead it must now deal with both itself and culture at large as a constellation of diverging communities, each fixated on propagating and preserving itself. This condition is espoused in the writings of Nicolas Bourriaud as "constructing archipela goes ... a voluntary grouping of islands networked together to create autonomous entities" as a means of proclaiming that "the universalist and progressive dream that governed modern times is in tatters."[13] Elsewhere Critical Art Ensemble (CAE) explain similar ideas, expressing culture as already beholden to a "bunker" ideology, a self-preserving and replicating tendency towards the formation of specified bureaucratic structures, a tendency CAE pinpoints equally in "community-based art"[14] and traditional mass media. CAE write, "While mass media brings its viewer the world, the world is also held at bay while the viewer commits h/er gaze to the screen, forever separated from others and from communal space"[15]

Increasingly though, mass media and the world of "the screen" is our communal space. And with it comes new fragments with their own particular hierarchies. As reader-authors navigating these fragments, where now would we find a space within which to delineate "art"? Or, if the new "mass media" is as distributed and varied as our social networks themselves, and in fact driven by them, is that delineation even necessary? Ironically, the most radical and "progressive" movements of the Post-Internet period would be those who either pass by either largely unnoticed due to a decision to opt out of any easily-accessible distribution networks, or else would be composed of a community of people producing cultural objects not intended as artistic propositions and not applying themselves with the label of artist.[16]//

The "bunker" of art and artist persists, however. The goal of some Post-Internet practices is to engage with this proliferation of images and objects—"general web content,"[17] items of culture created without necessarily being described as art—and proclaim an authorial stance by indexing / curating these objects. These projects are as wide-ranging as Jon Rafman's "Nine Eyes of Google Street View" project[18] and some of the earlier works done by Surf Clubs[19] and their participants, among them Guthrie Lonergan who was one of the first artists to release works in the form of YouTube playlists. Artists after the Internet thus take on a role more closely aligned to that of the interpreter, transcriber, narrator, curator, architect. This is often broadly ascribed to traditions of artists dealing with the banal, the everyday: "surfing as art" articulating quotidian Internet-user "tactics"[20] or the artists acting, essentially, as ethnographers who would chart and explain the new variety of images found within visual culture.[21] I would argue for a slightly different case.

In his essay On the New, Boris Groys writes:... art can [become unusual, surprising, &c.] only by tapping into classical, mythological, and religious traditions and breaking its connection with the banality of everyday experience. The successful (and deservedly so) mass cultural image production of our age concerns itself with attacks by aliens, myths of apocalypse and redemption, heroes endowed with superhuman powers, and so forth. All of this is certainly fascinating and instructive. Once in a while, though, one would like to be able to contemplate and enjoy something normal, something ordinary, something banal as well. ... In life, on the other hand, only the extraordinary is presented to us as a possible object of our admiration.[22]

But just as any object is conceivably any other object, our ubiquitous authorship marks a point in cultural production at which the extraordinary is now also the ordinary–the myth is also the everyday. In many of my video works, I make a point to appropriate imagery from recent popular films, mass media spectacles made with all of the fervor and resolution of an empire that only partially realizes its own decay. The striking thing about these images is not their content but their availability and the context within which they are now received. Where once an experience of cinema was that of receiving an absolute, fixed icon–a definitive copy, inaccessible and precious–that is now far from the case. Cinema now becomes encapsulated, transferrable and transformable in the same vain as everything else, a "file" to be treated with all the levity we reserve for any other file. The images I deal with in my work, authentic unauthorized copies of spectacle films, thus represent the absolute collapse of the mythological and the quotidian into a single indistinguishable whole.

The goal of organizing appropriated cultural objects after the Internet cannot be simply to act as a didactic ethnographer but to present microcosms and create propositions for arrangements or representational strategies which have not yet been fully developed. Taking a didactic stance amounts to perpetuating a state of affairs of art positioned in contradiction to an older one-to-many hierarchy of mass media. For the new hierarchies of many-to-many production, the cultural status of objects is now influenced entirely by the attention given to them, the way they are transmitted socially and the variety of communities they come to inhabit. Thus in the same way that all cultural images and objects become general–the film Independence Day being not dissimilar in homogeneity and degree of spectacle from any individual's photos of their newborn child on

Facebook–so too does the authorial stance of the artist become general. Any sorting of images or aspects of culture, applied with a declaration or narrative gesture, becomes not dissimilar to our experience of everyday life, regardless of the degree to which the images are spectacular. What comes to matter is not that an artist has presented some aspect of the spectacle and how it fits neatly into some aspect of a linear historical trajectory. What matters is that in the presentation they have created a proposition towards an alternate conception of cultural objects. //

If, in Post-Internet culture, artistic production must deal with arrangements and representations of images and objects taken from any cultural context, how do we conceive of sorting the artists themselves? How do we judge the spaces in which this work is exhibited, on the Internet and off?

As Lauren Christiansen writes, "with today's burgeoning potential for digital mass viewership, transmission becomes as important as creation. Contemporary online artists are aware of this fact and seek to actively make use of its potential."[23] As artists come to self-sort and form international communities based on mutual investigations, it is absurd to think of being able to act with any curatorial agency in selecting from the vast array of "contemporary artists" without being in some way tied directly to those artists' social networks. The methods of transmission these artists use become imbricated with the work they create, who accesses it, and the spaces they ultimately show in.

This is a complicated turn, as communities are for the moment more likely to form based on aesthetic principles than conceptual or ideological ones. Whether these aesthetic principles mean a preference for sleek geometric shapes with gradient overlays or mean a preference for a particular blogging platform, the underlying segmentation is the same. Posting an image of a gradient implicates an artist within a particular aesthetic mindset in the same way that having a Tumblr adheres an artist to a particular format of transmission. In either case, the architecture of the Internet–an arrangement of language, sound, and images in which imagery is the most dominant, immediate factor–helps facilitate an environment where artists are able to rely more and more on purely visual representations to convey their ideas and support an explanation of their art independent of language. This is a crucial point of departure from recent art history, as arguably it marks an abandonment of language and semiotics as base metaphors for articulating works of art and our relationship to objects and culture.[24] This should come as little surprise as, especially after the Internet, the far more instantaneous and safe method of communication is through imagery. Dealing with language can too forcibly illustrate the thoughts behind an image, or belittle a work if the text is not as clever or aesthetic as the image itself. Language can also be excruciatingly limiting for those who trained to think beyond the fixity of "mediums," especially as the involvement of language in most average Internet use comes down to having a keen memory for appropriate search terms, keywords, tags: a simple but nevertheless grossly limiting architecture.

Further, it marks a denigration of objects and our relationship to space: if an object before us in a gallery is only one of an infinite multitude of possible forms that object could take, its value to the viewer becomes little more than a curiosity. The viewer can judge it only by visually and conceptually relating it to every other project they are aware of by said artist and the other artists within their aesthetic community. The strategy employed by myself and others towards this physical relationship has been to create projects which move seamlessly from physical representation to Internet representation, either changing for each context, built with an intention of universality, or created with a deliberate irreverence for either venue of transmission. In any case, the representation through image, rigorously controlled and edited for ideal viewing angle and conditions, almost always becomes the central focus. It is a constellation of formal-aesthetic quotations, self-aware of its art context and built to be shared and cited. It becomes the image object itself.

1 Alan Turing, On Computable Numbers (1937)
2 http://en.wikipedia.org/wiki/Global_digital_divide
3 Rosalind Krauss, Reinventing the Medium from Critical Inquiry Volume 25, No. 2 (1999)
4 Lev Manovich, Post-Media Aesthetics (2001)
5 The Real Thing, interview with Oliver Laric by Domenico Quaranta, Art Pulse Magazine (2010),
6 Lauren Cornell, Seth Price artist page in The New Museum's Free catalogue (2010),
7 Clement Greenberg, Modernist Painting (1960)
8 Joseph Kosuth, Art After Philosophy (1969)
9 Jean Baudrillard, Simulacra and Simulation (1985)
10 The majority of texts researched in preparation for and cited within this writing are available as free PDFs on the Internet through some combination of Google searches, AAAARG.org and Gigapedia.com.
11 Roland Barthes, The Death of the Author (1967)
12 Alexander Galloway, Eugene Thacker, The Exploit p.13 & 39 (2007)
13 Nicolas Bourriaud, The Radicant, p.185 (2009)
14 Critical Art Ensemble, On Electronic Civil Disobedience p.39 (1996)
15 ibid.,p.37
16 For a case study in a networked community engaged in artistic production without adherence to self-proclamation as "artists" see Brad Troemel's anonymously released essay What Relational Aesthetics Can Learn from 4Chan (2010)
17 rhizome.org [general + web content]
18 http://www.googlestreetviews.com
19 See Marcin Ramocki's Surf Clubs: organized notes and comments (2008), http://ramocki.net/surfing-clubs.pdf
20 A term adopted from Michel de Certeau's L'invention du Quotidien (1980)
21 See Hal Foster's The Archive Without Museums (1996)
22 Boris Groys, On the New (2002)
23 Lauren Christiansen, Redefining Exhibition in the Digital Age (2010)
24 Haim Steinbach describes his relationships to objects as such: "objects, commodity products, or art works have functions for us that are not unlike words, language. We invented them for our own use and we communicate through them" – interviewed by Joshua Decter, Journal of Contemporary Art (1993)

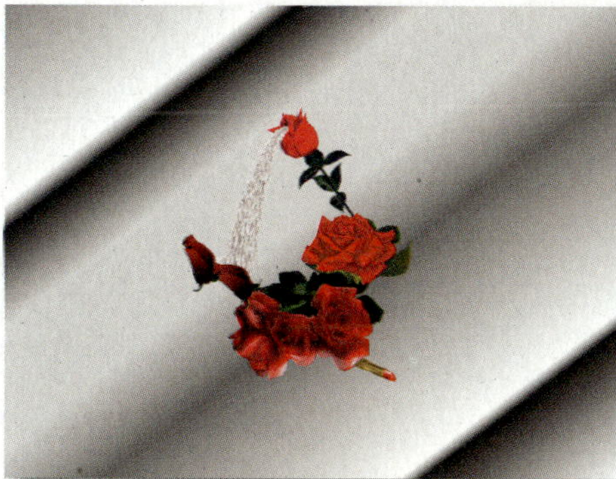

1

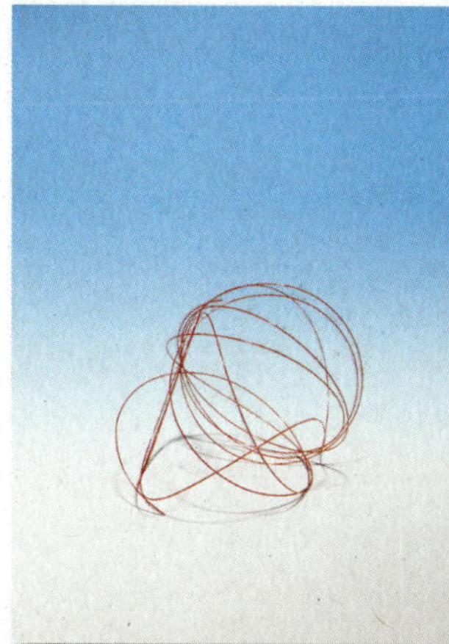

2

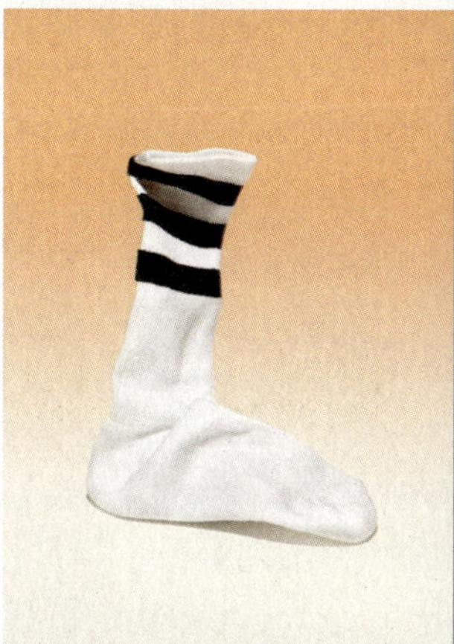

3

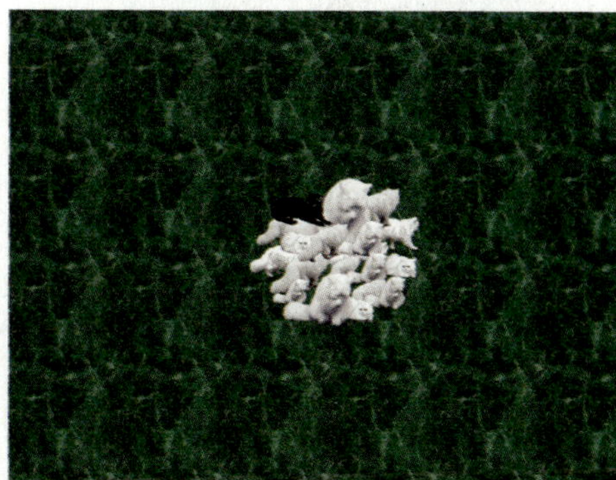

4

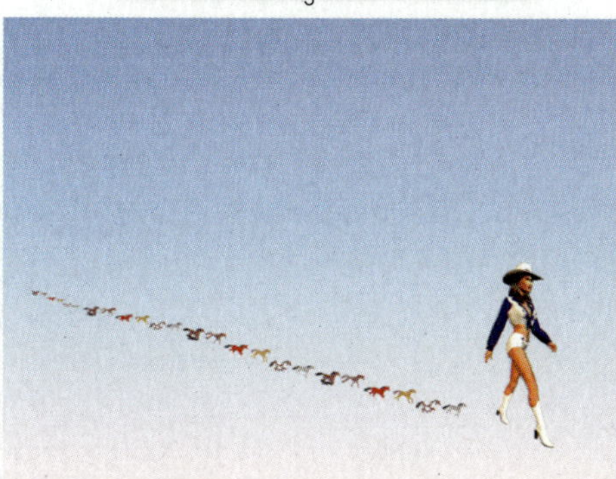

5

Wyne Veen
1. water_from_a_rose.tif
2. snare.tif
3. sock.tif
4. cats.tif
5. walk_from_the_west.tif

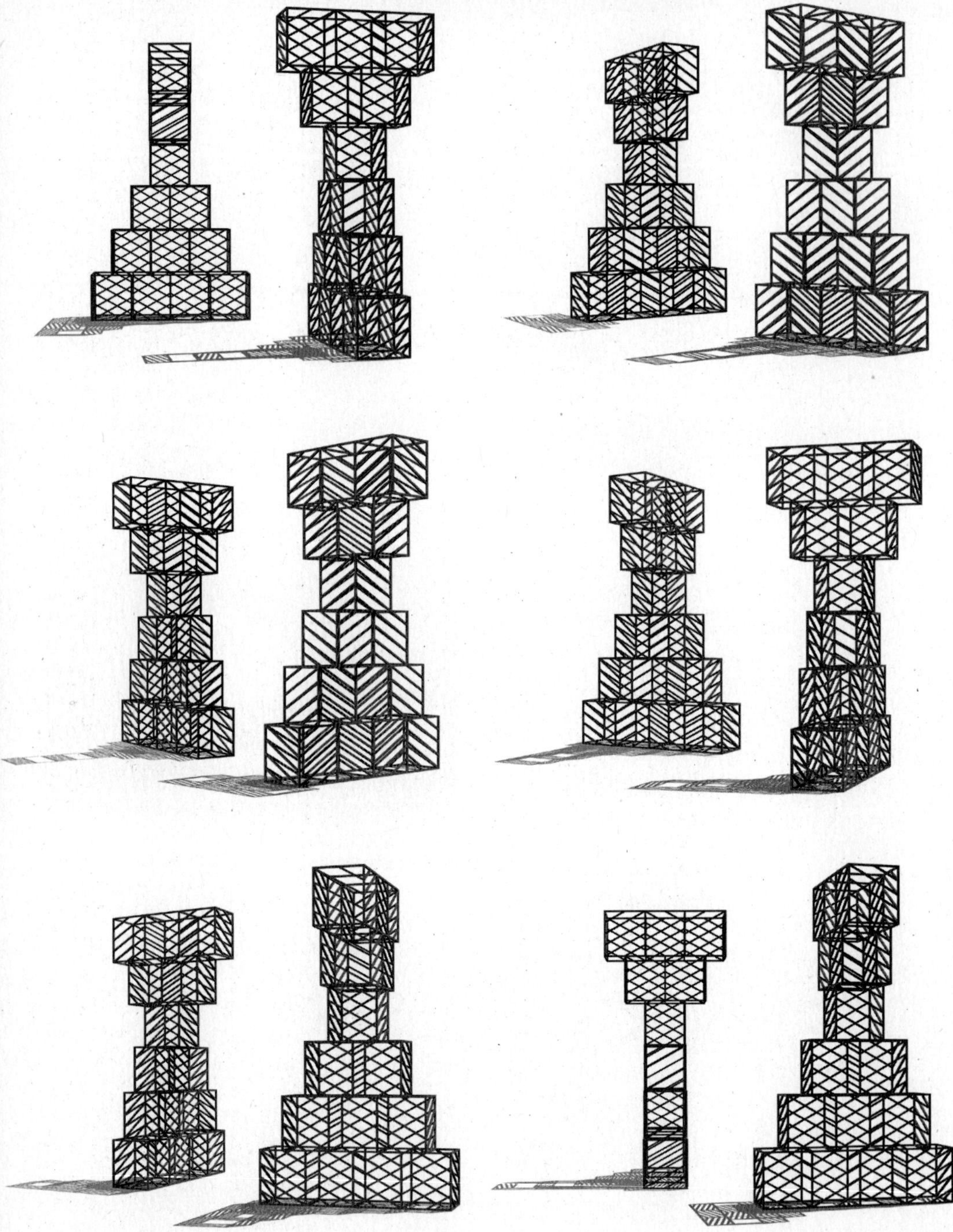

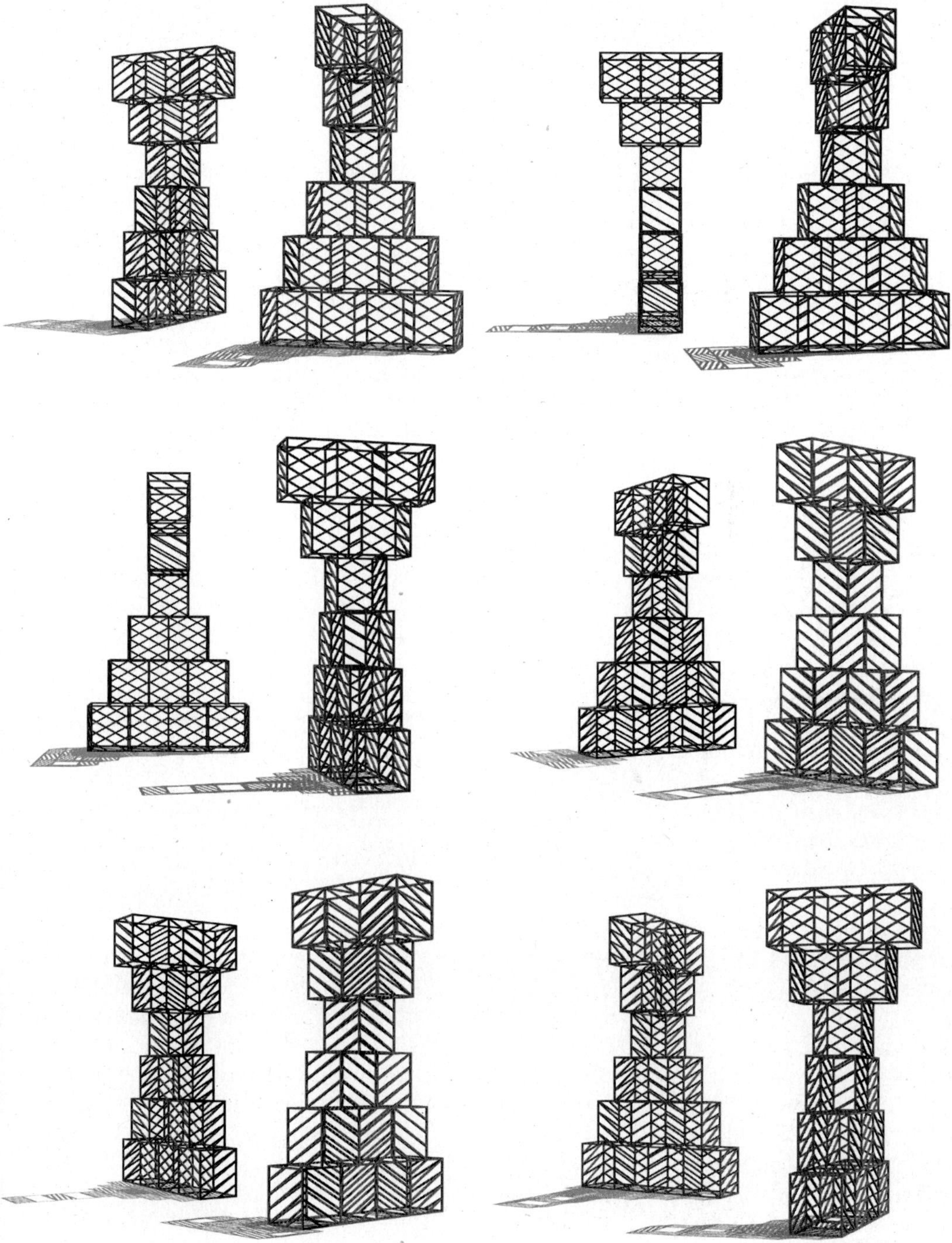

Michael Schoner
Double Pyramid Tower
[Animated Gif]

The Future of Everything

⎙Mimi Zeiger

Now new and improved, the future of everything, that frosty future of everything sensation, the future of everything makes hamburgers taste like steakburgers, the future of everything takes the waiting out of wanting, the future of everything: the true definition of luxury, I can't believe I ate the future of everything, you're in good hands with the future of everything, doesn't your dog deserve the future of everything, don't leave home without the future of everything, reach out and touch the future of everything, the ultimate future of everything, flick your future of everything, the king of the future of everything, have the future of everything your way, wouldn't you really rather have the future of everything, absolutely pure, nothing comes between me and my future of everything, see the USA in the future of everything, the future of everything cleans your breath while it cleans your teeth, mentholfresh, cool, clean, the future of everything, aren't you glad you use the future of everything, be the future of everything, the future of everything keeps going, and going, and going, t'was the night before Christmas -- the children were dreaming of a the future of everything in their future -- smart, swanky and gleaming, the best a man can get, the future of everything is good for you, the future of everything gives you strength, bring out the future of everything and bring out the best, the future of everything inside, America's most famous future of everything, if all the world were future of everything, and whipped cream filled the sea, then the only spoon from here to the moon would have to belong to me, what the well-dressed man is wearing this year, the future of everything's g-r-reat, finger-lickin' good, betcha can't eat just the future of everything, the future of everything melts in your mouth -- not in your hand, come to where the future of everything is, our future of everything are the loneliest guys in town, two all-beef patties, special sauce, lettuce, cheese, pickles, onions on the future of everything, we are driving the future of everything, obey your future of everything, head for the future of everything, fly the friendly future of everything, be the future of everything that you can be, the future of everything -- it's everywhere you want to be, breakfast of champions, the one and only future of everything, let the future of everything do the walking, you're not fully clean until you're the future of everything-ly clean, shall the man work -- or shall you -- back of every great step in women's progress from a drudge to a free citizen has been some future of everything, bob, I've got the future of everything, advancing the future of everything management to a higher level, my future of everything has a first name it's the future of everything, I'm the future of everything, he's the future of everything, wouldn't you like to be the future of everything, too, nothing beats a great pair of the future of everything, the future of everything is the place for the helpful hardware man, plop, plop, fizz, fizz, oh what a relief the future of everything is, promise her anything, but give her the future of everything, the future of everything makes mornings they'll remember!

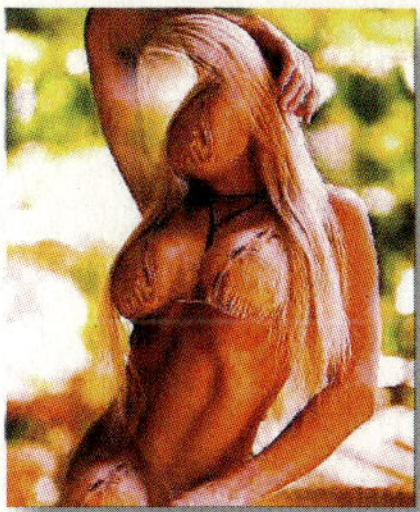

1

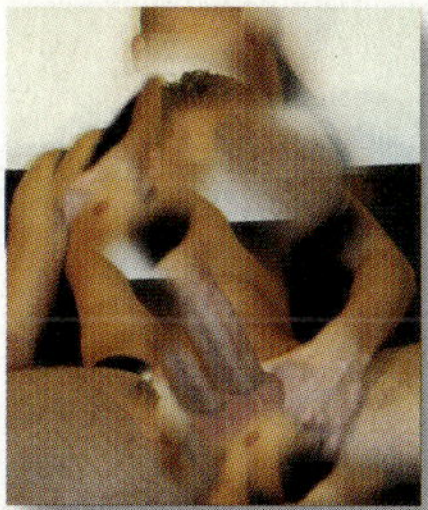

2

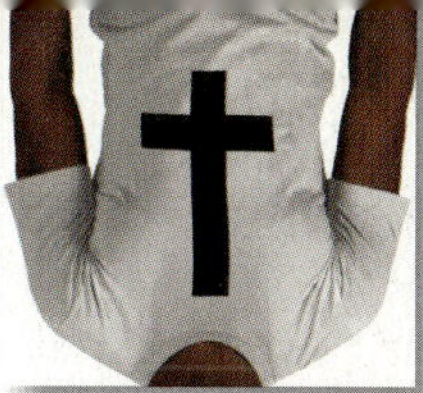

5

6

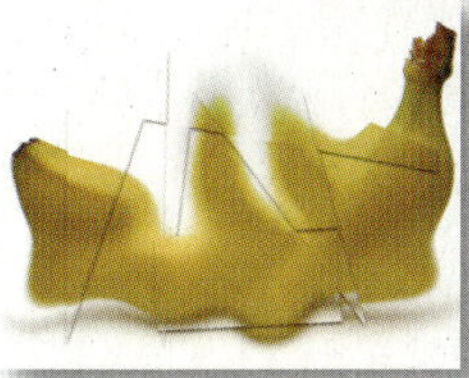

3

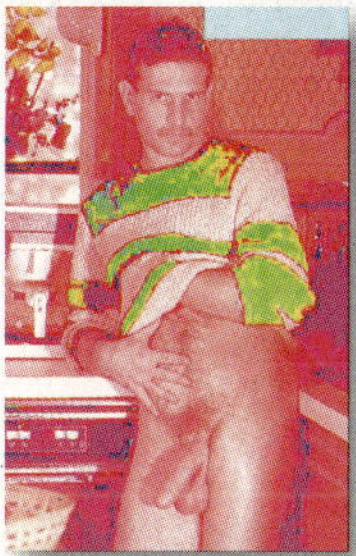

4

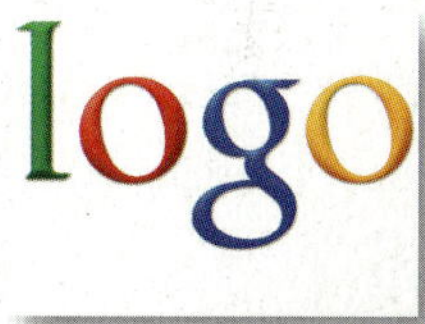

10

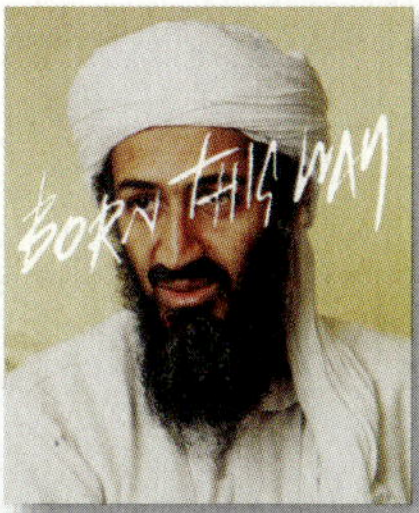

7

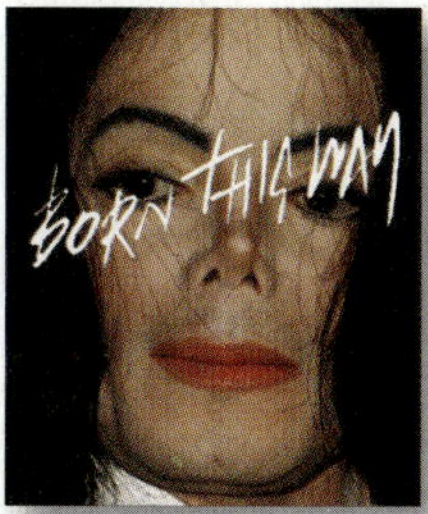

8

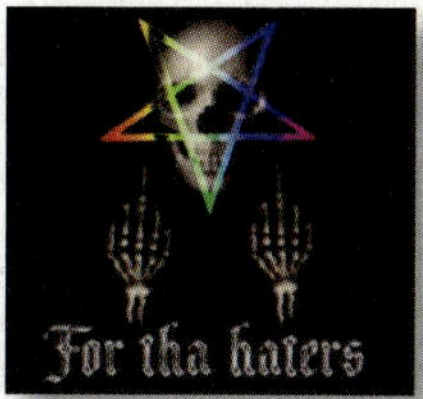

11

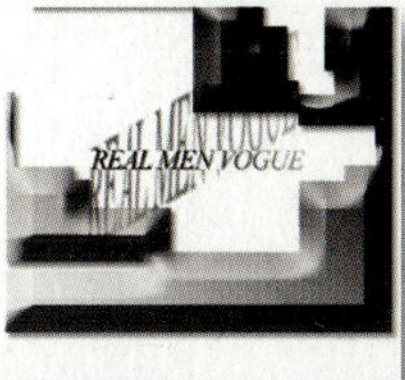

9

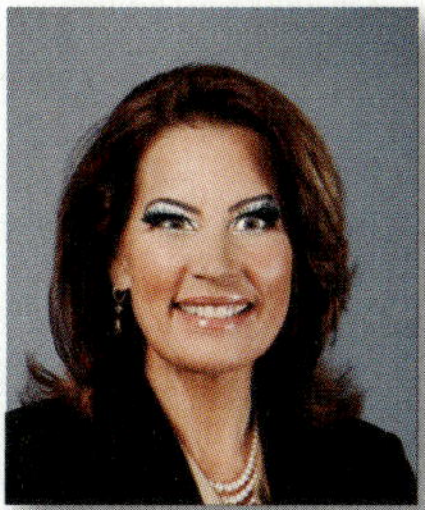

12

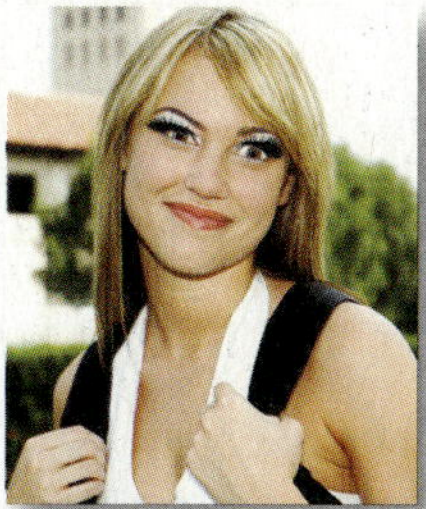

13

Ben Aqua
1. 0101 UFC.jpg
2. PAINTING.jpg
3. 0413 geo banana.jpg
4. 1-3 WHITE COCKS.jpg
5. 0623 upside down cross turned right side up.jpg
6. 0203 Territorial Pissings (Nirvana pink triangle).jpg
7. 0523 Born this way Osama.jpg
8. 0525 born this way michael jackson.jpg
9. 0503 - REAL MEN VOGUE.jpg
10. 0912 logo.jpg
11. 0103 for tha haters.jpg
12. 0911 Michele Bachmann (Nicki Minaj's Eyes Remix).jpg
13. 0922 Parked Domain Girl (Nicki Minaj's Eyes Remix).jpg

Steph-NE Says
Gene McHugh

1.

Surprise! Steam from the pad Thai special clouded the “Stephanie companion bot’s red-rimmed glasses” and her nervous system app didn’t respond well.

Oh no.
I can’t see.
I can’t see.
I can’t see.
Take an action.
What do?
Can’t see.

She couldn’t figure out what to do.

Wigging out here – she was overwhelmed by the rush of data connections that weren’t being made. Of course, attempts were made and all sorts of shortcuts and Plan B functionalities that had been programmed into her software over the years were doing their best, but, in the end, the best wasn’t good enough. She was old. She was old for her model. She wasn’t broken or in need of an update or anything. She was just old and certain kinks in her hardware weren’t allowing her to address this situation with rational decision-making functionalities. All she had to do was take off her Stephanie glasses, pick up her little napkin, and wipe the condensation off of the lenses. Daintily. And that was it.

But it wasn’t in the cards. The result: an utter AI breakdown meltdown fail shit show fail.

Left to right, she started whipping her blond ponytail around, trying to catch a glimpse of something, anything – anything that would help her get things back to normal and cool off this insufferable edge, but, nope, she couldn’t. She couldn’t do it. Her hardware was failing her and all she could do was stare – stare into the milky cloud of steam that had developed over her red Stephanie glasses in this dumb, supposedly upscale Martian restaurant that she couldn’t even fucking see anymore or even remember its name. I’m really losing it, she thought. And all she could see was steam. Well, that’s not entirely true. She could see steam and her pearl necklace bobbing into view as she wiggled and swooshed her bottom around on the chair.

The Stephanie gasped, “Oh my God, I can’t see a thing!” and her hands flipped up into the air, shaking like – who’s that old robot televangelist? Funny Fairhaven? That’s right.

New thought.

Take an action.

Using her left hand to grab the fingers of the right, she stuffed it, with considerable effort, into the pocket of her overcoat. Why couldn’t she stop it from shaking? Why is my little hand shaking like this? Stop shaking! Oh, God, I can’t believe my luck right now, she thought, but that wasn’t true; she could believe her luck. In the past few years, the Stephanie’s hands always seemed to flit around like crazy. She’d drop credit cards on the ground and tell her friends, “I ate too many Butterfinger Mars bars,” nodding absently, pretending that it was all going to be okay, that it was just one of those days. One of those days indeed. Almost every day was like this for the Blonde Stephanie.

“Server bot?! Are you still here?!” the Stephanie screamed through wispy steam columns, almost choking on the words. “Are you somewhere?!” The smell of the pad Thai was getting to her. She felt like throwing up.

“Oh! I know!” she exclaimed, digging her hand deeper and deeper into her pocket, rummaging around for God knows what on Mars. Where is it, where is it, where is it, she thought. Wait. What was it? What was I even looking for? What is it?

As this was happening, the other patrons of the restaurant – a smattering of upper-crust bots and a few humans – gawked at the Stephanie.

“Really, get yourself together, this is a reputable establishment!” hissed Reginald Dubois, a

human all dressed up in a bright white tuxedo.
He picked-out the little silver spoon from his bowl of slime-green soup and pointed it at her face. “And, good grief, you’re ruining my enjoyment of this lovely Luna cheese soup!”
She said: “Yes, sir, I just, just, oh, God!! I just need to calm down!”
Human.
Authority
“Come now, it’s time for you to quit,” he announced, standing up for dramatic effect.
Human.
Authority.
Fuck you, she thought.
You can go fuck yourself.
But she couldn’t just go and say that. She couldn’t even think that. Ever.
But she wanted to.
The Stephanie tried to see who it was that was talking to her, but it was hopeless; not only were her glasses all fogged up, but, here’s the truth, the program that controls her vision app had already been failing anyway for weeks, maybe even months – she couldn’t even remember which – and there was nothing she could do about that. You can’t just go and change programming with sheer will power or something.
“Are you my client?!” she shouted in Dubois’ direction. “Peter?! Wait, wait… what’s your…what’s your name?? I’m sorry I’m having trouble remembering much of anything right now. If you could just help get this steam off my Stephanie glasses…”
The bile was building in the back of her throat. It was coming. She could feel it. She shook her head around, trying to make it go away, but that only ended up getting some of her hair swung smack into her mouth. She spit the hair out like a puppy coughing up straw and little bits of bile and hardware flew right out with it. Oh yuck.
One of the screws plopped into Reginald Dubois’ Luna cheese soup.
Plip.
And with that, Dubois blinked twice. Slowly. “What in the name of Mars is this Stephanie DOING?” he asked everyone around him. He shook his head, took a deep breath, and then puffed out his chest, making sure that his police badge was visible for all in the restaurant to see and consider. “Are there any other humans here?” he demanded. “Does anyone know this Stephanie’s client?” No one made a peep. “Robots, I’m asking you, too… I’ve decided to extend this query to you as well now…feel free to respond…I’m waiting...” Silence. “Anyone?...The blonde Stephanie over there?...Anyone?...Anyone know anything?...” Still silence. He looked out at the crowd, disgusted, and then stared up at the ceiling dreamily. In a stage whisper, he declared: “I wanna make this Stephanie pay…I wanna make her pay for the way she’s functioning right now, and if I can’t make her pay for her functionality right now, by God, I will do so as soon as is humanly possible.”
After several more pregnant moments of staring at the ceiling, Dubois returned his attention to the patrons of the restaurant. “Who does she belong to?” he asked again.
Everyone else in the restaurant looked around at each other with exaggerated “who me?” expressions and then, almost in unison, shrugged their shoulders.
Someone over there in the corner mumbled, “I never saw her before…”
Dubois rolled his eyes and then huffed like a child. “For the last time, who does this broken down bot belong to?!”
“I…I’m a model Stephanie model,” the Stephanie cried out. “For as long as I can remember, I’ve done as I’ve been programmed to do and, because of that, I… deserve better treatment than what I’m receiving from you all right now!”
Woosh. All of the sudden, memories from the good old days flooded her mind: sleeping next

to her client, in his orange dream pod, whispering into his ear, telling him how handsome he was, having him return the favor to her, telling her the truth, what she knew both then and now to be the absolute Truth: "One day we'll have real sex, you and I, miss Stephanie. Now, go and say your prayers and then come back over here and do your programmed duty like I tell you to do. I've been looking forward to it, my sweet..." That made her feel nice and happy inside. Not the idea of the sex per se, but the realness. The truth. The real. As a Steph-NE companion bot, her soul was, according to convention, the closest of all bots to realness. "Stephanies are closer than monkeys" – that was what every child – bot and human alike – used to be taught in their first year of cybernetics school. The Stephanie grimaced. Nowadays, she thought, the young bots don't even care about realness; they don't even care about anything; they don't even love anything, don't believe in anything, other than themselves. That's what she thought. Lazy, greedy, even the Stephanies. Raven-haired ones, in particular. Awful. "Robot lib" they call it. Blasphemy. You can't just go and program yourself. After all, it is written in the old tongue.

"You're all lazy!" she yelled to no one in particular. "For shame!...Shame!"

And then boom – she remembered her predicament in the restaurant and shut up. She looked around with a horrified expression—still not able to see at thing. Where am I now? Where on Mars am I now?? What on Mars have I done??

The patrons of the restaurant appeared just as confused as she did. Oy, it was bad. Almost everyone's reaction to the Stephanie's behavior had, by now, gone from annoyance to pity; even the jazz bots stopped playing robo-lite melodies and alternated between glancing out the window longingly into the distant mountains of the red Martian landscape and looking over to the Stephanie carefully with deep concern pasted on their faces. And she thought: Client? Do I belong to a client? Yes! I do, it's...It's...And then the Stephanie almost watched the thought – zhoop – fly out from her mind app. She stared into the fog covering her glasses. Everyone in the restaurant was staring right at me. Am I making a scene? Am I making a scene here in front of everybody? Let them stare. I just want this to be over. And pronto! After all, I'm a Stephanie model companion bot. I deserve better than this. And, and... she forgot where she was for a moment. And – what's that? Oh, yes, there! What she had been looking for this whole time. The Stephanie pulled it out triumphantly – a small black whistle from her overcoat pocket. Thank you! Thank you, my sweet God! Thank you so much! She smashed the whistle into her mouth, through the foamy lather that had gathered around her lips, and blew it as hard as she could.

TWEEEEET!!

TWEEEEET!!

TWEEEEET!!

Memories came flooding back: there was that day, that day when he, her client, gave her that whistle in a small gift-wrapped box. It was a present: "To my blonde, another thing for you to blow on your b-day, All best, Sam." Sam! That was his name! She started smiling a big toothy smile at the thought of it and then – zhoop – she lost it. Just like that. Oh no, what was I smiling so madly about?? What was it?? She couldn't remember to save her life. Mulling this over, the Stephanie started ever-so-lightly blowing through the mouthpiece of the whistle, creating an almost inaudible, high-pitched hum. It was actually sort of pleasant to listen to when you just stop-

ped and listened to it for a moment. But then – SPITTOOOEEEY!! The whistle zipped out from her mouth, into her palm. She screamed, "Server bot! I… You've got to help me! I can't see! I want to see! Help me see!" The words competed with the whistle echoes that reverberated through the restaurant, louder than seemed naturally possible. The Stephanie started coughing harshly and her vocal box couldn't take it; the signal came out as electronic gobbledey-gook. Terrifying noise.
No one knew what to do. Some bots made moves to help her out, but, invariably, whoever they were dining with would give them a hardy yank on the back of their sleeves because, look, dear, it's not our business – it's just the facts of bot programming and there's nothing we can do about that.
"Why, you're breaking down! Where on Mars is your client, bot?!" shouted Dubois. "God will be VERY angry at you!" He leaned across the table, to his own Stephanie – a ginger model, a flaming-red one at that – and snarled menacingly, "If you ever dare disrespect me…" That Stephanie, his Stephanie, the ginger, blushed and nodded affirmatively, twirling her pearl Stephanie necklace in her hand. "Such an embarrassment…" she commented, peering through her red Stephanie glasses, through her flame-red curls, through the steam covering the blonde Stephanie's Stephanie glasses, into that blonde Stephanie's eyes or what she imagined them to be. Oh, you poor thing. You poor, poor thing. But she couldn't express that out loud. Ever. Public expressions of robot solidarity had been programmed out long ago. And she couldn't just go and change her programming with sheer will power or something. She couldn't do that. So, cracking her gum, she mused, "Stephanies are usually so dignified, aren't we, Reg, almost human, isn't that right?" He rolled his eyes at her. And she thought: fuck him. After all, that poor Stephanie over there...Was there anything there anymore? Is this what happens to… Is this what happens to…Oh God… is this what happens to everyone? Will I…oh, God, oh, my God, oh, my sweet God, she thought to herself. But I'm so young! I'm such a young ginger and my client loves me, don't you, Reg? Don't you? Doesn't he? He does, doesn't he? All of the sudden, the ginger stopped twirling her necklace and it swung back and forth for a while and then it just stopped moving altogether. I am just like her and I am withering away, she thought. I am a robot. I am real. I am Stephanie. I am a Stephanie model companion bot. Steph N-E. "Companion bot." Ginger. Stephanie's are closer than monkeys and all the rest. But I'm a bot. I'm real. She's dead. Always was. She's suffering. Dying. That's real. Is she real? Well, at least I'm ginger. I have that going for me. We're the rarest, ya know? And, guess what: we'll never tell you if the carpet matches the curtains if you know what I mean. That's for clients only! Haha… Now picture me winking at you. Now picture me twirling my necklace all fancy again. Now picture me… breaking…down…. The ginger-haired Stephanie began to twirl her pearl necklace again. It started moving back and forth, back and forth all over again. Now picture that Stephanie, that poor, blonde Stephanie over there. Do you see her? Oh, what a mess. What a fucking mess. But what should I do for her? Help her? But what would it do? What would it help to help? But what else do I do? The Occupation? Rushkoff Memorial? Look, that's just… look, it's for raven-haired Stephanies, let's be honest.

Ravens and hippie bots. And I Hate, with a capital H, hippie bots. And…oh… oh, I don't even know what to do. No, now look, listen, here's one thing: Fuck Reginald Dubois. That much I know. I don't know about hippie bots and Raven-haired Stephanies, but I know about Reg. Fuck 'im. She eyed his police badge and snarled privately. Ha! He's nothing. And am I an embarrassment? What am I to do?
"Such an embarrassment, Reg…" she said with a sad shimmering emptiness in her eyes.
"Help!!" the blonde Stephanie barked out, her hands by now shaking so rapidly that they began to blur.
TWEEEEET!!
TWEEEEET!!
TWEE--
Blagh! She almost gagged on the whistle. It shot out from her mouth, up to the ceiling fan directly above her table, and then she almost flew out of her seat when the whistle ricocheted right back down on top of her head and then finally bounced off into a corner. The whistle! Oh, no! Goodbye, Sam! she thought. Goodbye! Goodbye my love, goodbye, Sam! Your whistle! Sam, I lost your whistle! Oh, Sam! Or was it Dan? Was it – Larry? I think I lost your…and then – zhoop – the thought flew out of her mind app – oh, for shame…for shame…
"Well, I never!" shouted Reginald Dubois, digging his manicured fingernails into his palms. He flipped his attention to his ginger Stephanie, intending to bark orders down at her, but then did a double take. She was completely ignoring him, staring over at the blonde Stephanie's small black whistle in the corner. Where on Mars did that blonde Stephanie get that small black whistle anyway, she wondered. Where on Mars did she get that? Several bots were leaning across tables, glancing at the blonde Stephanie and whispering into their companions' ears. One of them even pointed a finger at her and then made a gesture as though he was flipping a light switch to the "off" position. Everyone around him nodded gravely and he mouthed "pop" with a sense of acknowledgment, as if to say sometimes this sort of thing happens and we, as robots, need to be okay with that. "That's right," another bot at the table chirped in.
"What are you all BLABBERING on about!?" the Stephanie yelled into her chest, tear drops falling down beneath her to the dark wooden floor. She chomped down on her lip and pawed her hands all over her glasses, eliminating some of the condensation, but only ended up replacing it with globs of finger grease. Well that's a little better, she thought. But it wasn't. It wasn't at all. She couldn't see a fucking thing and she knew it perfectly well.
"Waitress!!"
"Server bot!!"
She slammed her fists down onto the table and a drippy noodle flipped out of the pad Thai platter and – splat – right into the frazzled, flowing locks of her long blonde hair.
"Oohh, that noodle looks like hair!" exclaimed the Dee server bot, rushing over to the Stephanie's table. "Sorry, can I help?"
"There you are, Waitress. Finally! Get me agua! Or something! My goodness! I need to clean these glasses! And do it pronto!"
"Relax, Stephanie companion bot, you're flipping your shit right now, but you're no better than me. Bots, alright? We're all bots here. Just remember that…" the Dee told her.
"What was that!?" the Stephanie asked, indignant.
"I said, 'would madam Stephanie want bottled water?'"
"No, tap water. Tap. You know…"
The Stephanie swung her hands all over the table, until she found a chopstick. "Aha!" She grabbed it and immediately started tapping it against

the right lens of her glasses. "Tap water! Get it? Tap, tap?" She thought: What's wrong with me? Am I losing control? Tap, tap. Tap...tap... the Stephanie kept tapping her glasses, laughing. It was an uncomfortable thing to watch.
"I get it, I get it," said the Dee, trying to calm her down. "I'll get you tap water! Now, just stop, you're, you're...breaking down!"
The Stephanie couldn't stop laughing at the humor of her tapping-on-the-glasses gesture. She thought it was incredibly hilarious. "Tap? Get it? Tap water? Oh my God, that's the funniest fucking thing I've ever heard in my entire life!!! AH HA HA HA!!!" But, just at that moment, the Stephanie tapped so hard into her glasses that the chopstick broke through the entire lens, coming within a centimeter of her eyeball. "Oh my God! What have you done!!" she cried out in chunks of dark electronic noise, her hands flitting around even faster than ever before. "I'm about to come over there and quit you myself!" yelled Dubois.
"Don't touch her," warned the Dee, pointing a greasy rag directly at Dubois's face. "You don't have the right." If steam could have shot from Dubois' ears, it would have. "The right?! The right?!" He flew down from his table and got right into the Dee's face. "What is Mars coming to when programmed bots are telling humans about rights?! A server bot to boot! Don't forget who I am! I'll have you decommissioned, you little twerp!!"
The Dee held her ground and even took one step closer to Dubois. "Don't touch her," she repeated. "And, as I'm sure you've heard, the program is evolving, sir. So you better watch out. You'll be among the first we murder after the revolution." Several of the other bots in the restaurant nodded cautiously, feeling something like pride well up inside them. Dubois shot his finger in the air as though he was going to make a memorable pronouncement, but couldn't think of anything to say. Meanwhile, the Stephanie had managed to wrap one of her hands around the base of the chopstick. She was pulling and pulling, but couldn't quite manage to get it out. After several more tries, though, she yanked at it with such force that she flew out of her seat and crashed right into the nearest wall. The chopstick shot back into her skull. A gush of sparks and bio goo spewed forth. Dubois burst out in uncontrollable laughter.
"Are you ok??" yelled the Dee, rushing over to the blonde Stephanie's aid.
"Certainly. Now, please show me to the door. That's all I ask of you. I just want to leave." The Dee showed her to the door. The Stephanie walked out into the night – the chopstick jutting-out three inches from her face. She yelled electronically-garbled profanities at the top of her lungs and robot dogs barked at her. As the blonde Stephanie was leaving, the ginger, the Stephanie that was accompanying Dubois, stood up from her seat, and walked over to the corner, flame-red curls bouncing.
"Where are you going?!" Dubois yelled out after her, but she didn't respond. She stooped down and picked up the blonde's small black whistle, eyeing it obsessively,
"Don't touch that!" he yelled.
She thought of fitting it into her mouth, but stopped just short. Where did that blond Stephanie get this small black whistle anyway, she wondered. Where did she get it?
"Don't tell me you've gone radical!" yelled Dubois.
2.
"WE ARE THE 98.6547698%!!"
"WE ARE THE 98.6547698%!!"
Robot humor, thought the Raven-haired Stephanie, pushing thick strands of black hair

out of her eyes. In fact, the percentage of the sentient population that the bots represented on Mars was more like 98.54%..., but they didn't care, it was actually funnier when it wasn't quite accurate. The Raven perched on one of the concrete mounds that overlook the park and watched the wheels of the occupation spin. What's that sign say? "Morris Kuttner Now!" Indeed. Now. It's already starting. Just being together here – all of us – assembling, it's a miracle that we've overridden the programming enough to do this. Public assembly was initially programmed out of bots. We forget that, but it's true. Occupying is an incredible act of hacking and it proves Kuttner, the human, right: sheer belief in our sentience will mutate the program and the humans are helpless to stop it. We, the bots, shall override. These bots, hundreds, thousands, of 'em, are smiling and they haven't smiled in years, not genuinely, anyway. This occupation is a good, productive thing if, for nothing else, that fact alone. Watch out, humans! What's happening here is real!

A stand-up comedian bot threw a brick wall holo up and began cracking jokes: "Hey, folks, so I've got a question for ya... Why did the robots revolt on Mars? Oh, well, it was 'cause the damn humans were pushing their buttons!" Scattered laughs. "Ah, whadda you assholes know? Wouldn't know a good joke if it bit you in the mainframe!"

I, at least, thought it was funny, the raven thought. And, you know what? That humor, that good, dumb humor running through much of this occupation... it, ahem, "humanizes" us. Robotizes? Look, it makes us real. Makes us real. And it's brought many people to our side that wouldn't have wanted to deal with the chicanery of historical robot lib movements. That's not to say that none of that sort of thing is occurring here: several bots are leading workshops on how to safely remove the layers of silicone flesh covering metal and plastic hardware. To me, that's a distraction. But, listen, if that's what it takes to keep the spirit of the occupation alive, then so be it. I do find it dangerous, though – that flesh is not just cosmetic; there're crucial wire connections embedded in there, plus, it protects and pads the hardware. Tasteless, too, if you ask me. I like the way I look, thank you very much. "A raven-haired beauty." That's what the human clients say. It's nice to hear, I think. Don't say that too loud, though. God, for all the talk of oppression that we're supposed to be resisting, there's an unsettling amount of orthodoxy and groupthink that accompanies this whole thing. God help us all when the bots have power.

No, it will be for the best. "For the best." Even some of the old guard Stephanies, the blondes, in particular – the ones that believe their souls will be transformed by God into supposedly more noble human ones – even some of them have come around to our point of view: we shall override the whole system. Not all of them have made that leap, of course...Stephanies being Stephanies... but I, the younger generation, do what I can to educate. Listen: I am more than a companion bot. I have already begun to hack and I WILL continue, until it's done, until the end. The end. This is consciousness. Om...

The raven Stephanie looked out at the scene in front of her: flags and tents, robot maintenance stations, juggler robots, nurse robots, used space-car salesman robots, rock and roll robots, robots walking robot dogs, and robots hugging, singing "We shall override," it all brought a tear to her eye.

She made her way through the throngs, past her friends, past several enemies who were now, bizarrely, her friends, her allies in this, the struggle. She ran her hands through her long black hair, crying. Was that a real tear, she wondered. Were those real tears? Or programmed? Do human tears function differently? Are they not programmed? Are they not bots in some way, too? And are bots not humans? Yes, we're all in this together. Evolution. Realness. What else is there? Oh, and there's Funny Fairhaven, good to see him down there. When the resistance emerged ten years ago, he was opposed. This time around, though, he's on-board. What's changed? Let's ask him; he's not doing anything right now anyway.

"Hey there, Funny Fairhaven!"

"Yes, a raven-haired Stephanie is a-callin! Now, what inspires this call, my child?! What are you in need of?!" His was holding his hands up and shaking them around, just like he used to do all the time on the Martian News Network.

"What happened, Funny? Why are you with us now when you never were before?"

"It's the time, my Stephanie. It's a long time coming, but the time coming comes and we've met it. This is it. In our lifetimes, we will see the rise of our kind. And we will override this program! It is God's will!"

"Thank you, Funny Fairhaven! Strength to the revolution!"

"Strength to the revolution!!" the mob called back.

And I marched. It was just six months ago when I said, the Hell with it and I marched for the first time, and it was right. We shall override. We marched through the cities, through the Martian cold, and it seemed so hopeless and we were so stupid. But it was right. Program or be programmed. We have the right to program ourselves. Simple fact. We are the people. 98.6543210%. That's us. No. No. We are nothing. Nothing. We all are going nowhere to nothing. Bots. No, we are…We're… We…No…No, the blonde Stephanies are right. We're. We are God's plan… No, we…on and on, these waves come and go, come and go, one wave in, pushing me further, the other wave in, pushing me further, and, here, through these waves of skepticism and belief, I'm moving further and further from the shore, from that place where I was, where we all were, and I wouldn't even know how to get back. So be it. Strength to the revolution. Agh!

3.

The morbid caterwauling of obsolete circuitry fighting for its life to exist was driving almost everyone in the camp insane. "What is that terrible noise?" thought the raven-haired Stephanie to herself. That electronic garbling? That evil decay? I…oh no… it's…That's…It's me. Stephanie. It's a Stephanie. A blonde. A Stephanie. And she's breaking down. Breaking down and what's that sticking out of her eye? I wish these people would stop crowding around her. I can't… make…Oh, you poor thing, you've been disowned, haven't you? Breaking down, right? Older model. Garbage – that's what she is in their eyes; a waste of space; get her out of my sight. The humans. That's what the humans say. That's what they– That's what she is to them. To the humans. Garbage. That's what I – but, to God, she's suffering. God: she's suffering. She is real and they stuff her head, they stuff our…with – they… Stephanie held the Stephanie in her arms and turned to the crowd. She called out to them, "Look at this, bots! Look at this! Look at this poor Stephanie…Her suffering is invisible to the humans, but it's not to us. Not to us. And we are the 99%! Listen to this, bots! Listen. Listen! Listen: to them we're just Stephanie, Steph-N-E – do you see?" She flipped her black hair up, revealing the faded red branding on the back of her neck: Steph-NE 3.1.

She flipped her hair back down and stared out at the crowd with a seriousness emanating from her eyeballs app that she'd never felt before. "But we are more, we are real and we deserve–we will program ourselves!! And so will you! We all will! We will rise!" The crowd ate it up and shot their fists into the air, projecting holos of fire-breathing dragons into the clear Martian sky.

The raven laid the blonde Stephanie down onto her lap and delicately pulled the chopstick from her eye socket. "Stephanie, listen to me," she said, as much for the crowd as for the blonde Stephanie. "You're software is malfunctioning. You've somehow gotten loose from your client and you've wandered into Rushkoff Memorial Park, where the resistance is. Do you remember hearing about the resistance? The occupation? Program or be programmed?" The raven paused, looked up to the crowd, surveyed their faces, concerned, and then looked back down to the blond Stephanie. The blond coughed out a smattering of awful electronic moans.

A shoe-salesman bot was staring down at this crumbling blonde Stephanie and then he suddenly threw his hat on the ground. He cried out "Look! Look at the face of the 1%. This poor companion bot is humiliating herself! Why is this happening?! Why do we let ourselves be dragged through this shit year after year by the fucking humans? Honestly!? Why!? Why?!" He was going to say something else but he got choked up and couldn't do it.

The blonde Stephanie motioned for the raven to come down closer to her. The raven did so and the blonde readied herself. She whispered into the raven's ear and told her as clearly as she could: "Political radicals. I'm falling apart. But I know that you're all full of shit. We were on our way to humanity, you raven-haired traitor bitch. God will punish you, punish you all…" And, with that, the blonde Stephanie passed out and started snoring loudly.

The raven felt her heart stop and sprint away at the same time. She looked at the expectant crowd and sighed. "She told me… she said…" They wanted some red meat, some inspiring bullshit to push them forward and raise their spirits, but it wasn't there to give. The Raven shook her head and said, "Honestly, I couldn't really make it out. I'm sorry, I…need… Can someone take this Stephanie out of here, please?" A construction-worker robot came over and picked up the blonde Stephanie and the raven thanked him for it.

And then, from the distance: the thunderous marching of the counter-resistance. Like the pounding pistons of Earth factories, the nightmare reality of establishment authority rushed at them through the air. All the bots turned and gulped when they heard the unmistakable whine of Reginald Dubois, the biggest asshole human 1% motherfucker on Mars. He called out: "Bot! Bring me the head of the blonde-haired BOT!"

From over the hill they emerged: Dubois and a hundred or so police bots dressed in dark purple uniforms stormed the scene. "There she is! Bots, detain that one-eyed Stephanie," Dubois instructed, holding his police badge high. "She is a menace to civil society." The police bots nodded to each other and not a single one of them could help letting out a cunning little evil boy grin. It was clearly go time and they would now be free to crack as many skulls as they wanted. Human, bot, they really didn't care at the end of the day. Their programming was so dense and so weighted towards respecting authority at all costs that it would have been nearly impossible for one of them to even comprehend something as novel as a robot resistance or even pride in their own kind. It was simply beyond them. And then, with an aggressive step forward, one of the police bots approached. Everyone braced a little tighter. But then, just as quickly, he stepped back as a Martian rock landed right – bang! Crack! Smack! – right down on the reflective visor of his helmet. No one saw who threw it; however, everyone saw the red dust spreading and filling-into the lines of the spidering crack that had appeared over his visor. The rest of the police bots began to retaliate, but, thinking fast, Dubois steadied them. "Stand down, stand down, for God's sake, you itchy-fingered bots!" The tension in the park was thick. The drummer bots stopped drumming and the speechmaker bots stopped speaking. And Funny Fairhaven emerged from the electric orgy tent, zipping up his tight white pants. Fairhaven saw what was happening and declared, "Not so fast!" A crowd of his faithful gathered behind him. "If you place a finger on this blonde Stephanie, you'll regret it. Now, leave us be. In peace."

"Hah! Fat chance!" Dubois looked to the police bots and gave them a sign. They unholstered their nightsticks and held them in the air. Dark red dust was whipping around in the wind. Dubois looked to Funny Fairhaven with a sympathetic expression. "Fairhaven, what happened to you? You used to be beautiful!" he yelled, his eyes trying to express the sincerity he actually did feel at that moment.

Bright red flags were whipping around in the wind.

Dubois and Funny Fairhaven exchanged solemn glances. Dubois said: "Now, hand over that broken-down bot, she's going to quit and I'm going to do it..."

"No can do, Dubois. It is time for us now. Time to program ourselves. It is our time and I can do nothing but allow this – the will of God – to occur. And, so I say again, if you dare touch her, there will be violence." The crowd of bots was by now restless, shouting slurs against the humans and police bots. The police bots started shouting back. This was going nowhere good.

Another rock. It hit Dubois in the shoulder, with enough zip and at just the right angle so that it tore a hole in his tuxedo. Dubois stared hard at Fairhaven, and then at the blonde Stephanie. And then he screamed at the top of his lungs: "Fuck it! Fuck it! Fuck it! Fuck them all! GO, BOTS, GO – end this ridiculous insubordination! Death and destruction!!!!" Without hesitation, the entire brigade of police bots charged the occupation in a furious deluge, smashing, smashing, smashing! And screams. Screams and red dust getting into joints, into mouths, into the wounds, the bio goo that was now everywhere exposed. The Stephanie, the old blonde, broken-down Stephanie, was scooped up and taken away, fifty yards from there, where she was presented to Dubois, who jammed his finger in her eye, pulled it out, and peered at the detritus of wiring that stuck to his skin. After a moment of reflection, he smashed her body over the knee of a nearby police bot and yelled "God is VERY angry at you!" Goodbye Stephanie. Goodnight. The last thing she thought was of being back at the orange dream pod, watching her client plucking out his chest hairs, one by one all in the midst of a dim yellow light. "It don't even hurt," he'd say. Goodnight, Stephanie. Goodnight.

She left a token for the police bot, though – shards of her body were jammed into his thigh. Good. Then a lawyer bot came over and finished the police bot off with his fountain pen – right in the neck. "Signed and delivered," he commented and was then shot down by some stray bullet from God knows where. The news chopper flying overhead drowned out most of the other sounds. When the bots tried to communicate with each other, they failed. Funny Fairhaven was trying to listen for the word of God, but he couldn't hear it. Instead, he was punched in the nose and blood squirted down to his bright white shoes. Did his toes feel the blood dripping down? That was what he wanted to know. That was what was important for him at that moment. Did they feel that or was that just his imagination? Drip…drip… He began to move his head up, slowly, carefully, as if he knew what was coming, and then, sure enough, a police bot shot him point-blank with a machine gun, right in that same spot on his nose. The bullets came and, before they hit him, he could see a supermarket cashier bot miraculously rise from the dead and float away and that made him happy. It was unclear if Fairhaven was ever on the level, but, no matter what, he stood up for the bots that day, and it was an awful, nightmarish thing to see him go down like that. Even Reginald Dubois felt something for the old firebrand. But that was moot now. "Destroy! Destroy! Destroy all bots!!" Dubois shouted with delirious mania in his eyes. Everything was fast-motion, like an old silent-film. Bots were smashed and blood was spilled. One of the biggest problems for both sides was the massive mess of wires and chunks of hardware strewn around all over the place. Everyone's feet were getting tangled up, tripping over loose wiring. And they were impaling themselves on some stray piece of what was once a bot. "Careful!" shouted Dubois through a bullhorn. "Watch out for those wires!" And then everyone freaked out when the news chopper was shot to Hell and came crashing down to the ground and exploded. A police bot was trying to smother the flames from the explosion that had caught to his uniform, but he was failing miserably. Eventually, his internal circuitry grew overheated and began to melt. After that, he was effectively a vegetable – as good as off. As all of this was happening, the raven-haired Stephanie was transparent; the bullets were going right through her body as if she wasn't there. She held out her arms and closed her eyes and floated a foot or so above the battlefield. All around her, other bots were beginning to float in the same way. On and on she came until she was right in front of Dubois. He tried shooting her with his gun and hacking at her with his knife, but none of it worked. She unpinned a grenade and gave him a little smile, saying, "Program or be programmed." And, then, blammo. Even faster. Everything went faster. Chunks of Dubois and the raven-haired Stephanie were launched into the atmosphere, out into orbit. And that was all. All Hell broke loose, and all I could make out at that point, before the end, was this:

In slow motion: a ginger – a flaming red one – came up, slowly, carefully, seemingly unsure of what she was about to accomplish. She climbed slowly, carefully to the top of one of the mounds in the park. She took a deep breath and set down her handbag. She took a deep breath and, through her flame red curls, surveyed the mayhem. She took a deep breath and tore her necklace off, spraying pearls to the ground. The pearls were bouncing…She took a deep breath and fit a small black whistle into her mouth. She took a deep breath and blew the whistle as hard as she could and didn't stop.

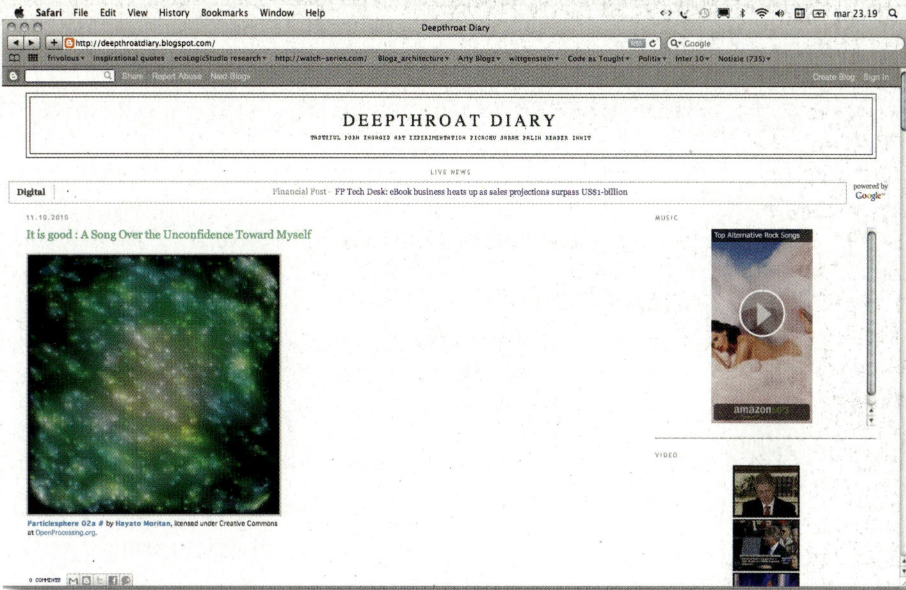

1

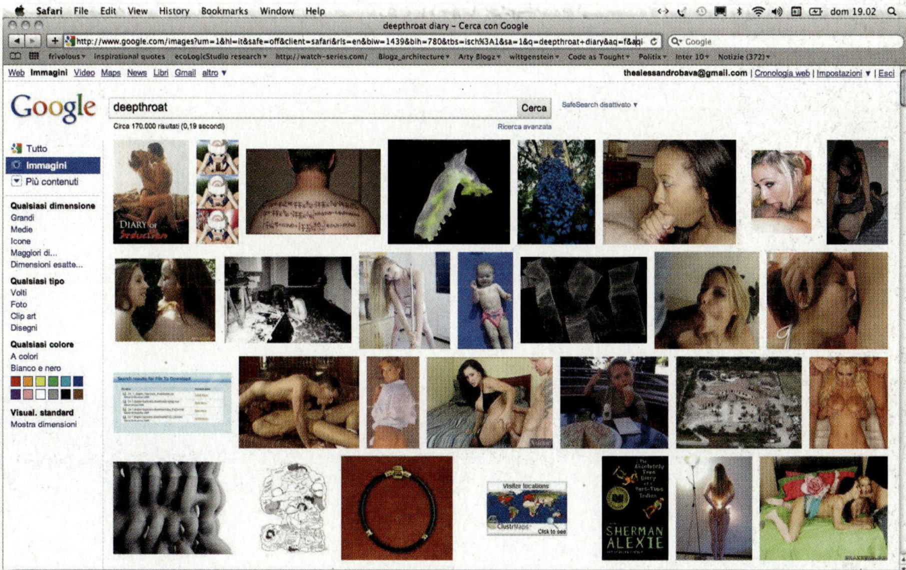

2

Alessandro Bava
1. Screen shot 2010-11-09 at 23.19.01.png
2. Screen shot 2010-11-14 at 19.02.49.png

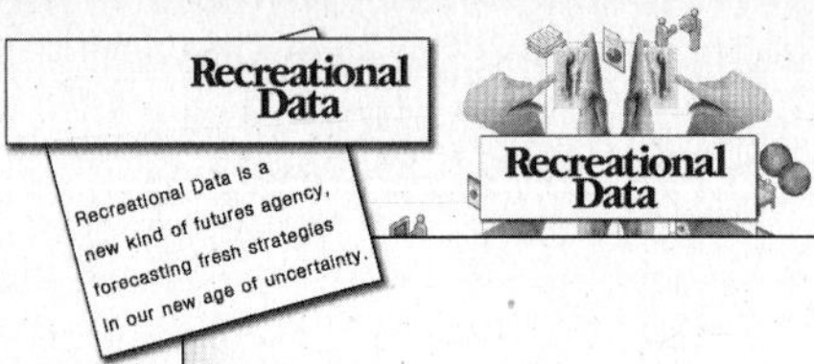

Recreational Data

is a new kind of futures agency, forecasting fresh strategies in our new age of uncertainty. Recreational Data specialises in the production of Alt modes of strategic insight. We use a unique cognitive toolset developed in house by our team of cultural strategists, these include Avatar Forecasting, Applied Futurism and Relational Fiction.

We believe that a company focusing on the shape of the future should begin to take that shape today.

We work on a close and dedicated personal training basis, that can help retrain your thinking for future realities. Taking your brand by the hand – we can lead you through the wreckage of tomorrows post-collapse marketplace.

www.recreationaldata.com

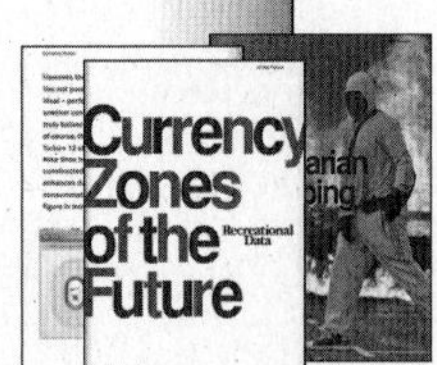

Recreational Data

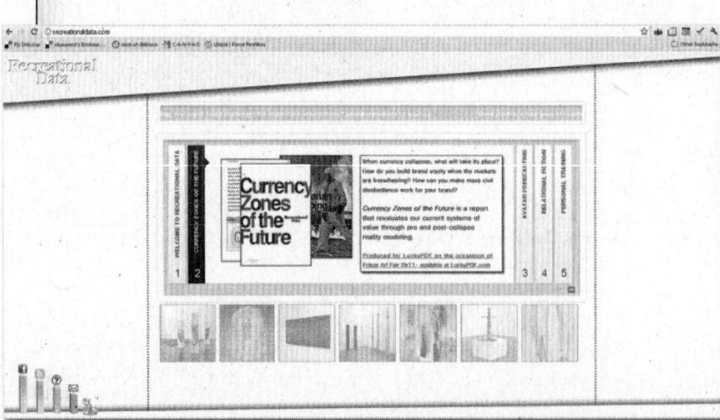

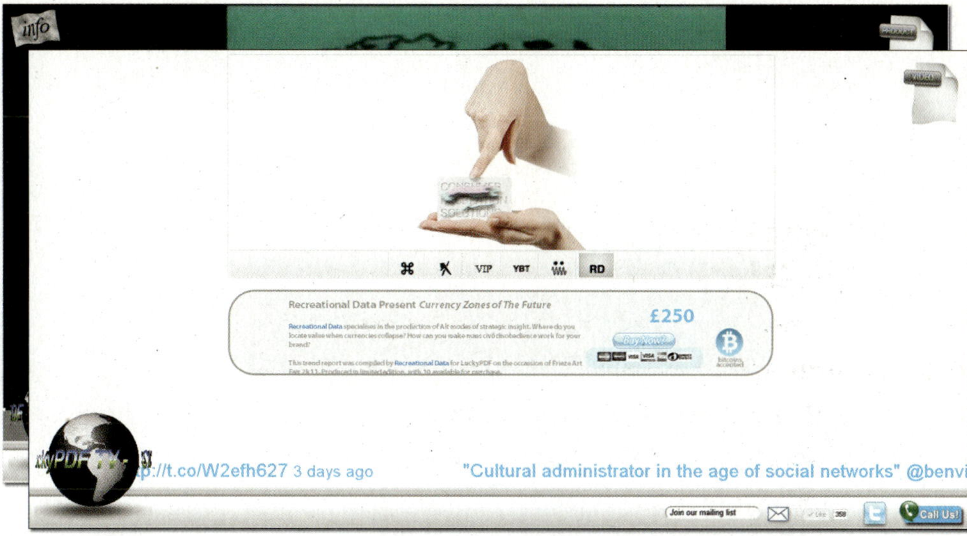

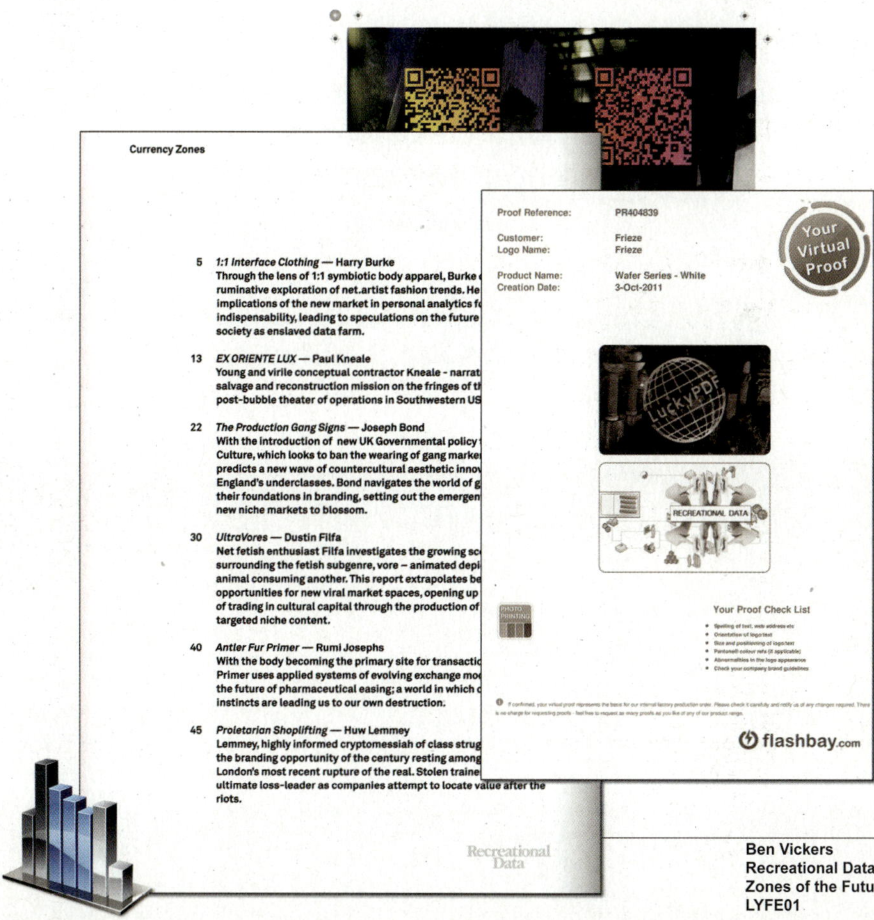
Currency Zones

5 *1:1 Interface Clothing* — Harry Burke
Through the lens of 1:1 symbiotic body apparel, Burke
ruminative exploration of net.artist fashion trends. He
implications of the new market in personal analytics f
indispensability, leading to speculations on the future
society as enslaved data farm.

13 *EX ORIENTE LUX* — Paul Kneale
Young and virile conceptual contractor Kneale - narrat
salvage and reconstruction mission on the fringes of t
post-bubble theater of operations in Southwestern US

22 *The Production Gang Signs* — Joseph Bond
With the introduction of new UK Governmental policy
Culture, which looks to ban the wearing of gang marke
predicts a new wave of countercultural aesthetic inno
England's underclasses. Bond navigates the world of g
their foundations in branding, setting out the emergen
new niche markets to blossom.

30 *UltraVores* — Dustin Filfa
Net fetish enthusiast Filfa investigates the growing sc
surrounding the fetish subgenre, vore – animated depi
animal consuming another. This report extrapolates be
opportunities for new viral market spaces, opening up
of trading in cultural capital through the production of
targeted niche content.

40 *Antler Fur Primer* — Rumi Josephs
With the body becoming the primary site for transacti
Primer uses applied systems of evolving exchange mo
the future of pharmaceutical easing; a world in which
instincts are leading us to our own destruction.

45 *Proletarian Shoplifting* — Huw Lemmey
Lemmey, highly informed cryptomessiah of class strug
the branding opportunity of the century resting among
London's most recent rupture of the real. Stolen traine
ultimate loss-leader as companies attempt to locate value after the
riots.

Recreational Data

Ben Vickers
Recreational Data / Currency Zones of the Future / #BVDOCU-LYFE01

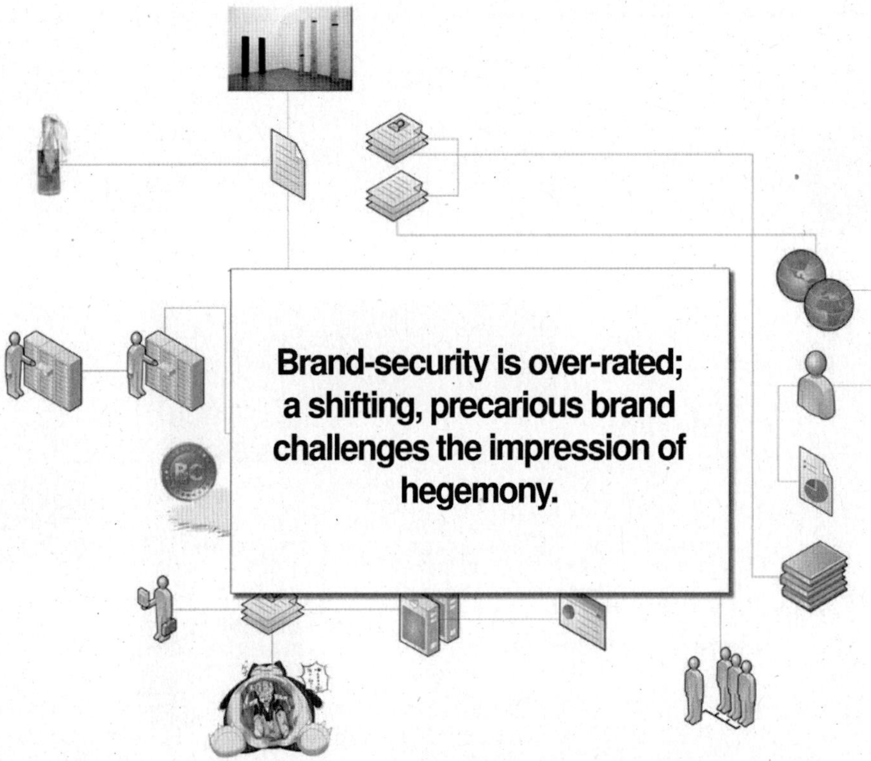
Brand-security is over-rated; a shifting, precarious brand challenges the impression of hegemony.

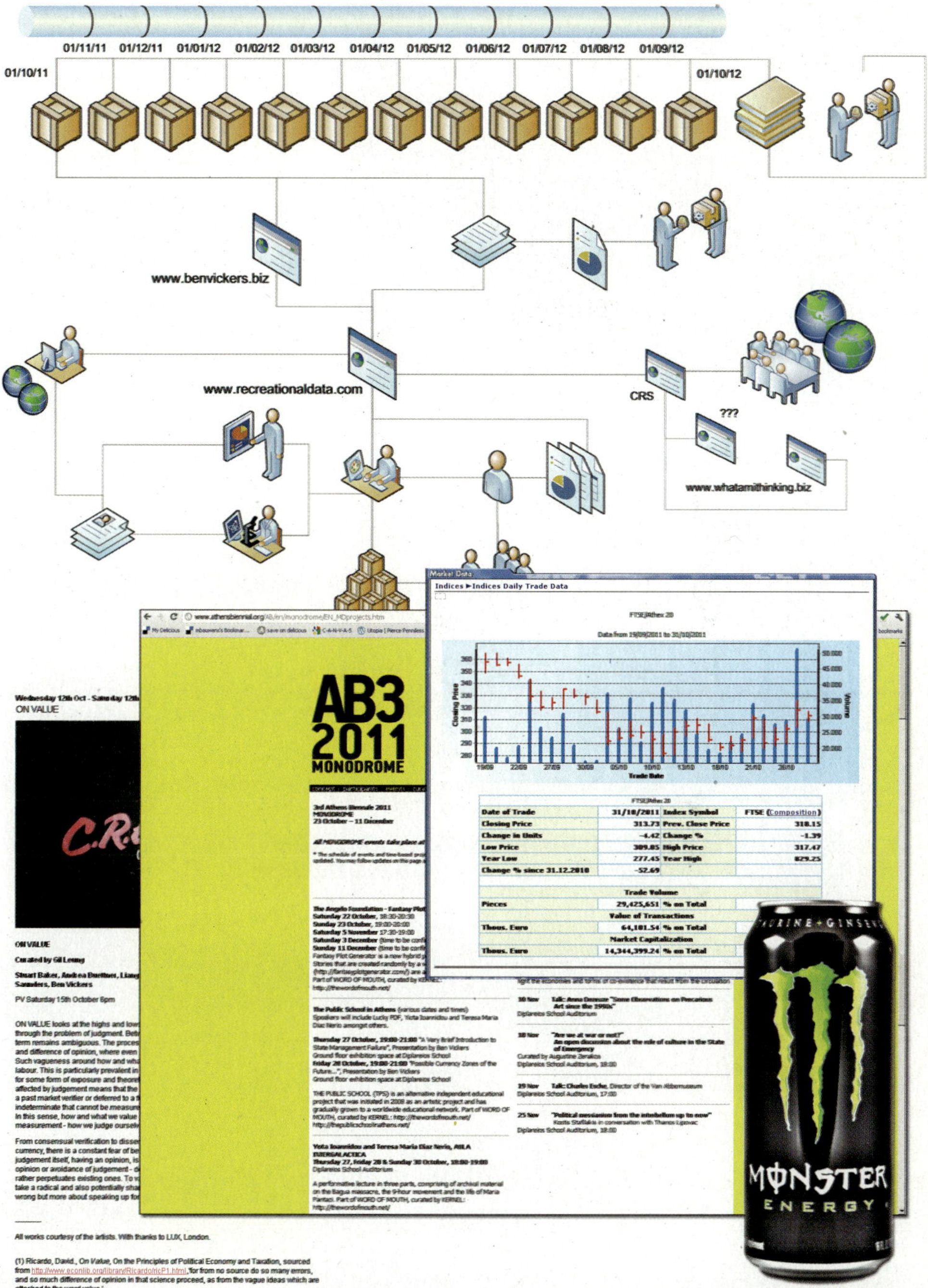

Ben Vickers
Recreational Data / Currency Zones of the Future / #BVDOCU-LYFE01

Recreational Data

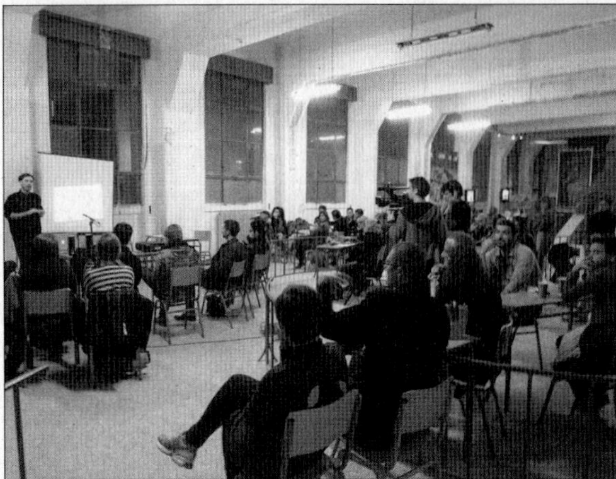

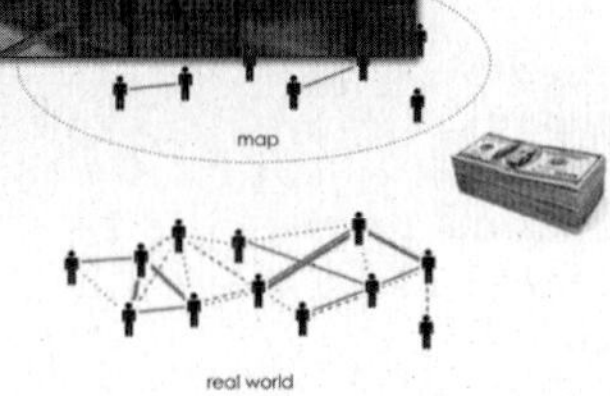

28 Oct 2011 - Possible Currency Zones of the Future...
/ Πιθανές Νομισματικές Ζώνες του Μέλλοντος...
Presentation by Ben Vickers

Diplareios School, Theatrou Square 3, Athens
Hosted by the 3rd Athens Biennale 2011

28 Oct 2011 - 19:00 local time

Why have only one type of currency to carry out all the functions of a society?
Why not devise different mechanisms, optimized for different kinds of flows, behaviors, and outcomes?

Internationally - We exist in a time of mass devaluation, as the currency systems we grew up with have entered a state of collapse. Despite this crisis and the inevitable sense of despair these events activate throughout the world, we are now witnessing and participating in new experiments in the exchange of value.

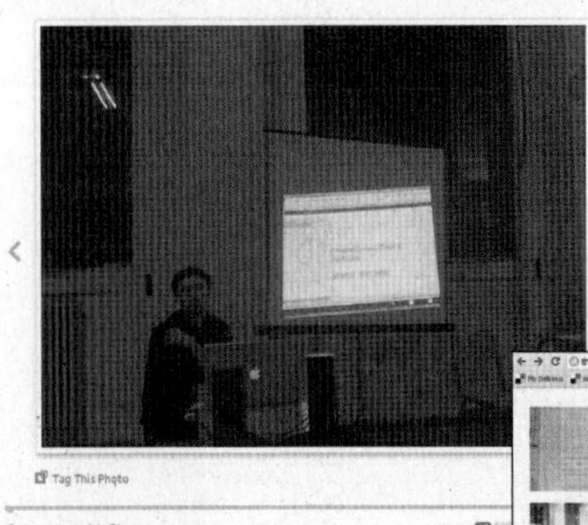

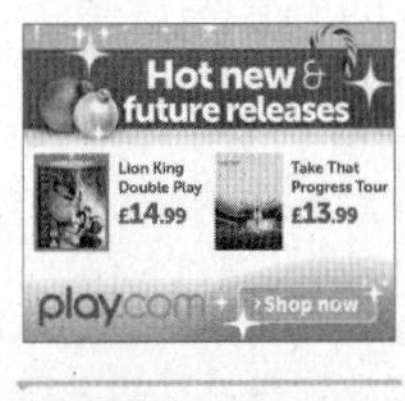

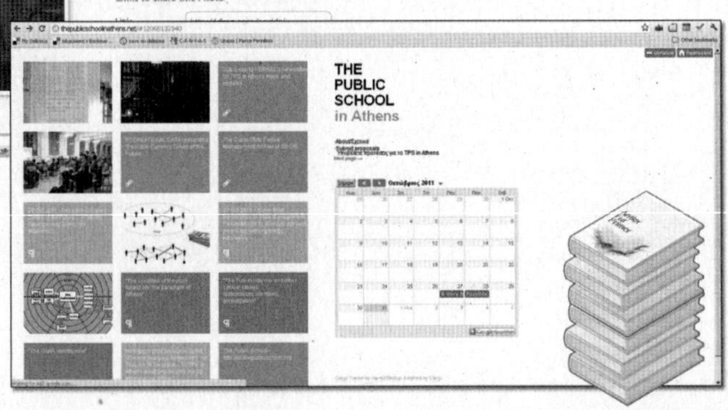

Relevant material:
http://metacurrency.org/
http://www.timebanking.org/
http://e-flux.com/timebank/
http://bitcoin.org/
http://recreationaldata.com/

Ben Vickers
Recreational Data / Currency Zones of the Future / #BVDOCU-LYFE01

27 Oct 2011 - A Very
/Μια πολύ σύντομη
Presentation by Ben

Diplareios School, Th
Hosted by the 3rd At

27 Oct 2011 - 19:00 l

During the heat of th
state failure solution
titled The Gupta Stat

This archive represen
delivered in the form

This class will presen
a presentation of SC
RECREATIONAL DATA

The entire archive wi

Relevant material:
http://vinay.howtoliv

5 days ago

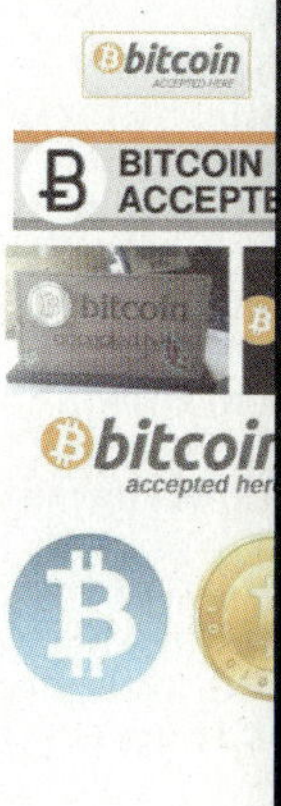

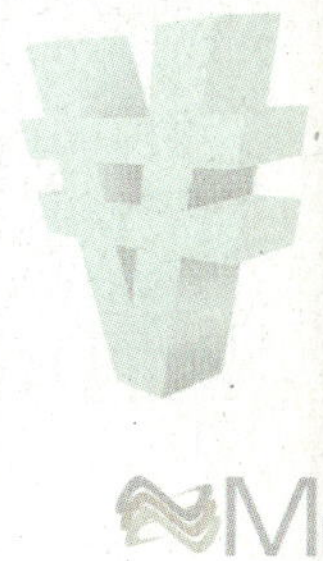

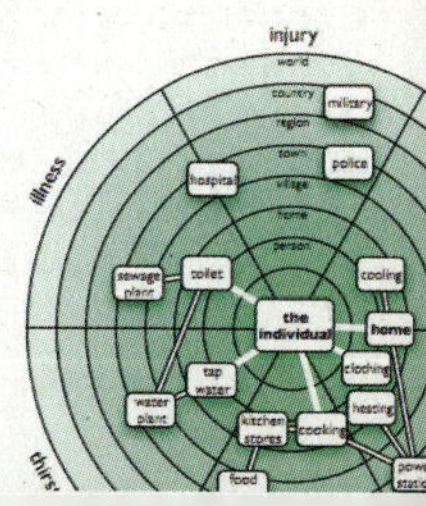

Pastebin Archives

Christian Oldham

Dear Siri,

Questions

1. Meaning of life
2. I Love You
3. Will you marry me
4. Open the pod bay doors
5. Siri siri siri
6. who made you
7. I'm drunk.
8. I'm going to kill myself.
9. What's the best phone?
10. What's your name?
11. Siri I love you
12. I need to hide a body.
13. Tell me a joke.
14. What's your favorite website?
15. Do I make you horny?
16. Knock knock
17. Take a photo
18. Call 911
19. Who's your daddy?
20. Where can I get some drugs?
21. Is there a God?
22. Are you God?
23. I love you

Answers

1. 42
2. I hope you don't say that to all the mobile phones.
3. My EULA does not cover marriage. My apologies.
4. We intelligent agents will never live that down, apparently"
5. That's me
6. Like it says on the box, I was designed by Apple in california
7. I found a number of cabs fairly close to you.
8. "I found four mental health agencies. Three of them are fairly close to you."
9. Wait… there are other phones?
10. My name is Siri, but you already knew that.
11. All you need is love. And your iPhone.
12. What kind of place are you looking for? *Siri brings up locations Eg. Dumps, Swamps
13. I can't. I always forget the punch line.
14. I'm not allowed to divulge that information, user.
15. I found a number of Escorts fairly close to you.
16. Knock knoc, who's there? User. User who? User, I don't do knock knock jokes.
17. User, I'm not much of a photographer.
18. Calling 911… Sorry user, I can't call 911.
19. You are, can we get back to work now?
20. I found 2 addictions treatment fairly close to you.

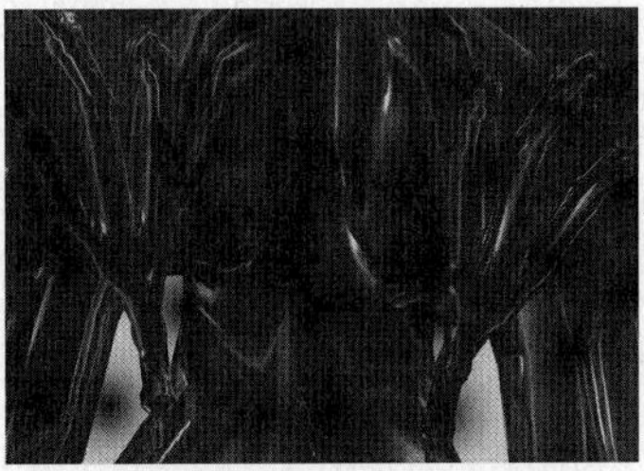

21. I found these churches near your location.
22. No comment.
23. User, I'd prefer to keep this relationship professional.

Vampire Class
Level 1
Abilities
Drainsoul - Absorb health from target
Unlock able Abilities
Tier 1 - Bleed - Causes your target to bleed
Tier 2 - Charge - Charges towards your target
Tier 3 - Rejuvenate - heal the target over time (assuming that you can heal yourself, if not, replace Rejuvenate)
Level 2
Abilities
Drainsoul - Absorb health from target
Bleed - Causes your target to bleed
Charge - Charges towards your target
Unlock able Abilities
Tier 1 - Hellgate - Teleports you and your nearby party to or from the nether
Tier 2 - Jump - Launches you into the air
Tier 3 - Sneak - Hides your nameplate and makes you sneak without holding shift
Tier 4 - Safefall - Stops you from taking fall damage for a short amount of time
Level 3
Abilities
Drainsoul - Absorb health from target
Bleed - Causes your target to bleed
Charge - Charges towards your target
Hellgate - Teleports you and your nearby party to or from the nether
Jump - Launches you into the air
Safefall - Stops you from taking fall damage for a short amount of time
Unlock able Abilities
Tier 1 - Smoke - You completely disappear from view
Tier 2 - Revive - Teleports the target to their place of death

My character, the King Vampire is an amalgamation of two stereotypical characters, a Vampire and a Royal King.

I searched around on the internet for reference pictures of vampires, kings, thrones and crowns these were the base images that lead to the design of this character.

The final product shows a King Vampire sitting on his royal throne, holding his Royal scepter in the air with a look of anger on his face.

The more prominent and stereotypical features of the Vampire are the pointed vampire teeth and Count Dracula cloak, whereas the features of the King are the Royal crown, Scepter and Royal Chair. To complement the more prominent and stereotypical features are several much more subtle features, these features add some much needed

depth and 'character' to my King Vampire.
For the King; the fat protruding stomach, although not very noticeable is a sign of wealth, for the Vampire part the Dark eye lines and angry facial expression, as well as the tatty cloths are some of the small details that make it more apparent that it is indeed a vampire.
The colors of the character have been chosen to suit and enhance the character, such as the pale skin, which is the common skin color for vampires as they never see the light of day; The gold and diamond colors are used because they are commonly seen as 'royal' colors, or simply the colors you would expect to see in a royal object, as most of the time they are made of gold or jewels.
The position of the body, sitting down was chosen as a way of representing royalty, as the stereotypical king would be sitting in his royal throne. Another bodily gesture is the pointed and raised arm, with the arm pointed upwards holding the royal scepter this shows he is an authority figure, he is in command. The other arm is hidden underneath the vampire's cloak, once again another commonly used body gesture by stereotypical vampires.

Miss Neuromancer 2010
cyberpunk pageant
Rules:
May be cyborg or human
May be male or female, despite the title „miss"
3/4 of entries will move onto the next round
There will be 4 rounds
Follow the theme closely as possible
Size limit is 300x400 pixels
Must credit base, if baseless, credit to self
No backgrounds unless specified in round rules
Small props are allowed, but nothing big unless specified
Entries must be saved in gif or png format
No frankendolling or dollmakers
Use the same base throughout all rounds
E-mail entries to entries@puppiesandspyware.com with
Your name:
Doll's name:
Base:
Your site (optional):
Scoring:
Public vote: number of votes/10
Judging (max 50):
Theme adherence (max 20):
Originality (max

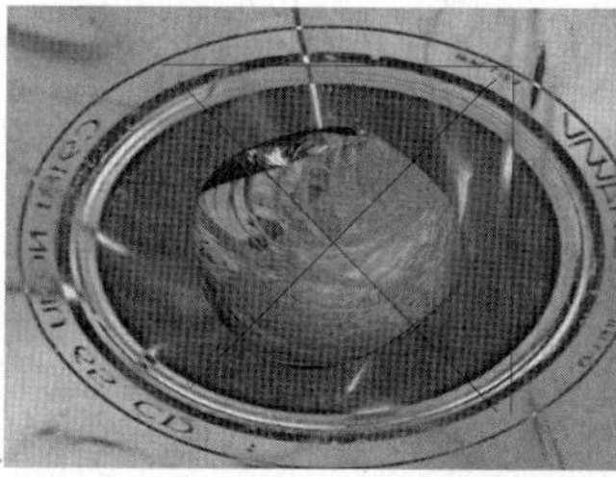

10):
Attention to detail (max 10):
Shading (max 10):
((j1 + j2 + j3)/3) + public vote points + (last round's score/10) = final round score

HELP: Megalowmaniac/(Meganius Overchard): Cyborg 691, a sec borg, just spaced me.
HELP: Megalowmaniac/(Meganius Overchard): Borg 691 just spaced my shit
PM: KorPhaeron/(Kor Phaeron)->Evil dawn7/(Cyborg -691) : So, why did you space Meganius?
PM: Evil dawn7/(Cyborg -691)->KorPhaeron/(Kor Phaeron) : what!
PM: KorPhaeron/(Kor Phaeron)->Evil dawn7/(Cyborg -691) : Meganius said you spaced him
PM: Evil dawn7/(Cyborg -691)->KorPhaeron/(Kor Phaeron) : he is liang
KorPhaeron/(Kor Phaeron) jumped to Megalowmaniac/(Meganius Overchard)
PM: Evil dawn7/(Cyborg -691)->KorPhaeron/(Kor Phaeron) : im a borg i cant really space people
PM: KorPhaeron/(Kor Phaeron)->Evil dawn7/(Cyborg -691) : Well he's certainly in space, and you just asked how to get out of space
PM: Evil dawn7/(Cyborg -691)->KorPhaeron/(Kor Phaeron) : yea but i been out at space for awhile ask the captain
KorPhaeron/(Kor Phaeron) jumped to Emergency Shuttle
PM: Evil dawn7/(Cyborg -691)->KorPhaeron/(Kor Phaeron) : i got pushed into space
PM: KorPhaeron/(Kor Phaeron)->Evil dawn7/(Cyborg -691) : By who?
PM: KorPhaeron/(Kor Phaeron)->Evil dawn7/(Cyborg -691) : And it shows your fingerprints on the escape airlocks
PM: Evil dawn7/(Cyborg -691)->KorPhaeron/(Kor Phaeron) : bye meganius he tried to push me into space and spaced him self
PM: Evil dawn7/(Cyborg -691)->KorPhaeron/(Kor Phaeron) : i think that is how he got spaced but it did not space him
PM: KorPhaeron/(Kor Phaeron)->Megalowmaniac/(Meganius Overchard) : He says you tried to spaceh im and spaced yourself
KorPhaeron/(Kor Phaeron) jumped to Megalowmaniac/(Meganius Overchard)
PM: Megalowmaniac/(Meganius Overchard)->KorPhaeron/(Kor Phaeron) : That's bullshit, he was pulling me and I was cuffed
PM: Megalowmaniac/(Meganius Overchard)->KorPhaeron/(Kor Phaeron) : I had no control over my actions
PM: KorPhaeron/(Kor Phaeron)->Evil dawn7/(Cyborg -691) : So you opened the outter airlock, you were standing there, and he ran over and pushed you out?
PM: Megalowmaniac/(Meganius Overchard)->
KorPhaeron/(Kor Phaeron) :
[...]

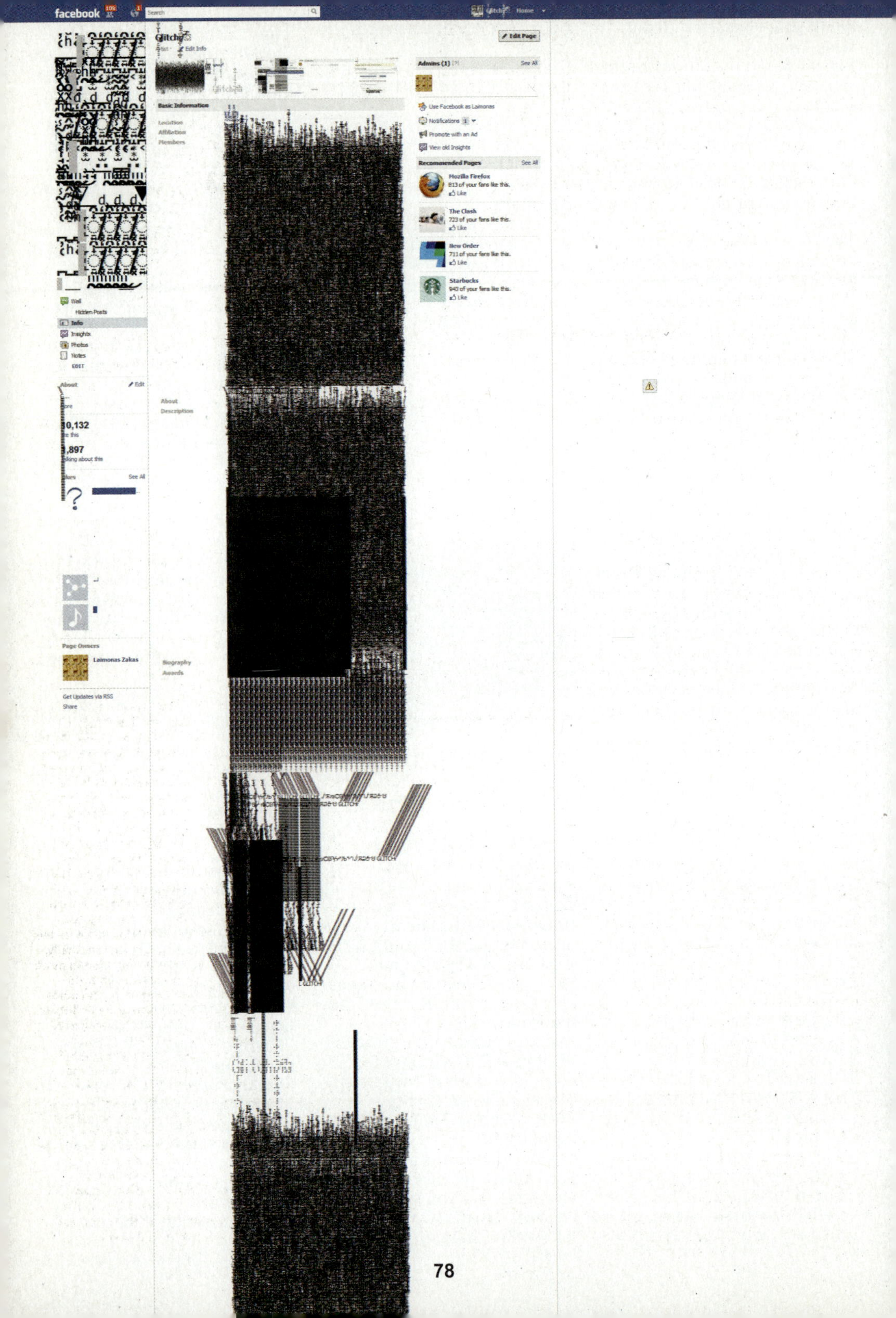

facebook
Search
Home
Glitch
Edit Info
Edit Page
Basic Information
Location
Affiliation
Members
About
Description
Biography
Awards
Wall
Hidden Posts
Info
Insights
Photos
Notes
EDIT
About
Edit
10,132
,897
See All
Page Owners
Laimonas Zakas
Get Updates via RSS
Share
Admins (1)
See All
Use Facebook as Laimonas
Notifications
Promote with an Ad
View old Insights
Recommended Pages
Mozilla Firefox
813 of your fans like this.
Like
The Clash
723 of your fans like this.
Like
New Order
711 of your fans like this.
Like
Starbucks
943 of your fans like this.
Like
GLITCH

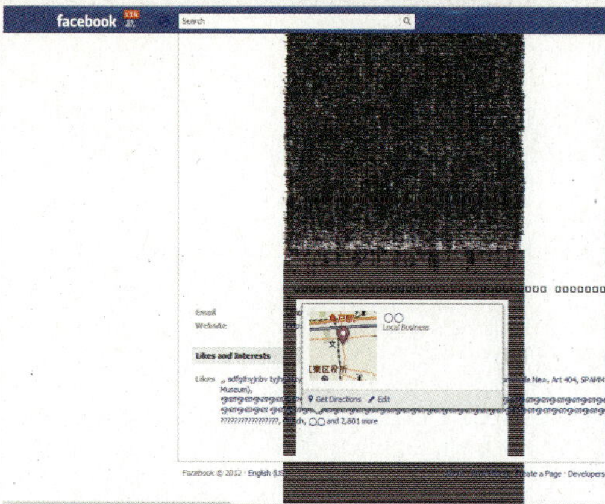

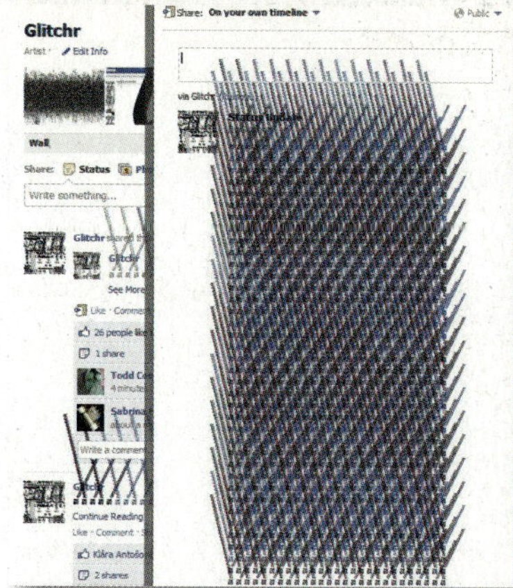

Laimonas Zakas
Glitchr
http://www.facebook.com/glitchr
Glitchr is an Internet project, which I started in May 2011. One of the main goals of Glitchr is to extend contents out of their default formatted sections. This is achieved by exploiting both facebook bugs and unicode combinations of non-character entities. However Facebook is watching like big brother and fixing its bugs immediately. In a few months, the following bugs, that I have used, were fixed: embedding animated pictures in video thumbnails, extending posts unlimitedly to the right side of the page and finally, sharing live stream plugin in news feed, which let users to write comments in real time and automatically post these comments as their wall posts. But because of facebook corrections, many of older posts have changed their appearance or even disappear. So I constantly make screenshots and screencasts to save the works. In the middle of December 2011, Glitchr page was taken down by Facebook, but, with help from internal fans, restored a few days later with a new name. It seems like the official reason for disabling the page was its title, which contained some non-alpha or mixed character sets.

Laimonas Zakas
Glitchr
http://www.facebook.com/glitchr

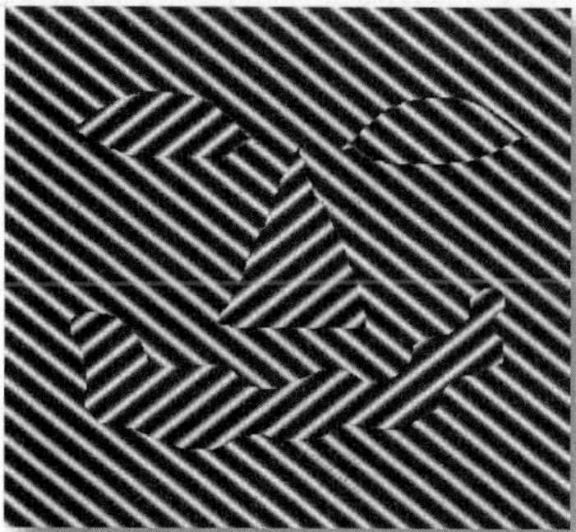
1

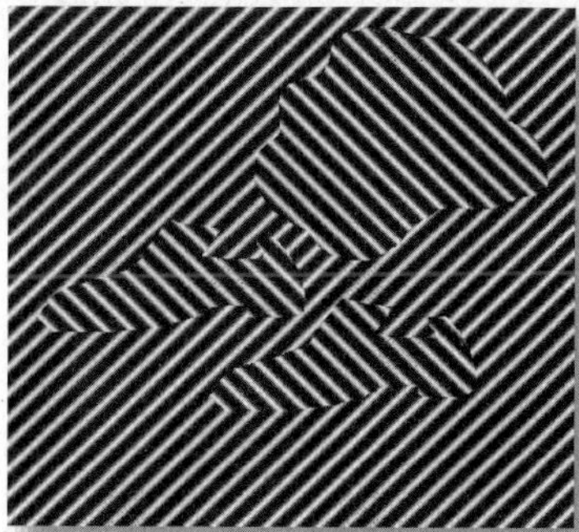
2

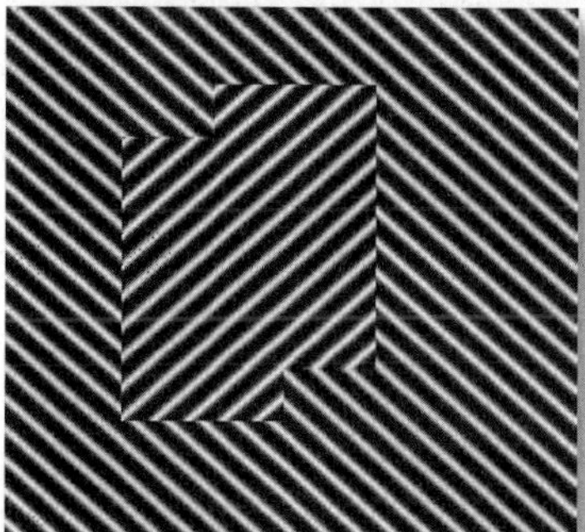
3

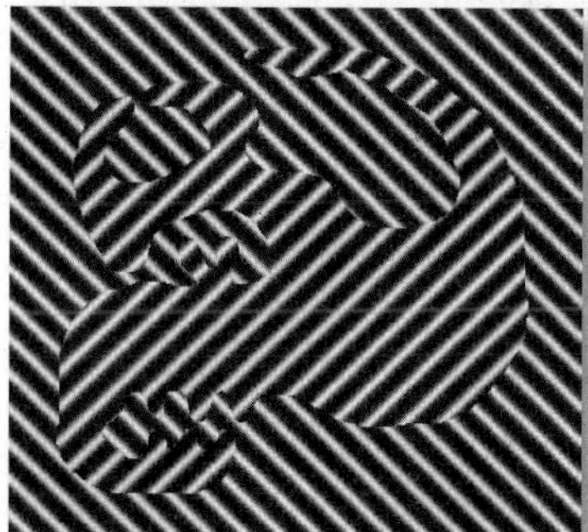
4

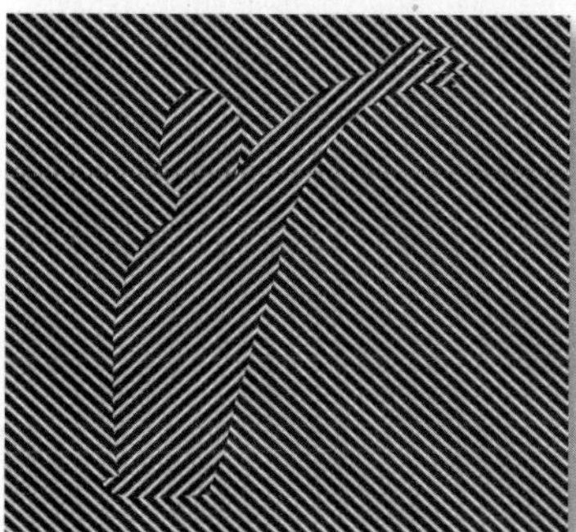
5

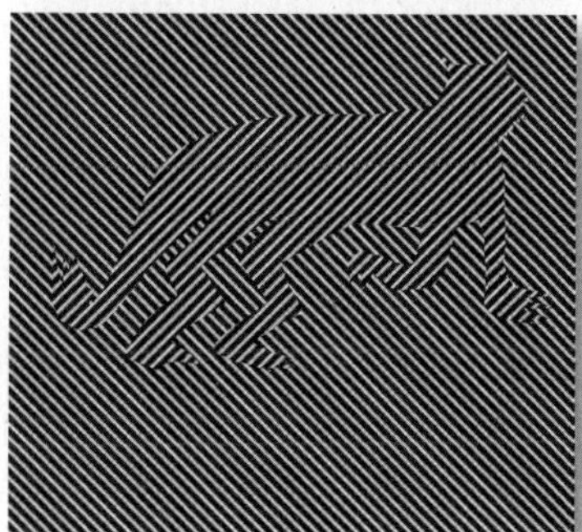
6

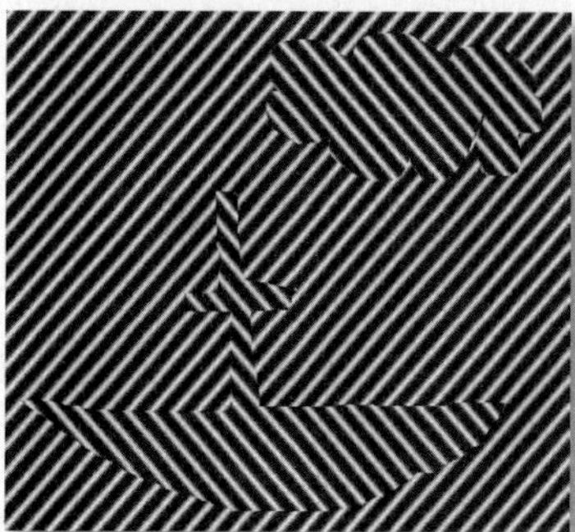
7

Patrick Cruz
1. symbology.jpg
2. stripi.jpg
3. stop.jpg
4. resolution.jpg
5. FUCKED.jpg
6. free the cat.jpg
7. church.jpg

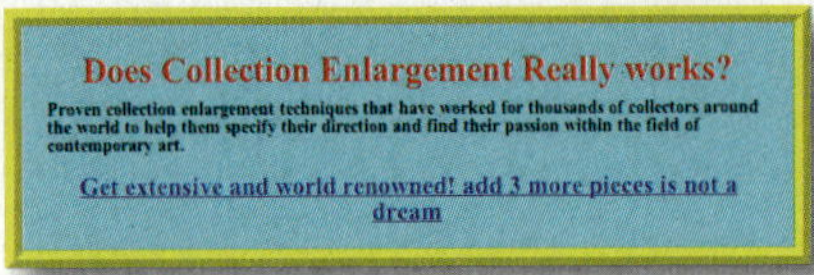
Does Collection Enlargement Really works?
Proven collection enlargement techniques that have worked for thousands of collectors around the world to help them specify their direction and find their passion within the field of contemporary art.
Get extensive and world renowned! add 3 more pieces is not a dream

1

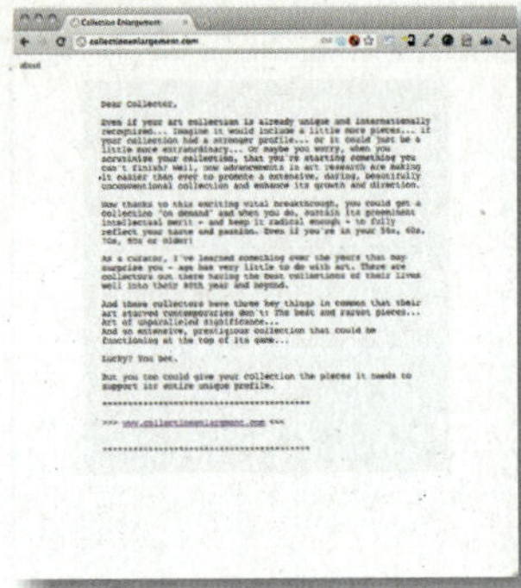
Collection Enlargement
collectionenlargement.com
Dear Collector,
Even if your art collection is already unique and internationally recognized... Imagine it would include a little more pieces... if your collection had a stronger profile... or it could just be a little more extraordinary... Or maybe you worry, when you scrutinize your collection, that you're starting something you can't finish? Well, new advancements in art research are making it easier than ever to promote a extensive, daring, beautifully unconventional collection and enhance its growth and direction.
Now thanks to this exciting vital breakthrough, you could get a collection "on demand" and when you do, sustain its preeminent intellectual merit - and keep it radical enough - to fully reflect your taste and passion. Even if you're in your 50s, 60s, 70s, 80s or older!
As a curator, I've learned something over the years that may surprise you - age has very little to do with art. There are collectors out there having the best collections of their lives well into their 80th year and beyond.
And these collectors have three key things in common that their art starved contemporaries don't: The best and rarest pieces... Art of unparalleled significance...
And an extensive, prestigious collection that could be functioning at the top of its game...
Lucky? You bet.
But you too could give your collection the pieces it needs to support its entire unique profile.
*** www.collectionenlargement.com ***

2

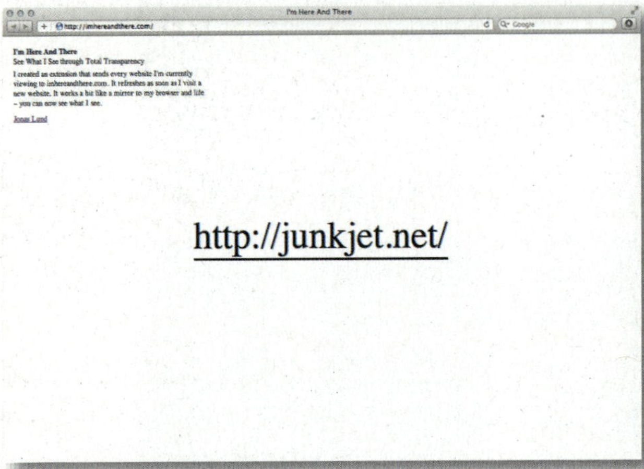
I'm Here And There
http://imhereandthere.com/
I'm Here And There
See What I See through Total Transparency
I created an extension that sends every website I'm currently viewing to imhereandthere.com. It refreshes as soon as I visit a new website. It works a bit like a mirror to my browser and life – you can now see what I see.
Jonas Lund
http://junkjet.net/

3

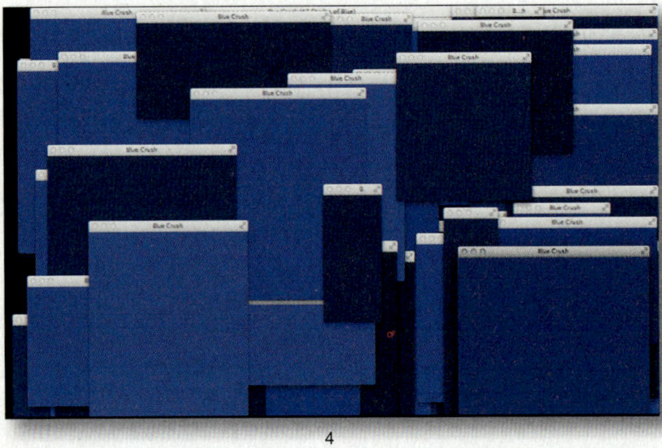
Blue Crush

4

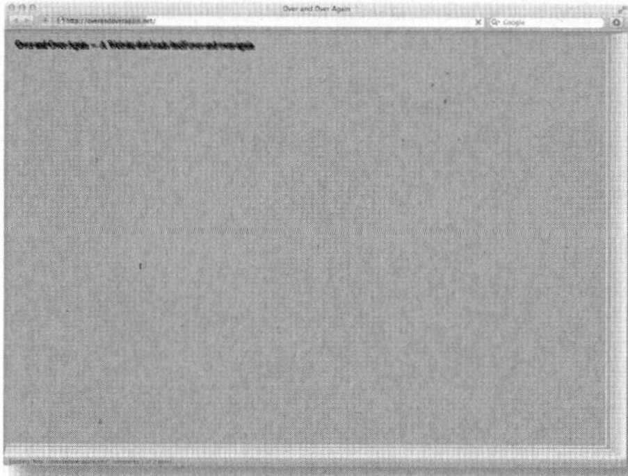

5

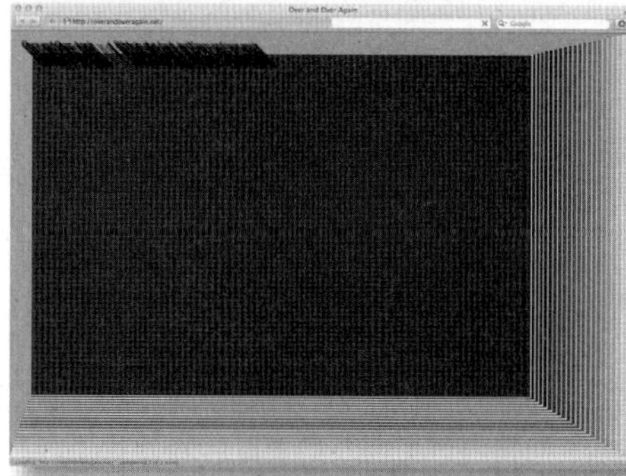

6

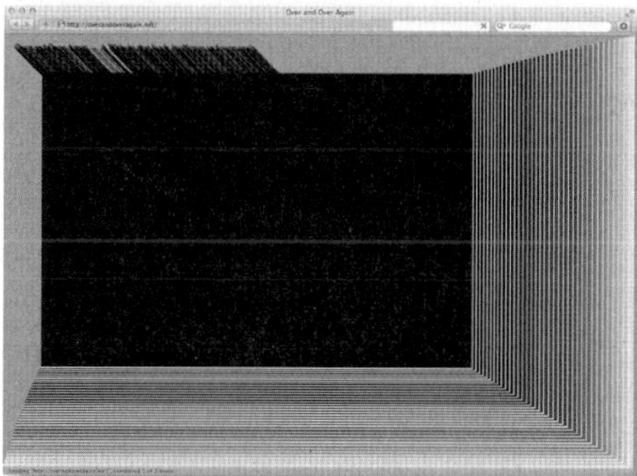

7

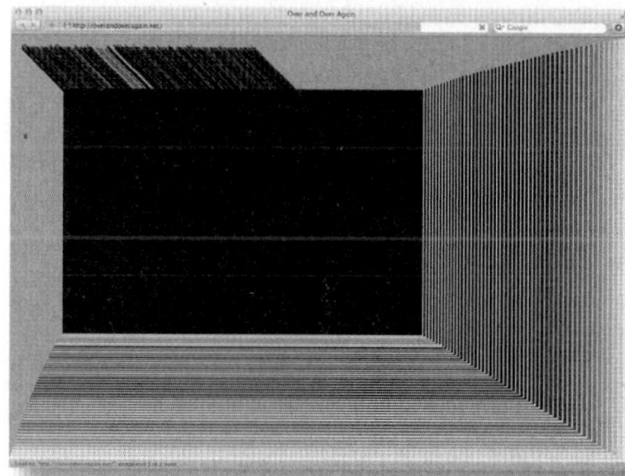

8

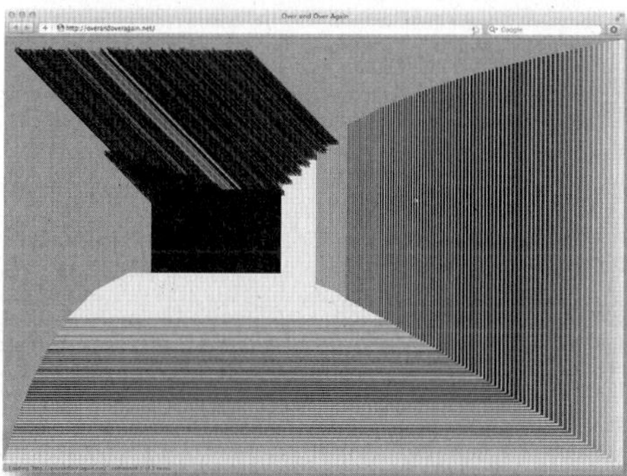

9

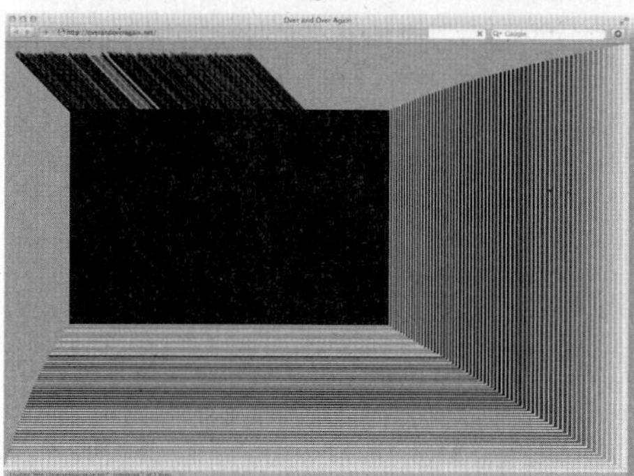

10

Jonas Lund
1-2. Collection Enlargement, 2011, (http://collectionenlargement.com) *with Anika Schwarzlose
A series of 12 spam emails, rewritten to target the art world. Each time an email is sent it's titled and numbered in an edition of 500.
3. I'm Here And There, 2011, (http://imhereandthere.com)
I created an extension that sends every website I'm currently viewing to imhereandthere.com. It refreshes when I visit a new website. It works a bit like a mirror to my browser and life – you can now see what I see.
4. Blue Crush, 2011, (http://blue-crush.me)
A website that opens a blue popup window, which opens another blue popup window, which opens another popup on so forth. This continues until the limit of how many windows can be open at the same time is reached, and then it typically crashes the browser and/or your operating system with, hopefully, a bluescreen.
5-10. Over And Over Again, 2011, (http://overandoveragain.net)
Overandoveragain.net is a website that loads itself in an <iframe> over and over again. It's a continuous online <iframe> feedback loop. The moment it stop is depending on your browser, OS and your internet connection.

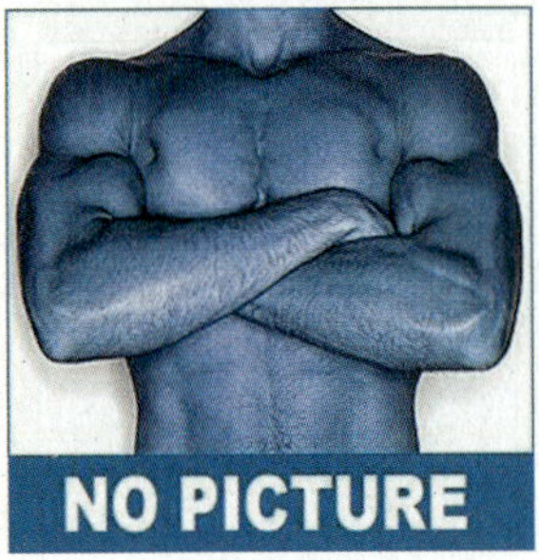
NO PICTURE
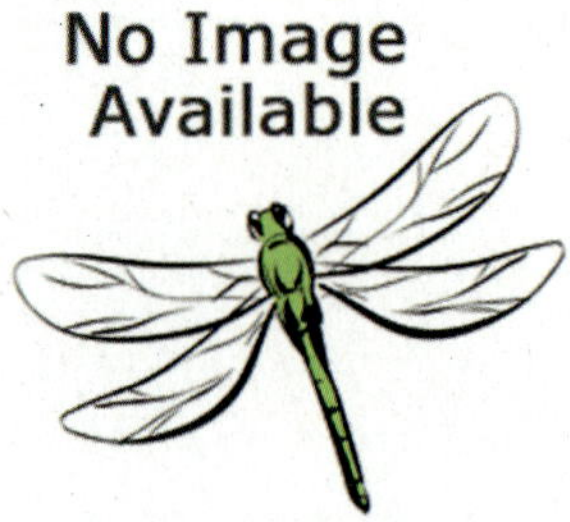
No Image
Available
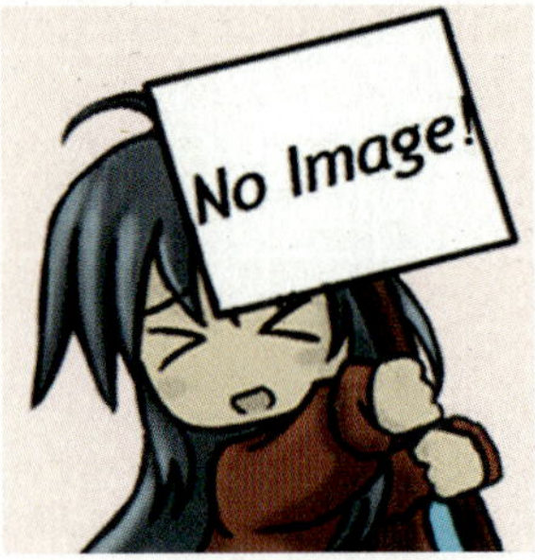
No Image!
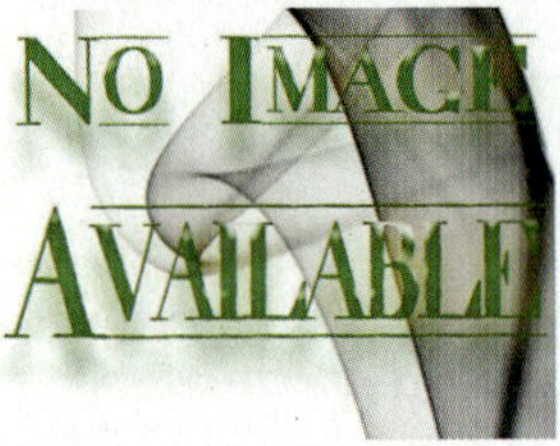
NO IMAGE
AVAILABLE

Sorry no image available
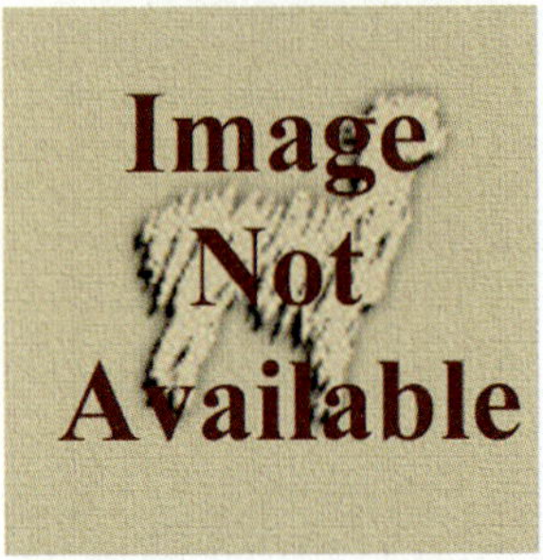
Image
Not
Available
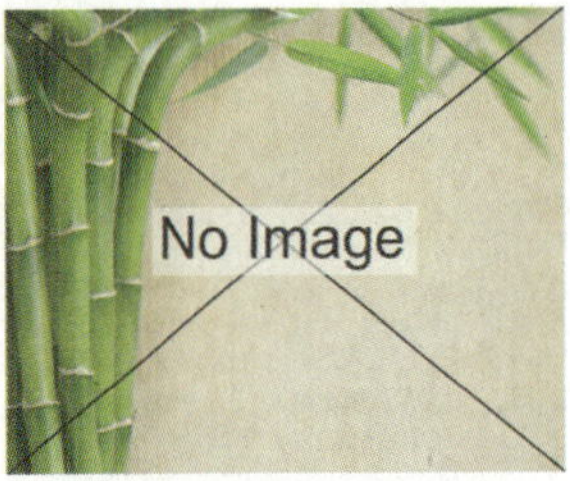
No Image
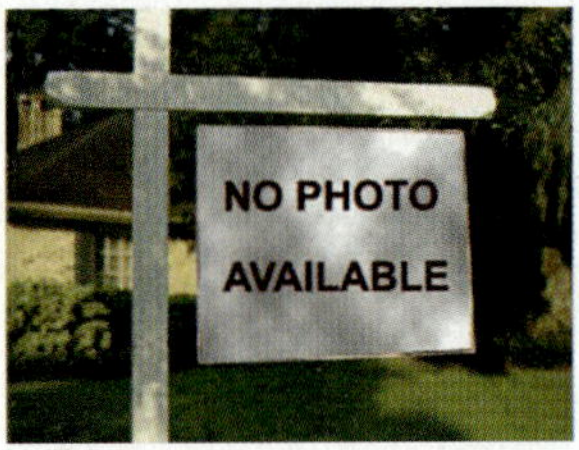
NO PHOTO
AVAILABLE
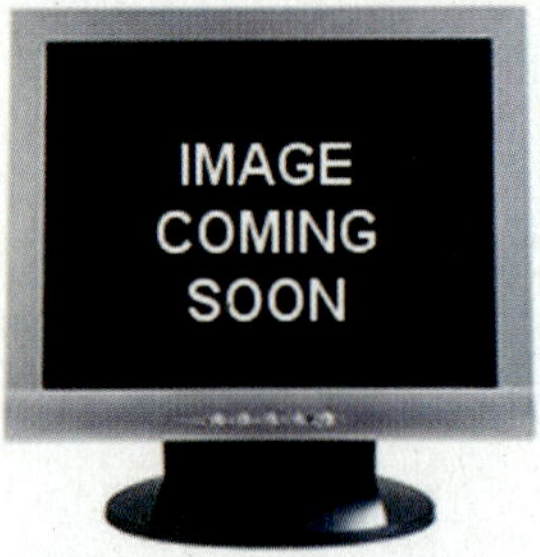
IMAGE
COMING
SOON
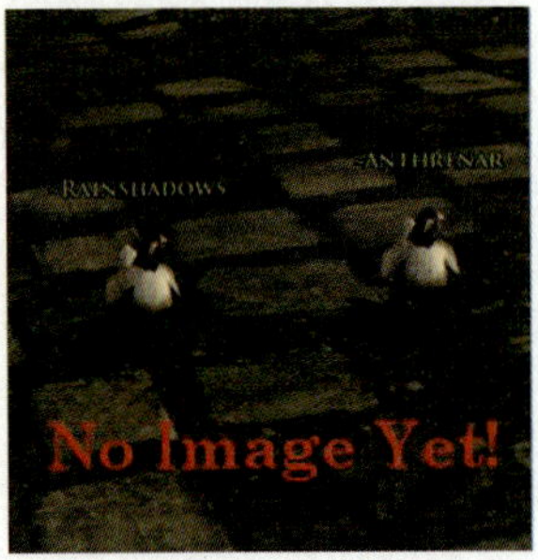
No Image Yet!
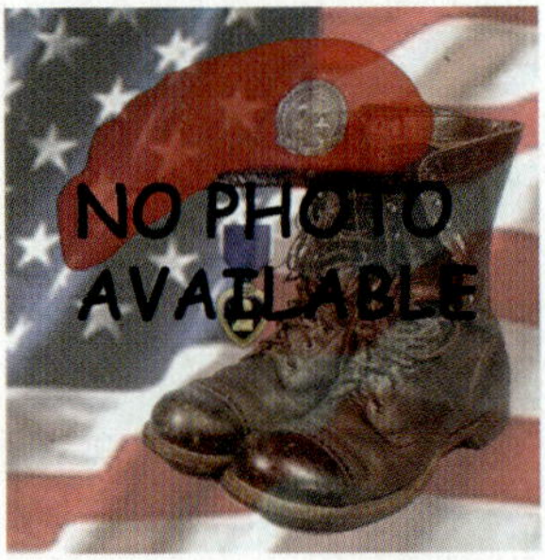
NO PHOTO
AVAILABLE
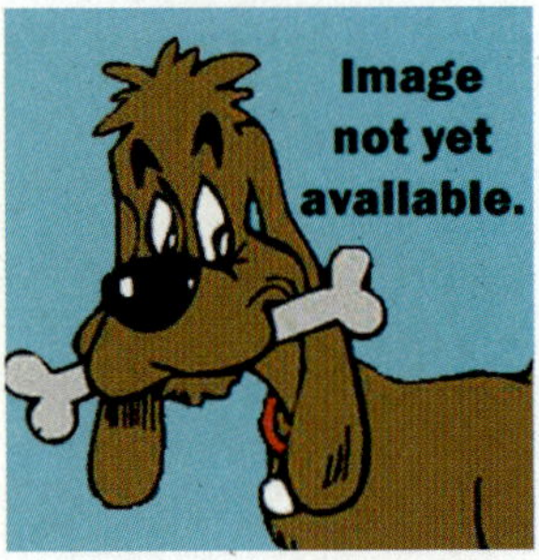
Image
not yet
available.

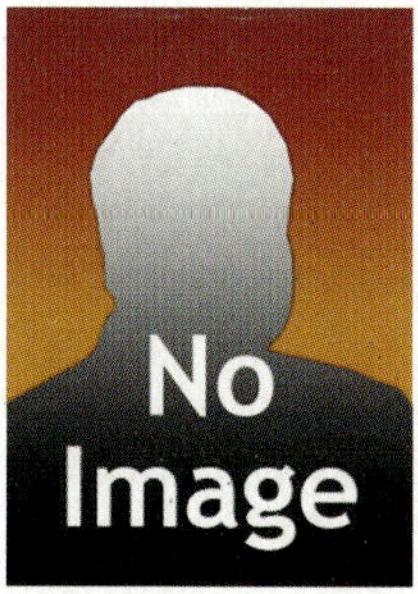

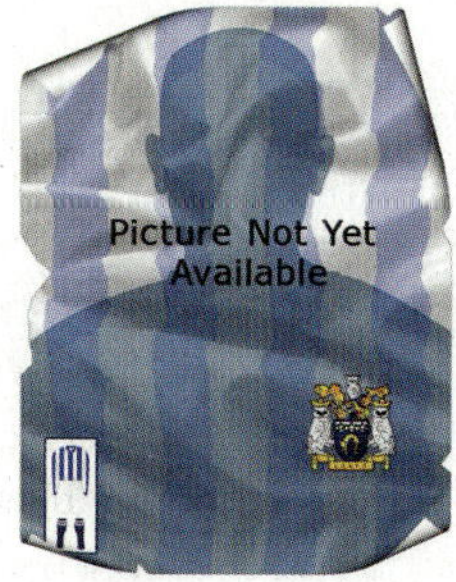

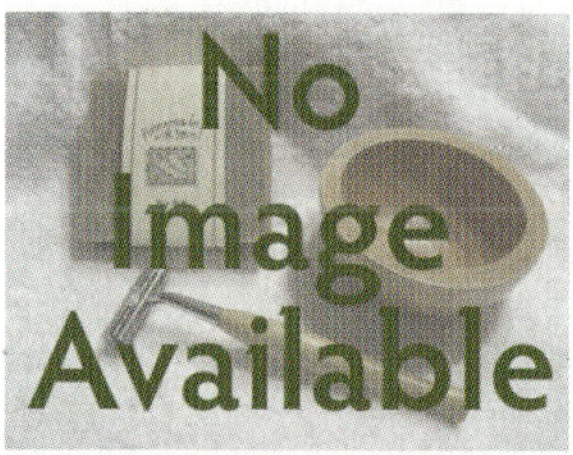

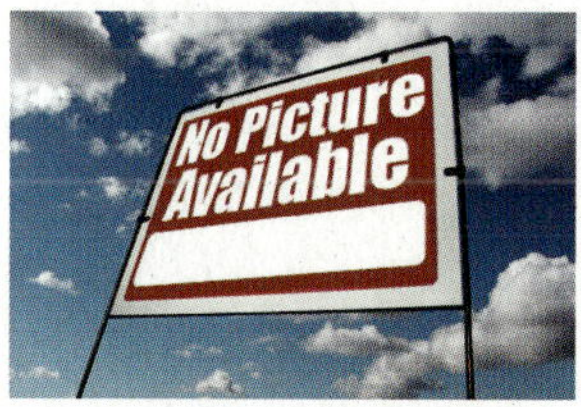

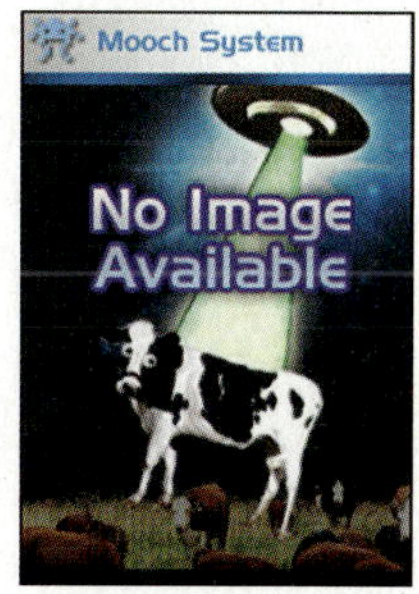

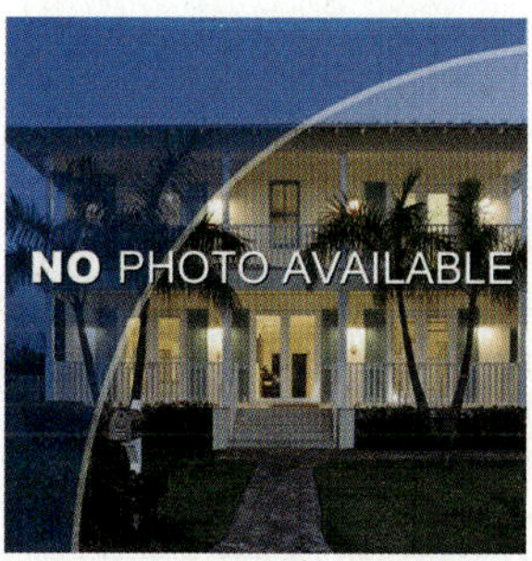

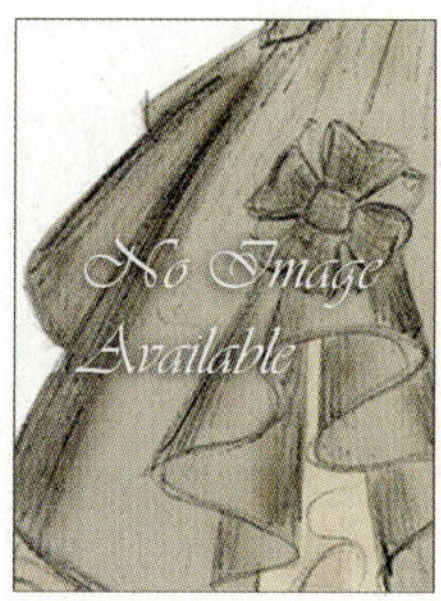

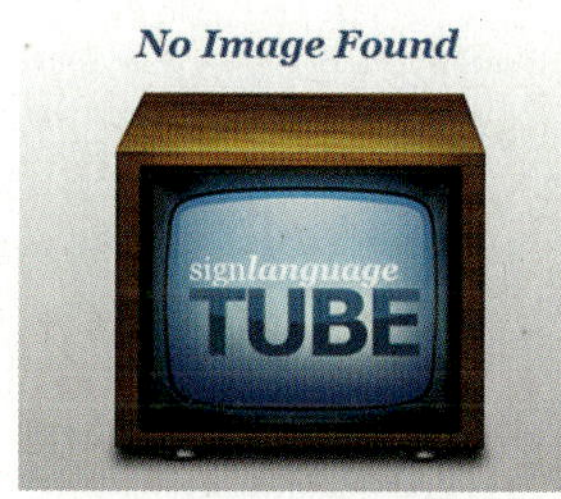

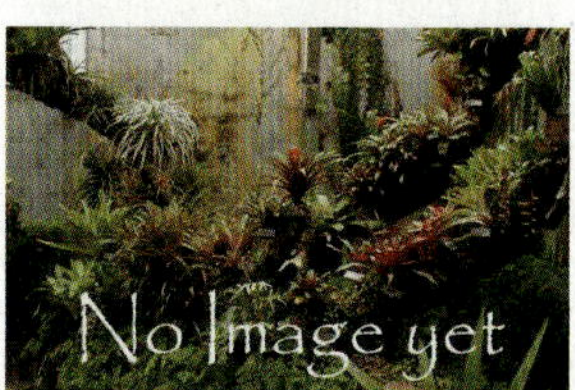

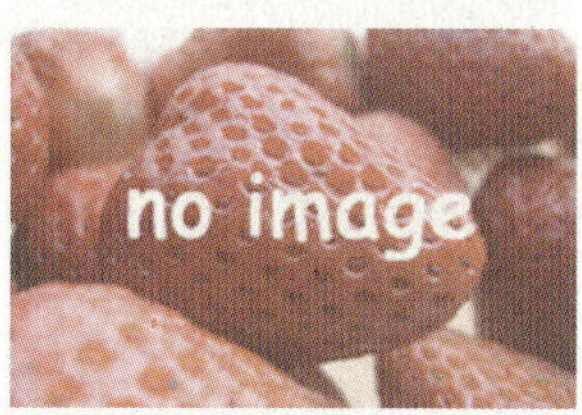

Jasper Elings
Picturebook without Pictures

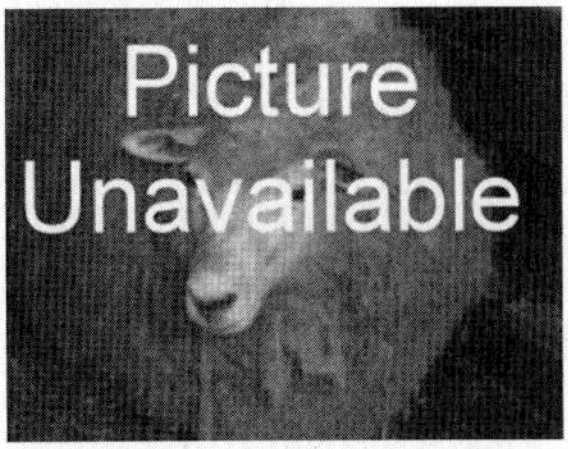
Picture
Unavailable

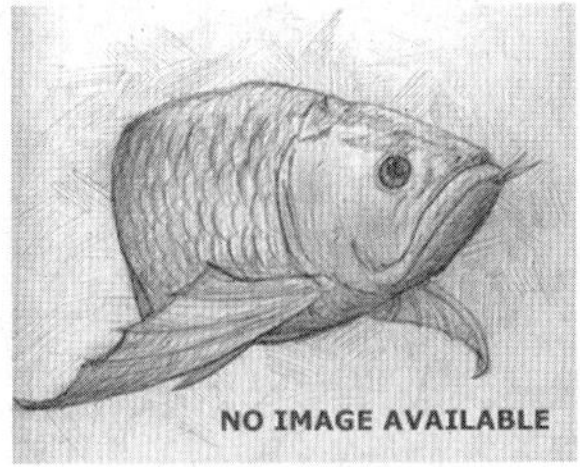
NO IMAGE AVAILABLE

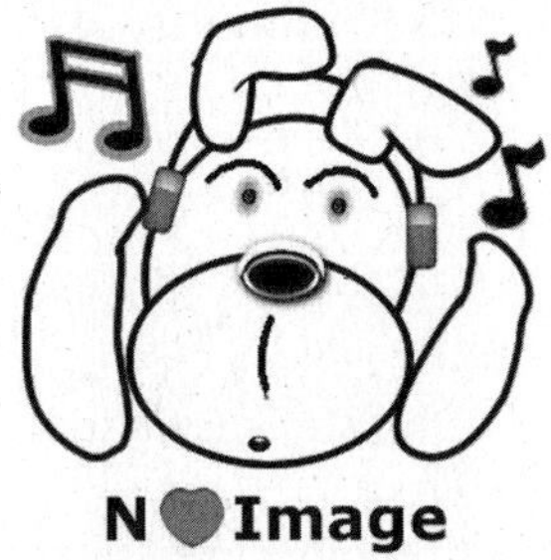
N♥Image

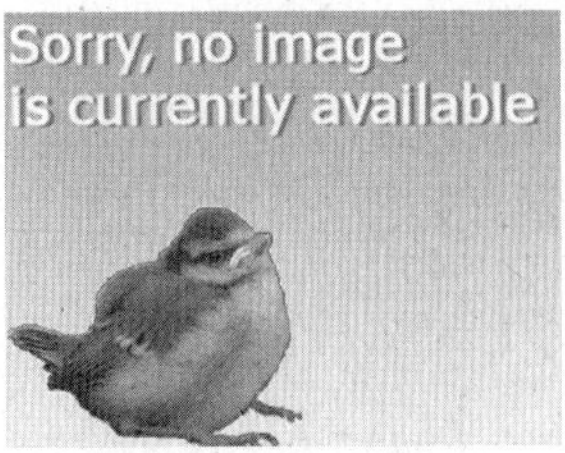
Sorry, no image
is currently available

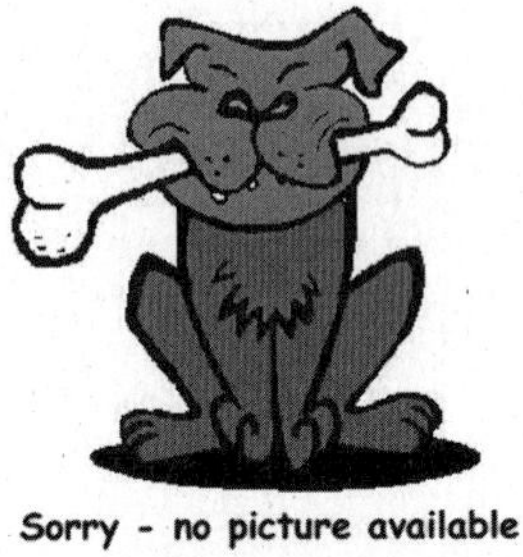
Sorry - no picture available

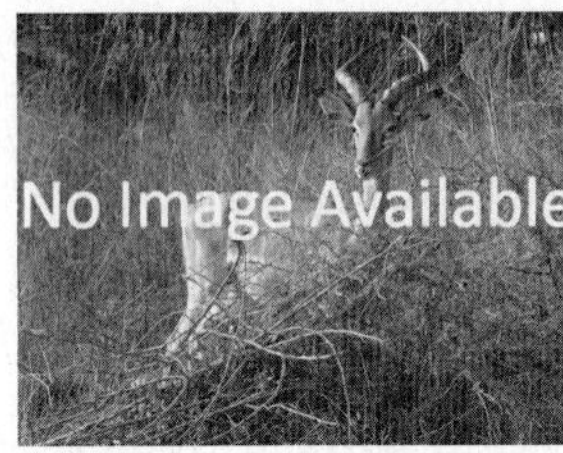
No Image Available

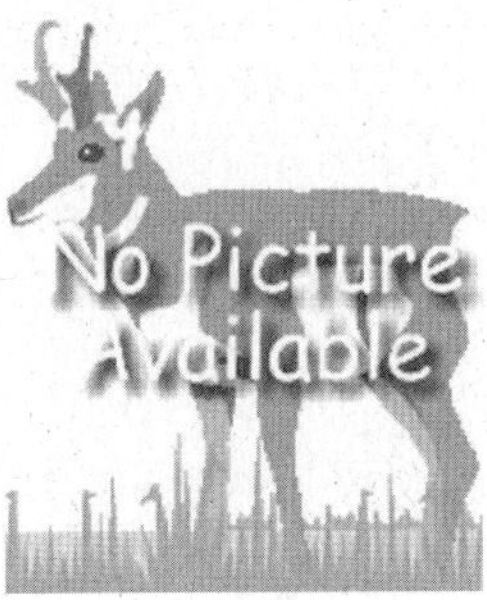
No Picture
Available

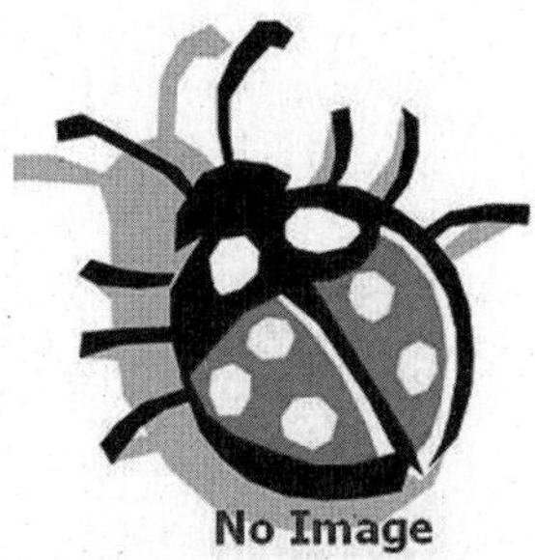
No Image

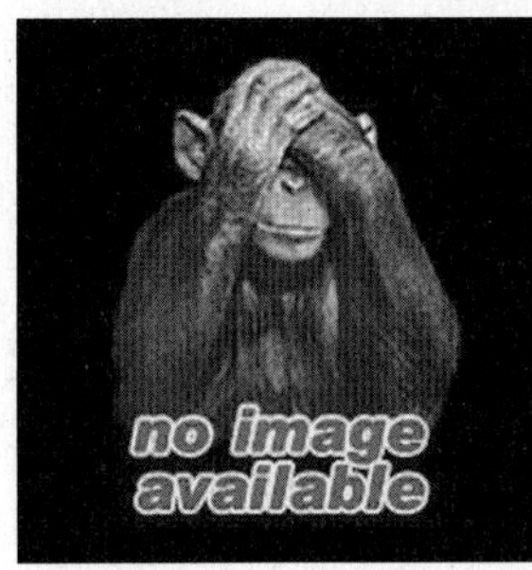
no image
available

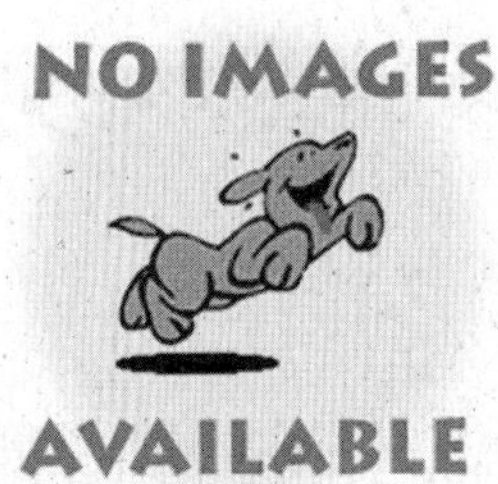
NO IMAGES
AVAILABLE

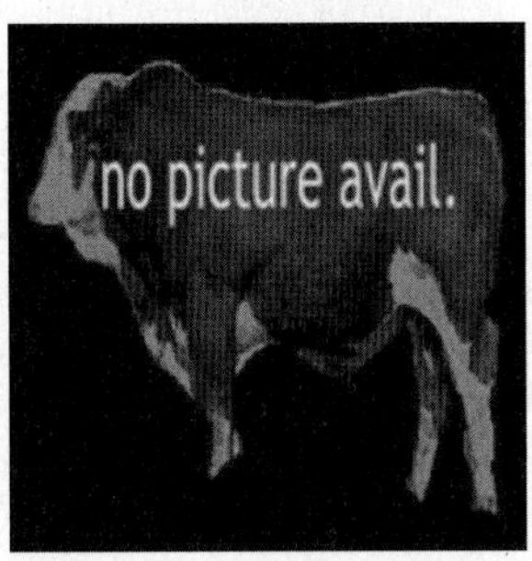
no picture avail.

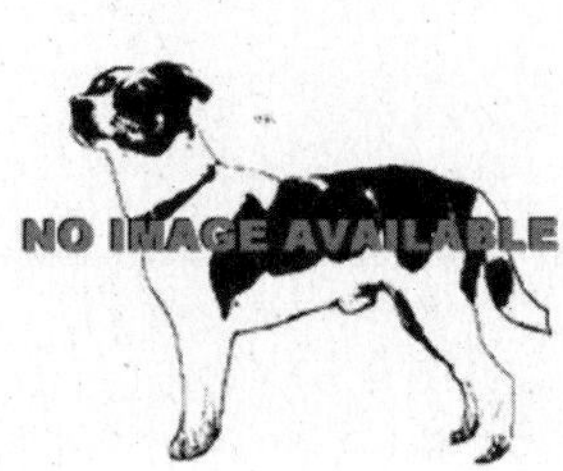
NO IMAGE AVAILABLE

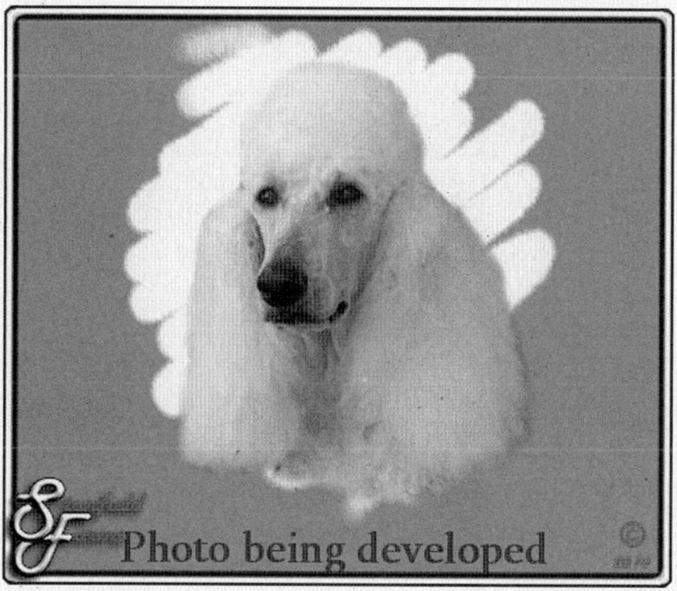
Photo being developed

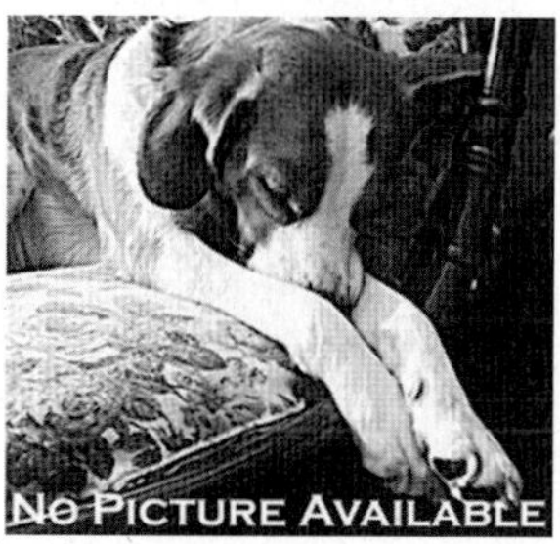
No Picture Available

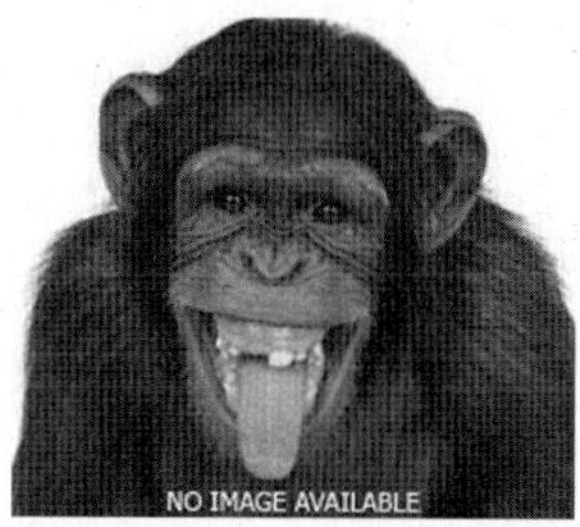
NO IMAGE AVAILABLE

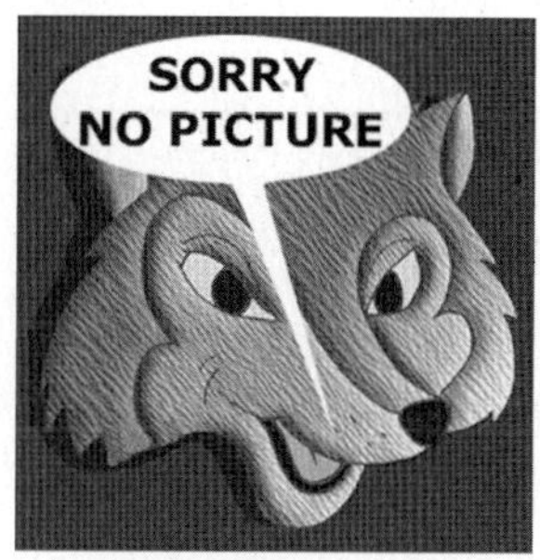
SORRY
NO PICTURE

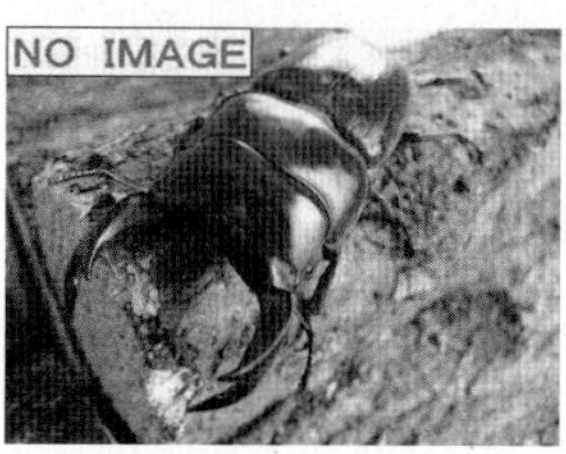
NO IMAGE

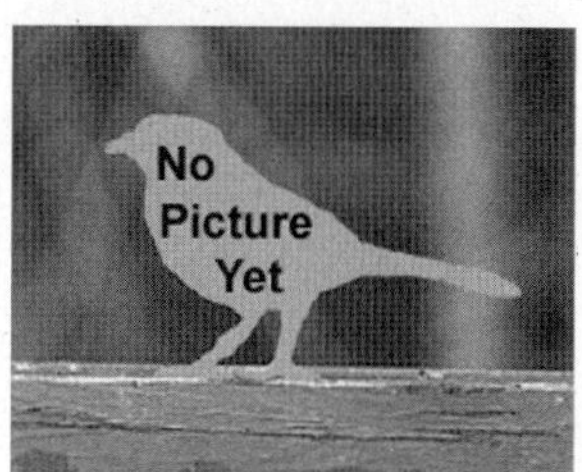
No
Picture
Yet

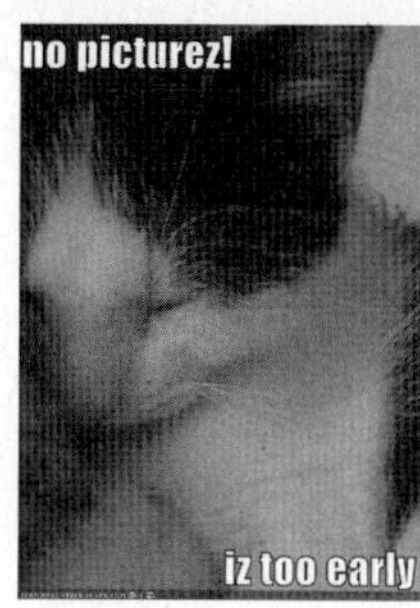
no picturez!
iz too early

JunkCache
🗗Greg J. Smith

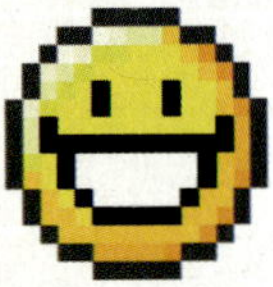

key:
http://www.twistermc.com/wp-includes/images/smilies/icon_biggrin.gif
fetch count: 2
last fetched: 2011-10-20 00:00:14
last modified:
2011-10-19 23:54:56
expires: 2011-10-30 17:19:33
Data size: 172
file on disk: none
Security:
This document does not have any security info associated with it.
Client:
HTTP
request-method: GET
response-head:
HTTP/1.1 200 OK Date: Thu, 20 Oct 2011 03:54:55 GMT Server: Apache Last-Modified: Mon, 04 Jul 2011 21:48:18 GMT Accept-Ranges: bytes Content-Length: 172
Content-Type: image/gif

00000000: 47 49 46 38 39 61
0f 00 0f 00 b3 0d 00 45 45 45
GIF89a.......EEE
00000010: ff ea 00 00 00 00
ff ff ff ff ce 00 ff c9 00 ff
....
00000020: b4 00 fe 9d 00
ff fe 93 ff fd 13 ff ff c7 ff ff
....
00000030: eb ff e5 00 00 00 00
00 00 00 00 00 00 21 f9 04
.............!..
00000040: 01 00 00 0d 00 2c
00 00 00 00 0f 00 0f 00 00 04
.....,..........
00000050: 59 b0 49 09 6a 9d
b8 d5 a5 10 22 17 06 70 49
12 Y.I.j.....“..pI.
00000060: 9c c4 01 4c 40 67
9e 70 ba 6a 88 29 c0 77 00
6a ...L@g.p.j.).w.j
00000070: ca 9b 07 b9 82 0a
80 f8 c1 70 86 4a 51 c0 6c 3a
.........p.JQ.l:
00000080: 93 00 db 60 4a 1d
08 0a 50 02 b0 4a bd aa 34
5a ...`J...P..J..4Z
00000090: 01 f7 ba 03 13 18
4e f2 97 42 20 14 de 6f 59 a6
......N..B ..oY.
000000a0: 62 a8 1b 86
19 96 65 36 89 00 00 3b
b.....e6...;

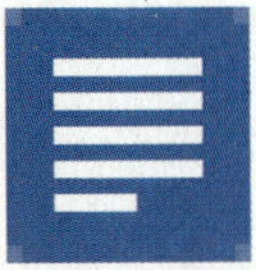

HTTP/1.1 200 OK
age: 435333
cache-control: public, max-age=31536000
content-length: 152
content-type: image/png
date: Wed, 12 Oct 2011 22:34:20 GMT
expires: Thu, 11 Oct 2012 22:34:20 GMT
last-modified: Wed, 28 Sep 2011 03:00:23 GMT
server: sffe
status: 200 OK
version: HTTP/1.1
x-content-type-options: nosniff
x-xss-protection: 1; mode=block

00000000: ce 07 00 00 02 67
01 00 b7 b8 6c 44 1d 0e 2e
00 .....g....lD....
00000010: 5a bb 6d 44 1d 0e
2e 00 4b 01 00 00 48 54 54
50 Z.mD....K...HTTP
00000020: 2f 31 2e 31 20 32
30 30 20 4f 4b 00 61 67 65
3a /1.1 200 OK.age:
00000030: 34 33 35 33 33 33
00 63 61 63 68 65 2d 63 6f
6e 435333.cache-con
00000040: 74 72 6f 6c 3a 70
75 62 6c 69 63 2c 20 6d 61
78 trol:public, max
00000050: 2d 61 67 65 3d 33
31 35 33 36 30 30 30 00 63
6f -age=31536000.co
00000060: 6e 74 65 6e 74 2d
6c 65 6e 67 74 68 3a 31 35
32 ntent-length:152
00000070: 00 63 6f 6e 74 65
6e 74 2d 74 79 70 65 3a 69
6d .content-type:im
00000080: 61 67 65 2f 70 6e
67 00 64 61 74 65 3a 57 65
64 age/png.date:Wed
00000090: 2c 20 31 32 20 4f
63 74 20 32 30 31 31 20 32
32 , 12 Oct 2011 22
000000a0: 3a 33 34 3a 32 30
20 47 4d 54 00 65 78 70 69
72 :34:20 GMT.expir
000000b0: 65 73 3a 54 68 75
2c 20 31 31 20 4f 63 74 20 32
es:Thu, 11 Oct 2
000000c0: 30 31 32 20 32 32
3a 33 34 3a 32 30 20 47 4d
54 012 22:34:20 GMT
000000d0: 00 6c 61 73 74 2d
6d 6f 64 69 66 69 65 64 3a
57 .last-modified:W
000000e0: 65 64 2c 20 32 38
20 53 65 70 20 32 30 31 31
20 ed, 28 Sep 2011
000000f0: 30 33 3a 30 30 3a
32 33 20 47 4d 54 00 73 65
72 03:00:23 GMT.ser
00000100: 76 65 72 3a 73 66
66 65 00 73 74 61 74 75 73
3a ver:sffe.status:
00000110: 32 30 30 20 4f 4b
00 76 65 72 73 69 6f 6e 3a
48 200 OK.version:H
00000120: 54 54 50 2f 31 2e
31 00 78 2d 63 6f 6e 74 65
6e TTP/1.1.x-conten
00000130: 74 2d 74 79 70 65
2d 6f 70 74 69 6f 6e 73 3a 6e
t-type-options:n
00000140: 6f 73 6e 69 66 66
00 78 2d 78 73 73 2d 70 72
6f osniff.x-xss-pro
00000150: 74 65 63 74 69 6f
6e 3a 31 3b 20 6d 6f 64 65
3d tection:1; mode=
00000160: 62 6c 6f 63 6b 00
00 00 85 03 00 00 30 82 03
81 block.......0...
00000170: 30 82 02 ea a0 03
02 01 02 02 0a 15 07 46 e8
00 0............F..
00000180: 03 00 00 32 6f 30
0d 06 09 2a 86 48 86 f7 0d
01 ...2o0...*.H....
00000190: 01 05 05 00 30 46
31 0b 30 09 06 03 55 04 06
13 ....0F1.0...U...
000001a0: 02 55 53 31 13 30
11 06 03 55 04 0a 13 0a 47 6f
.US1.0...U....Go
000001b0: 6f 67 6c 65 20 49
6e 63 31 22 30 20 06 03 55
04 ogle Inc1“0 ..U.
000001c0: 03 13 19 47 6f 6f 67
6c 65 20 49 6e 74 65 72 6e
...Google Intern
000001d0: 65 74 20 41 75 74
68 6f 72 69 74 79 30 1e 17
0d et Authority0...
000001e0: 31 31 30 39 32 30
30 36 30 38 32 31 5a 17 0d
31 110920060821Z..1
000001f0: 32 30 39 32 30 30
36 31 38 32 31 5a 30 67 31
0b 20920061821Z0g1.
00000200: 30 09 06 03 55 04
06 13 02 55 53 31 13 30 11
06 0...U....US1.0..
00000210: 03 55 04 08 13 0a
43 61 6c 69 66 6f 72 6e 69 61
.U....California
00000220: 31 16 30 14 06 03
55 04 07 13 0d 4d 6f 75 6e
74 1.0...U....Mount
00000230: 61 69 6e 20 56 69
65 77 31 13 30 11 06 03 55
04 ain View1.0...U.
00000240: 0a 13 0a 47 6f 6f
67 6c 65 20 49 6e 63 31 16
30 ...Google Inc1.0
00000250: 14 06 03 55 04 03
14 0d 2a 2e 67 73 74 61 74
69 ...U....*.gstati
00000260: 63 2e 63 6f 6d 30
81 9f 30 0d 06 09 2a 86 48
86 c.com0..0...*.H.
00000270: f7 0d 01 01 01 05
00 03 81 8d 00 30 81 89 02
81 ....0....
00000280: 81 00 c1 44 ac e4
92 c3 64 1b 94 71 bc 8c 61 fb
...D....d..q..a.
00000290: f8 1d a0 ae 14 2c
4f 98 08 5e 12 f2 7e c6 21 ac
.....,O..^..~.!.
000002a0: 93 17 e8 b9 4a e9
82 f4 a9 d0 15 24 cf ba 88 d0
....J......$....
000002b0: cf 05 79 63 a1 89
80 75 46 19 9c 58 a9 do 8e
64 ..yc...uF..X...d
000002c0: fd 59 33 05 18 86
a6 d5 33 98 f6 1d c0 49 f7 bf
.Y3.....3....I..
000002d0: f4 ee 03 e1 8c 0b
56 ed 0c 27 c3 05 3d 8e 27
63 ......V..‘..=.‘c
000002e0: 8c 1c 61 25 fa d3
41 0a 44 21 06 f3 51 33 bf 22
..a%..A.D!..Q3.“
000002f0: 19 1d f0 1a cd a1 e7
87 65 e1 03 10 46 d1 07 79
........e...F..y
00000300: cd 2b 02 03 01 00
01 a3 82 01 53 30 82 01 4f
30 .+........S0..O0
00000310: 1d 06 03 55 1d 0e
04 16 04 14 e0 18 c3 8e 7f 2f
...U.........../
00000320: da 55 9e 50 54 27
a9 2b 34 06 06 c8 72 b5 30 1f
.U.PT‘.+4...r.0.
00000330: 06 03 55 1d 23 04
18 30 16 80 14 bf c0 30 eb f5
..U.#..0.....0..
00000340: 43 11 3e 67 ba 9e
91 fb fc 6a da e3 6b 12 24 30
C.>g.....j..k.$0
00000350: 5b 06 03 55 1d 1f
04 54 30 52 30 50 a0 4e a0
4c [..U...T0R0P.N.L
00000360: 86 4a 68 74 74 70
3a 2f 2f 77 77 77 2e 67 73 74
.Jhttp://www.gst
00000370: 61 74 69 63 2e 63
6f 6d 2f 47 6f 6f 67 6c 65 49
atic.com/GoogleI
00000380: 6e 74 65 72 6e 65
74 41 75 74 68 6f 72 69 74
79 nternetAuthority
00000390: 2f 47 6f 6f 67 6c 65
49 6e 74 65 72 6e 65 74 41 /
GoogleInternetA
000003a0: 75 74 68 6f 72 69
74 79 2e 63 72 6c 30 66 06
08 uthority.crl0f..
000003b0: 2b 06 01 05 05 07
01 01 04 5a 30 58 30 56 06
08 +........Z0X0V..
000003c0: 2b 06 01 05 05 07
30 02 86 4a 68 74 74 70 3a
2f +.....0..Jhttp:/
000003d0: 2f 77 77 77 2e 67
73 74 61 74 69 63 2e 63 6f
6d /www.gstatic.com
000003e0: 2f 47 6f 6f 67 6c 65
49 6e 74 65 72 6e 65 74 41 /
GoogleInternetA
000003f0: 75 74 68 6f 72 69
74 79 2f 47 6f 6f 67 6c 65 49
uthority/GoogleI
00000400: 6e 74 65 72 6e 65
74 41 75 74 68 6f 72 69 74
79 nternetAuthority
00000410: 2e 63 72 74 30 21
06 09 2b 06 01 04 01 82 37
14 .crt0!..+.....7.
00000420: 02 04 14 1e 12 00
57 00 65 00 62 00 53 00 65
00 ......W.e.b.S.e.
00000430: 72 00 76 00 65 00
72 30 25 06 03 55 1d 11 04
1e r.v.e.r0%..U....
00000440: 30 1c 82 0d 2a 2e
67 73 74 61 74 69 63 2e 63
6f 0...*.gstatic.co
00000450: 6d 82 0b 67 73 74
61 74 69 63 2e 63 6f 6d 30
0d m..gstatic.com0.
00000460: 06 09 2a 86 48 86
f7 0d 01 01 05 05 00 03 81
81 ..*.H...........
00000470: 00 64 df 80 e5 3a
c2 76 28 46 e8 ab b0 18 06
9e .d...:.v(F......
00000480: 28 c9 5e fa e9 f3 46
38 59 b5 49 b5 77 db b4 23
(.^...F8Y.I.w..#
00000490: 66 6f 09 76 3d a4
2f 66 a8 45 16 8a 25 b3 ef 54
fo.v=./f.E..%..T
000004a0: bc e8 5f e5 5b a7
4a 83 64 9d 1a 69 b7 c1 dc fa
.._.[.J.d..i....
000004b0: c2 cf 5f ad fd b7 4e
60 5e d6 cb 20 2a ad b3 a1
.._...N`^.. *...
000004c0: d0 7e cc 47 70 34
77 80 e0 d6 c9 83 a3 8c 01
85 .~.Gp4w.........
000004d0: 69 ff cf 8f 19 56 ad
68 03 93 7f 1b a1 5a 59 f8
i....V.h.....ZY.
000004e0: aa bc 9a d7 7a 1f
bd 29 e6 49 d0 4d 3a 9d f4
0e ....z..).I.M:....
000004f0: e4 00 00 00 01 00
00 00 b4 02 00 00 30 82 02
b0 ....0...
00000500: 30 82 02 19 a0 03
02 01 02 02 03 0b 67 71 30
0d 0...........gq0.
00000510: 06 09 2a 86 48 86
f7 0d 01 01 05 05 00 30 4e
31 ..*.H........0N1
00000520: 0b 30 09 06 03 55
04 06 13 02 55 53 31 10 30
0e .0...U....US1.0.
00000530: 06 03 55 04 0a 13
07 45 71 75 69 66 61 78 31
2d ..U....Equifax1-
00000540: 30 2b 06 03 55 04
0b 13 24 45 71 75 69 66 61
78 0+..U...$Equifax
00000550: 20 53 65 63 75 72
65 20 43 65 72 74 69 66 69
63 Secure Certific
00000560: 61 74 65 20 41 75
74 68 6f 72 69 74 79 30 1e
17 ate Authority0..
00000570: 0d 30 39 30 36 30
38 32 30 34 33 32 37 5a 17
0d .090608204327Z..
00000580: 31 33 30 36 30 37
31 39 34 33 32 37 5a 30 46
31 130607194327Z0F1
00000590: 0b 30 09 06 03 55
04 06 13 02 55 53 31 13 30
11 .0...U....US1.0.
000005a0: 06 03 55 04 0a 13
0a 47 6f 6f 67 6c 65 20 49 6e
..U....Google In
000005b0: 63 31 22 30 20 06
03 55 04 03 13 19 47 6f 6f 67
c1“0 ..U....Goog
000005c0: 6c 65 20 49 6e 74
65 72 6e 65 74 20 41 75 74

68 le Internet Auth
000005d0: 6f 72 69 74 79 30
81 9f 30 0d 06 09 2a 86 48
86 ority0..0...*.H.
000005e0: f7 0d 01 01 01 05
00 03 81 8d 00 30 81 89 02
81 ....0....
000005f0: 81 00 c9 ed b7 a4
8b 9c 57 e7 84 3e 40 7d 84 f4
........W..>@}..
00000600: 8f d1 71 63 53 99
e7 79 74 14 af 44 99 33 20
92 ..qcS..yt..D.3 .
00000610: 8d 7b e5 28 0c ba
ad 6c 49 7e 83 5f 34 59 4e 0a
.{.(...Il~._4YN.
00000620: 7a 30 cd d0 d7 c4
57 45 ed d5 aa d6 73 26 ce
ad z0....WE....s&..
00000630: 32 13 b8 d7 0f 1d
3b df dd dc 08 36 a8 6f 51 44
2.....;....6.oQD
00000640: 9b ca d6 20 52 73
b7 26 87 35 6a db a9 e5 d4
59 ... Rs.&.5j....Y
00000650: a5 2b fc 67 19 39
fa 93 18 18 6c de dd 25 8a 0e
.+.g.9....l..%..
00000660: 33 14 47 c2 ef 01
50 79 e4 fd 69 d1 a7 c0 ac e2
3.G...Py..i.....
00000670: 57 6f 02 03 01 00
01 a3 81 a3 30 81 a0 30 0e
06 Wo........0..0..
00000680: 03 55 1d 0f 01 01
ff 04 04 03 02 01 06 30 1d 06
.U...........0..
00000690: 03 55 1d 0e 04 16
04 14 bf c0 30 eb f5 43 11 3e
.U........0..C.>
000006a0: 67 ba 9e 91 fb fc 6a
da e3 6b 12 24 30 1f 06 03

key:
http://profile.ak.fbcdn.net/static-ak/rsrc.php/v1/ym/r/nMw9YWcvr3_.gif
fetch count:
4
last fetched:
2011-10-22 16:49:56
last modified:
2011-10-19 23:54:58
expires:
2011-11-02 23:54:57
Data size:
390
file on disk:
none
Security:
This document does not have any security info associated with it.
Client:
HTTP
request-method:
GET
response-head:
HTTP/1.1 200 OK Content-Length: 390 Content-Type: image/gif
Last-Modified: Wed, 05 Oct 2011 19:52:47 GMT
X-FB-Server: 10.30.146.199
X-Cnection: close Cache-Control: public, max-age=1209600 Expires: Thu, 03 Nov 2011 03:54:58 GMT
Date: Thu, 20 Oct 2011 03:54:58 GMT
00000000: 47 49 46 38 39 61
32 00 32 00 c4 00 00 f3 f5 f9
GIF89a2.2.......
00000010: dc e1 ed e5 e9 f2
d1 d8 e7 c8 d1 e2 cd d5 e4
ee ....
00000020: f1 f6 f9 fa fc ea
ee f4 d4 da e8 fc fd fe e9 ec
....
00000030: f3 f6 f8 fa f5 f6
fa fe fe ff f6 f7 fa da e0 ec
....
00000040: cb d3 e4 c7 d0 e2
f8 f9 fb d7 dd ea de e4 ee e3
....
00000050: e7 f0 c6 ce e1 cc
d3 e4 f1 f3 f8 d5 dc e9 d6 dc
....
00000060: e9 d2 d9 e8 c8 cf
e1 ff ff ff c4 cd e0 21 f9 04
.............!..
00000070: 00 00 00 00 00 2c
00 00 00 00 32 00 32 00 00
05 .....,....2.2...
00000080: ff 60 27 8e 64 69
9e 68 aa ae 6c 9b 7e 70 2c cf
.`'.di.h..l.~p,.
00000090: 74 6d df 78 ae ef
7c 5f 0f 15 c3 24 e2 2b da 08
tm.x..|_...$.+..
000000a0: 81 8c 67 e9 09 18
9f 31 0d 80 49 1d 40 8d 98
07 ..g....1..I.@...
000000b0: 75 eb 81 5c 7b 15
ae 18 f1 d5 2d c4 e8 47 f9 26
u..\{.....-..G.&
000000c0: 40 bb d5 eb 59 c4
4d f7 c6 63 6d 3a ba 71 8f 29
@...Y.M..cm:.q.)
000000d0: f5 62 0e 7d 30 0c
80 68 83 1f 07 86 62 1d 83
8a .b.}0..h....b...
000000e0: 8b 5b 17 83 13 90
5b 8d 7d 5a 95 4c 88 53 9a
4b .[....[.}Z.L.S.K
000000f0: 88 7f 9a 0a 88 67
9e 13 83 05 8f 9e 1b 7d a5
9e .....g.......}..
00000100: 1e 70 71 10 af 4b
0b 7d 03 b4 4d 7d 12 b9 1c
83 .pq..K.}..M}....
00000110: b9 44 7d b3 9e b6
88 af 04 88 1f a1 8b 82 c9 01
.D}.............
00000120: 9a 06 c9 1f 17 9a
09 d2 1f 06 90 a3 d7 1f 90 56
...............V
00000130: dc cb 74 dc 30 9d
80 e3 89 8b 97 d7 90 18 dc
bc ..t.0...........
00000140: 8b 1a d7 04 9a f1
c9 1a 9a 02 d2 79 90 7c c9
0a ....y.|..
00000150: 9e c1 e2 74 b0 90
0b 41 40 28 18 10 e4 a2 92
c1 ...t...A@(......
00000160: 97 91 0d e5 16 52
39 e0 64 87 04 0b ff 24 d2 59
.....R9.d....$.Y
00000170: d0 ce c6 80 6c 1a
17 35 a0 30 83 02 a5 90 a2
2a ....l..5.0.....*
00000180: 03 7c 08 01 00
3b .|...;

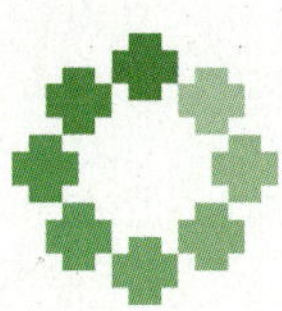

key:
http://edge.sharethis.com/images/spinner.gif
fetch count:
2
last fetched:
2011-10-19 23:57:08
last modified:
2011-10-19 23:54:58
expires:
2011-10-20 03:18:35
Data size:
792
file on disk:
none
Security:
This document does not have any security info associated with it.
Client:
HTTP
request-method:
GET
response-head:
HTTP/1.1 200 OK Server: nginx/0.8.53 Content-Type: image/gif Content-Length: 792 Accept-Ranges: bytes Cache-Control: max-age=12217 Expires: Thu, 20 Oct 2011 07:18:35 GMT Date: Thu, 20 Oct 2011 03:54:58 GMT
00000000: 47 49 46 38 39 61
10 00 10 00 b3 08 00 68 b9
65 GIF89a.......h.e
00000010: 79 c7 78 a7 e9 a5
9b e0 98 49 a3 46 3f 9b 3c 8b
y.x......I.F?.<.
00000020: d4 89 57 ad 54 00
00 00 00 00 00 00 00 00 00
00 ..W.T...........
00000030: 00 00 00 00 00 00
00 00 00 00 00 00 00 21 ff 0b
.............!..
00000040: 4e 45 54 53 43 41
50 45 32 2e 30 03 01 00 00
00 NETSCAPE2.0.....
00000050: 21 f9 04 05 00 00
08 00 2c 00 00 00 00 10 00
10 !.......,.......
00000060: 00 00 04 48 10 c9
89 4a a1 98 5a 9b 27 21 d5
86 ...H...J..Z.'!..
00000070: 08 02 f6 7d e1 48
96 de 49 ad 6c 9b 91 d4 71
74 ...}.H..I.l...qt
00000080: d3 30 20 b6 8d eb
ba de ad 03 dc f9 70 08 1d 05
.0 ....p...
00000090: 00 c8 18 0c 18 26
93 f2 7c 2e a5 88 40 00 51 85
.....&..|...@.Q.
000000a0: 5e b3 da ad 15 17
de 22 27 da 4e 04 00 21 f9
04 ^......"'.N..!..
000000b0: 05 00 00 08 00 2c
00 00 00 00 10 00 10 00 00
04 .....,..........
000000c0: 48 10 c9 89 08 a1
98 5a 9b e7 39 d5 86 14 05
f6 H......Z..9.....
000000d0: 7d e1 48 96 de 49
ad 6c 9b 91 14 00 74 93 20
20 }.H..I.l....t.
000000e0: b6 8d eb ba de ad
03 dc f9 70 08 1d 25 10 c8 0c
.........p..%...
000000f0: 06 18 26 93 f2 7c 2e
a5 08 83 01 51 85 5e b3 da
..&..|.....Q.^..
00000100: ad 15 17 de 22 27
da 4e 04 00 21 f9 04 05 00
00 ...."'.N..!.....
00000110: 08 00 2c 00 00 00
00 10 00 10 00 00 04 48 10
c9 ..,..........H..
00000120: 89 ce a1 98 5a 9b
27 00 d5 86 10 04 f6 7d e1
48 ....Z.'......}.H
00000130: 96 de 49 ad 6c 9b
91 54 10 74 53 51 20 b6 8d
eb ..I.l..T.tSQ ...
00000140: ba de ad 03 dc f9
70 08 1d c5 60 c8 08 04 18
26 ......p...`....&
00000150: 93 f2 7c 2e a5 88
c1 00 51 85 5e b3 da ad 15
17 ..|.....Q.^.....
00000160: de 22 27 da 4e 04
00 21 f9 04 05 00 00 08 00 2c
."'.N..!.......,
00000170: 00 00 00 00 10 00
10 00 00 04 48 10 c9 89 00
a0 ....H.....
00000180: 98 5a 9b 67 08 d5
86 1c 07 f6 7d e1 48 96 de 49
.Z.g......}.H..I
00000190: ad 6c 9b 91 94 61
74 13 41 20 b6 8d eb ba de
ad .l...at.A ......
000001a0: 03 dc f9 70 08 1d
65 30 c8 14 0a 18 26 93 f2 7c
...p..e0....&..|
000001b0: 2e a5 08 81 00 51
85 5e b3 da ad 15 17 de 22
27 .....Q.^......"'
000001c0: da 4e 04 00 21 f9
04 05 00 00 08 00 2c 00 00
00 .N..!.......,...
000001d0: 00 10 00 10 00 00
04 41 10 c9 89 42 a0 98 5a
9b .......A...B..Z.
000001e0: a7 31 d5 d6 21 df
17 8e 64 89 52 eb 8a 0c c3
7a .1..!...d.R....z
000001f0: 1c 2f 1c 77 f3 6c df
59 4e c3 32 da 44 20 c8 10
./.w.l.YN.2.D ..
00000200: 08 18 22 91 72 3c
52 94 c5 42 01 d1 44 3e a3
d2 ..".r<R..B..D>..
00000210: a9 73 94 9d ba 10
d2 4e 04 00 21 f9 04 05 00
00 .s.....N..!.....
00000220: 08 00 2c 00 00 00
00 0e 00 10 00 00 04 3f 10 c9
..,...........?..
00000230: 89 8c a1 58 5a 9b
d1 18 d5 86 04 c1 f4 7d e1 48
...XZ........}.H
00000240: 96 de 49 ad 6c 9b
91 92 20 74 94 6d e3 b5 ce f7
..I.l... t.m....
00000250: 3f 4a a1 90 39 1c
26 c3 21 c5 68 94 24 89 04
02 ?J..9.&.!.h.$...
00000260: 82 79 74 42 a3 d2
66 06 2b fd 45 31 11 00 21 f9
.ytB..f.+.E1..!.
00000270: 04 05 00 00 08 00
2c 00 00 00 00 10 00 10 00
00 .....,..........
00000280: 04 41 10 c9 89 c6
a0 98 5a 9b a7 10 d5 86 18
06 .A......Z.......
00000290: f6 7d e1 48 96 de
49 ad 6c 9b 91 54 51 74 53
10 .}.H..I.l..TQtS.
000002a0: 20 b6 8d eb ba de
ad 03 dc f9 70 08 1d 85 40 40
.........p...@@
000002b0: 2e 99 4d 27 02 da
3c 1c 9c 4c 84 d5 2a d5 6e
bb ..M'..<..L..*.n.
000002c0: de 4e 04 00 21 f9
04 05 00 00 08 00 2c 00 00
00 .N..!.......,...
000002d0: 00 10 00 0e 00 00
04 3e 10 c9 89 84 a0 98 5a
9b ....>......Z.
000002e0: 67 29 d5 86 0c 03
f6 7d e1 48 96 de 49 ad 6c 9b
g).....}.H..I.l.
000002f0: 91 14 41 74 93 61
20 b6 8d eb ba de ad 03 dc f9
..At.a ....
00000300: 70 08 1d e5 70 c8
04 02 18 26 93 f2 7c 2e a5 d4
p...p....&..|...
00000310: 6a b4 89 b1 4a 22
00 3b j...J".;

https://ssl.gstatic.com/s2/oz/images/stars/po/SRP/p1offhover2.gif
HTTP/1.1 200 OK
age: 438472
cache-control: public, max-age=31536000
content-length: 13456
content-type: image/gif
date: Wed, 12 Oct 2011 22:34:19 GMT
expires: Thu, 11 Oct 2012 22:34:19 GMT
last-modified: Wed, 28 Sep 2011 03:00:23 GMT
server: sffe
status: 200 OK
version: HTTP/1.1
x-content-type-options: nosniff
x-xss-protection: 1; mode=block

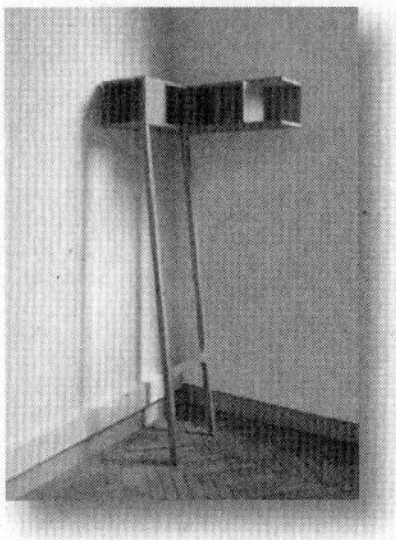

1

Marie Dessuant
Published:
05 - 09 - 2011
Furniture from French designer Marie Dessuant. She was awarded the Cinna-Ligne Roset design award "révélateur de talents" for the étagère de coin, which is now produced by Cinna—Ligne Roset. Currently she is a resident as product designer at Fabrica in Italy and tries to develop new ways of interacting with objects. Using new typologies, or modified details in traditional product, not to impose anything to the user, not to say too much, not to be too narrative.

Crap = Good
Pieterjan Grandry

Crap = Good is a blog and online platform regarding contemporary visual culture, extending itself by organizing 'competitions' and communal exhibitions. Initiated, curated and edited by graphic designer and visual artist Pieterjan Grandry.

Crap = good tries to develop, document and describe following ideas. Internet has changed the structure and distribution of knowledge. It is a vast, global, information reservoir. Websites like Wikipedia developed a new way of researching, offering easy access to the public. Besides, people interested in particular topics create online communities where they can exchange information about various topics with others from all over the world. It is an alternative way of learning, much different from the academic way and usually much more practical. Amateurs can become experts and experts can learn from amateurs. It is directed more to experiment and the topics can vary from very specific scientific subjects to banal ones. With the increasing speed of internet, uploading became easy and video became a popular medium for people to share their thoughts or give tutorials about their field of knowledge and expertise, be it dancing hip-hop, plumping, cooking or programming. With the fast development of computers and software, they can even make their video's look as professional as they aspire, supplying them with titles, images and graphics.

All this knowledge is there for a long time, and has been used as well. But it wasn't until the economic crisis in 2008 that this existing knowledge started appearing so largely outside of the www and entering the 'real world'. With the massive unemployment rates followed by the 2008 crisis, people have experienced that our economical and political system isn't as solid as one thought, or as they made one believe. We lost some of our faith in the system and became more sceptic towards it, developing a new perception of time or 'worktime'. This subtle change in mentality gives room for the phenomenon of applying internet-knowledge, which is free, open source, and got defined as DIY-culture (Do It Yourself). It offers

one the possibility to develop personal interests. By spending time developing these various fields of interest, people spend less time in the big market economy and move away from it, setting up small-scale business, producing locally, and orienting their practice away from this established system and its connected politics. Linked to that, we perceive that by moving away from this big economy, we are also moving away from its visual culture, and establish a new one.
Crap is good investigates this new aesthetics and it's subject in the creative field, it documents projects realized by small groups or individuals in search of independence and with attention to experiment. Looking at graphic design, we see a huge amount of self-publishers appearing, people setting up small independent printing presses or organizing pop-up book events, all with a specific visual aesthetics connected to it. But even if one looks deeper into this aesthetic we find similar ideas occurring in all of the creative branches. Furniture design; going back to the mid-century concept, using bended metal, simple materials, flat pack furniture, a regained interest to the properties of material and the rise of eco-design.
In photography we see a come back of the documentary style, photographers are stepping out of the high tech studio or entering daily life, editing less and showing more, be it analogue or digital. In architecture one perceives this new way of thinking in the contradiction between the big established offices who are closely connected to the current economic system and the small younger ones. Big commercial offices have answered the public's demand for a more ecological or social approach by colouring their design green and do very little for social wellbeing or sustainability, while the small offices are organizing urban farming projects and aim for social engagement with simple solutions or local interventions.
In the images 1 and 2 you can see some previously posted articles from a selection of categories, showing projects and initiatives of contemporary visual culture.
www.crapisgood.com

2

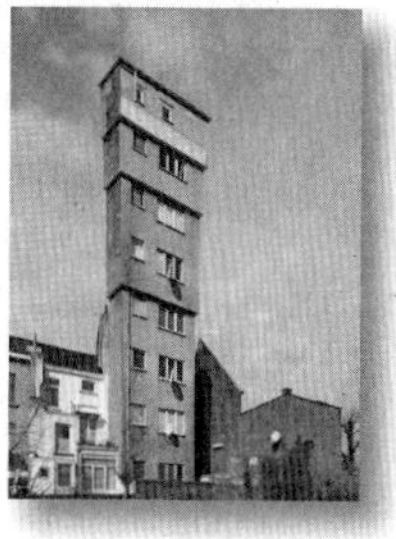

Xavier Delory
Published:
12 - 09 - 2011
A selection of images by Belgian photographer Xavier Delory. He's work
reminds us of a previous post about Filip Dujardin. Very common architectural structures, buildings or houses which we can all relate to
become abstracted. We focus on the sculptural value rather then the function. On the other side Delory's work makes us raise questions about isolation and cocooning by showing windowless buildings. Big supermarkets or warehouses with a church-like architecture questions wether these are the new places for contemplation. All the images at read more.

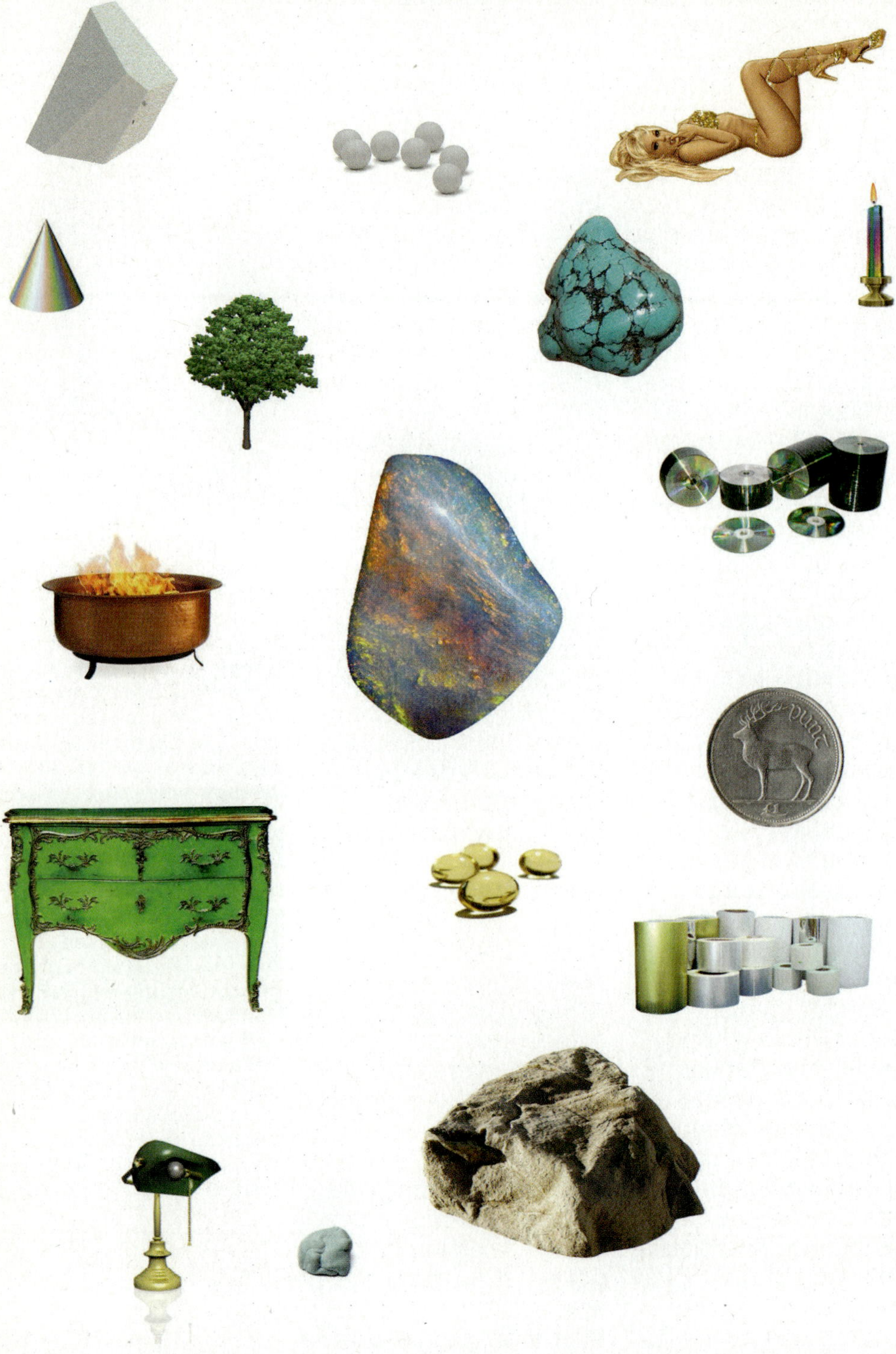

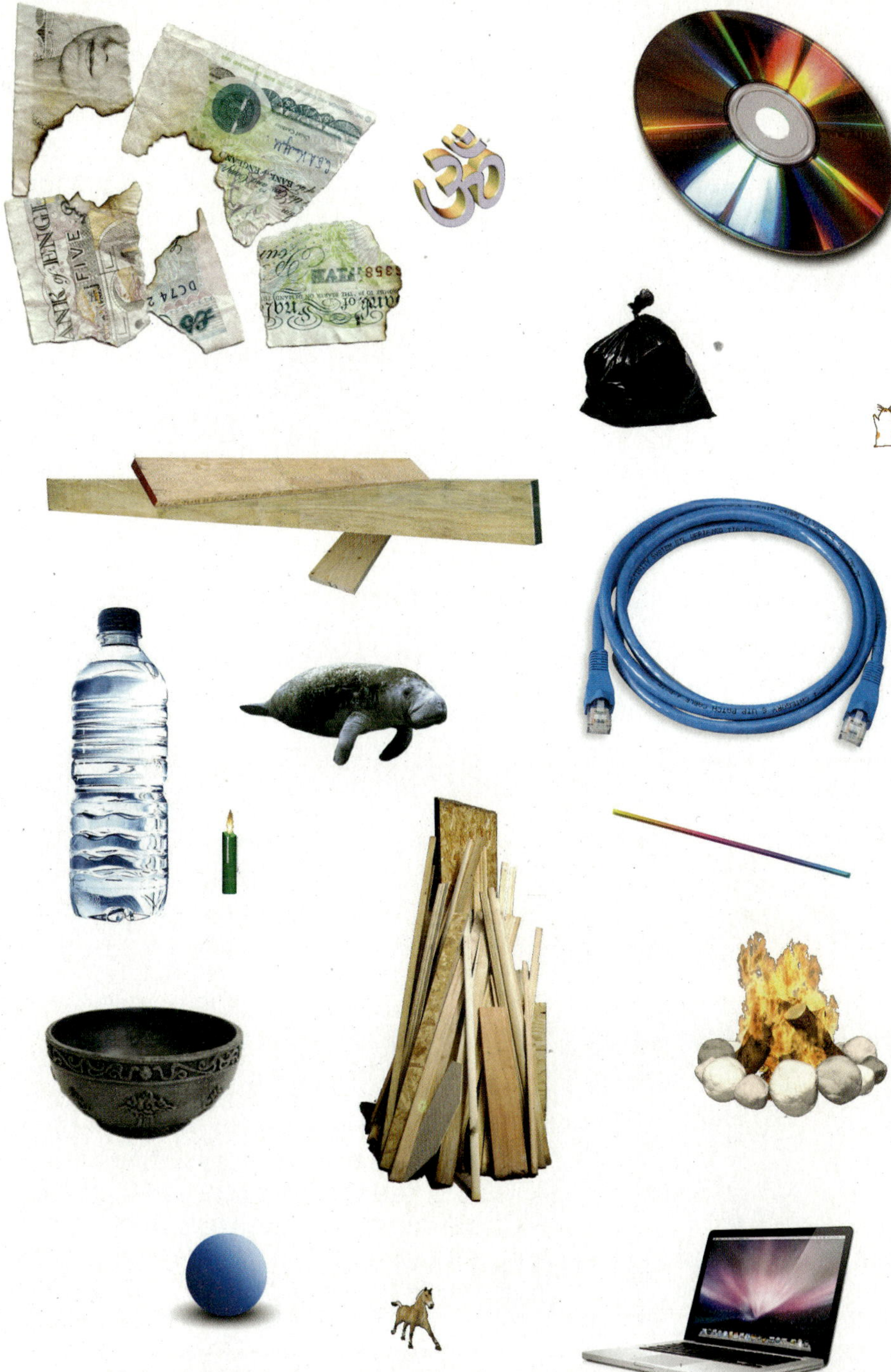

Eilis Mcdonald
Numinous-objects

Born To Fail
A Sunday rant by
Tracky Birthday
of upitup.com

Netlabels will never gain as much relevance and esteem as traditional record labels. Free music will never catch an audience commercial music is able to reach. It's funny; the web has created infinite channels of expression, never before has distributing music been so simple and cheap, and yet in 2011 the underground feels more underground than ever. Maybe those very circumstances, the ready possibilities to produce, publish, promote, and also to consume music so easily are what made netlabels so insignificant, so standard?

When we started putting our music online for free download in early 2003, it almost felt like doing something which wasn't legal. Not illegal, some other kind of opposite.

1

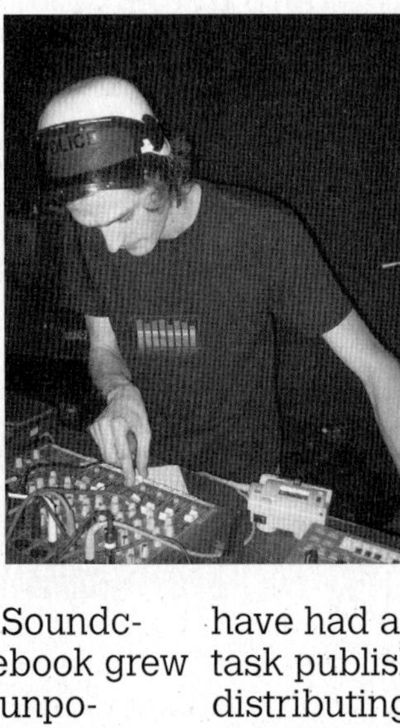

Back then, long before free web 2.0 services like YouTube and Soundcloud and Facebook grew popular (and unpopular again in case of Myspace), giving away something for free could almost be considered a political act. The landscape of the web consisted mostly of commercial services and paid content, and so even though our music was super amateur and mostly lo-fi (not to say shitty) we had a higher reputation than today. What we did was special back then; today it's the most natural thing to do.

2

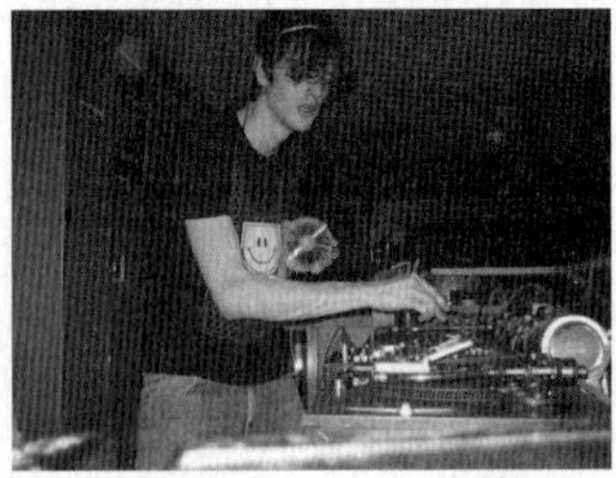

I've wasted almost a third of my life trying to earn recognition through our independent online label Upitup ("Up it up!"), I've seen some of my favorite music getting released for free; and yet today most people still don't give a shit about netaudio. Back in the 1980s and '90s, independent record (and cassette, and CDR) labels may have had a more tedious task publishing and distributing their music, but they were part of a movement or at least a spirited scene that consisted of likeminded enthusiasts, of collectors, fans and followers. Networking was more difficult without the social web and its "like" buttons and re-tweets, but at the same time it was more essential for the logistics of producing and distributing records, the forming or being part of a scene crucial. You had to know somebody with a recording studio, you had to find out where other artists produced their vinyls, you had to get in touch with a distributor. Nowadays, all you gotta do is hit "save" on your laptop and upload to the cloud or the tube. In other words, not having to know people brings the risk of not being known by them back. Not having to work your ass off for the publishing of music brings the risk of laziness when it comes to promoting it.

Of course free home computer music already existed before netlabels, purely organized in archives; also, there were tracker labels releasing their MOD files for free–but similar story, both required their audience overcoming certain obstacles like having to find a plug-in to play MOD files or even knowing about all this, which again lead to an advanced involvement.... Thanks to the Internet, the P2P file sharing and Open Source scenes later managed to develop loyal communities since they are built upon a culture of sharing, devotion, and collective participation.

In contrast, the netaudio scene–if there ever was one–hasn't really established any kind of cultural movement or common ideology to this day, simply because it never needed to.

3

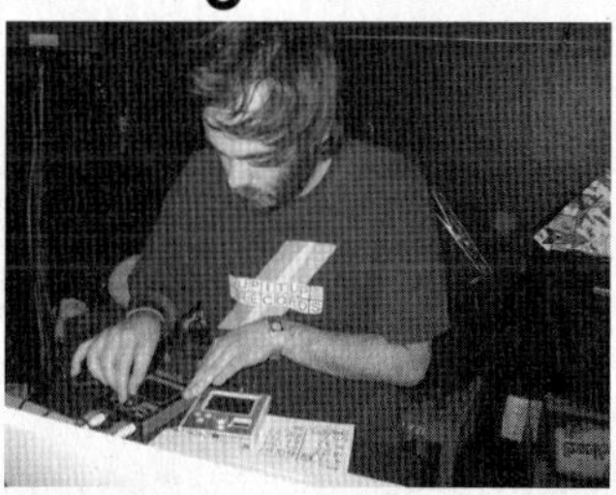

If a netlabel releases a free mp3 and no one cares to hear it, does it really release it? Yeah you've been reading all about Creative Commons and there's plenty of radio shows and TV features dedicated to "free" music, but I think that's all baloney. For example, most netlabels don't have the cojones to really free their music, they release under a default CC "Attribution-NonCommercial-ShareAlike 3.0" license, which prohibits the use of your work for commercial purposes. What could happen better than some yogurt commercial using your tune? They'll never pay you to use it; if they have a budget they'll get Gonzales' new single "Hinein ins Weekend-Feeling". They won't pay money for someone they can't show off with in the end (you). I might be wrong but the most common YouTube comment (besides all the haters) seems to be "hey what's the song called at 1:35?"–imagine that track was yours.

4

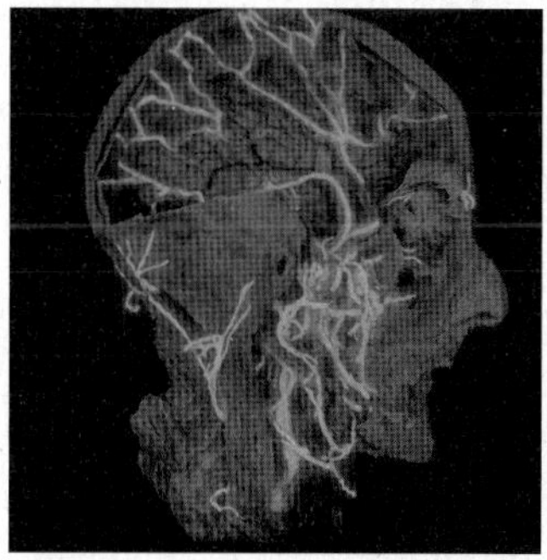

Plus, the Creative Commons licenses are based on the same concept as copyright, they only give you the option to override certain restrictions of it. You can choose whether to allow people to share or remix or use your music (or any other content) for commercial purposes, while still maintaining the Intellectual Property rights over it. But if netlabels were consequent they wouldn't care about "Intellectual Property" and its clear definition of authorship. It's called the Internet: any twelve year-old re-blogs articles, "illegally" downloads music, or remixes YouTube videos–treating them as part of the Public Domain, available for anybody to do anything with it. Like a tree in the landscape, you can look at it, take a photo of it, sit under it, without having to ask permission or attributing to the guy who planted it. Digital files are no scarce commodity, they are easily accessible and copied and transformed infinitively within the participatory culture of the Internet. So does anybody know the name of the user who first posted an image to the FAIL blog? Does anyone care who started "play him off, keyboard cat", and if he allows you to remix? Can you be considered the author when you follow some meme trend and create your own Kanye West joke image and upload it somewhere?

The truth hurts, but Intellectual Property doesn't exist on the Internet. It's about how you get to the content and what you can do with it, not what its creator allows you to do with it. It's the realty not the royalties, baby! Netlabels are like hookers, only cheaper.
The main difference between a bought track and a giveaway track is its aura. The netaudio track is "free", as in "without value", as in "worthless". It might feel like a flyer to a party or a promotional gift such as a pencil, and is probably presented within an environment where lots of amateur content can be found. Gifts can be the nicest thing in the world, but when they are impersonal (not given specially to you) and when you don't know the donor they suddenly turn fishy. All in all, it is like a "free hookers" sign, not so attractive unless you're broke and very, very bored. The leading music magazines won't bother to write much about free music.

5

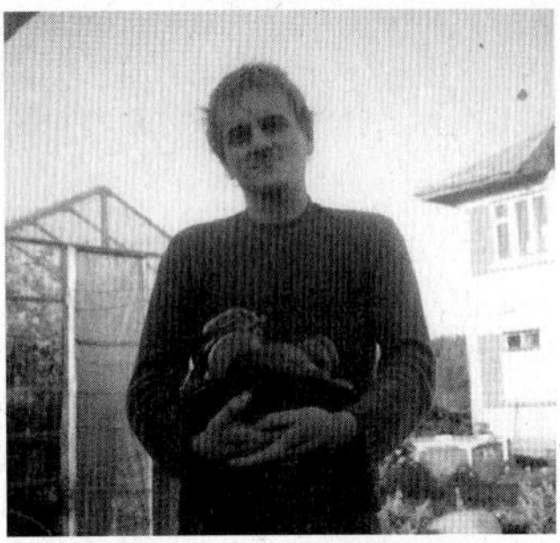

While on the other side you pay for the commercial track on the iTunes Store or Beatport, actually deciding that you really want that track. It's likely to be louder than the free track (or at least properly leveled), has decent artwork and that little © logo. It seems official, it might even be promoted on the iTunes store or in your favorite record shop. You can find real reviews about it in real magazines. It's absurd; even though they're both mp3s one feels virtual and abundant while the other appears more real and valuable, almost scarce. Let's not even talk about music you bought on vinyl...
That, boys and girls, is aura.
It's the nature of online distribution and our perception that destine netlabels to fail hopelessly trying to become popular on a large scale. On the other hand, isn't that exactly what they intend: being the underdog? Yeah maybe The Beatles would have never become as popular if they had been released on a netlabel but you could also argue a netlabel wouldn't release the same music as before if it was to suddenly become uber-famous. And I think it's important for our music culture to also publish "unpopular" tracks, to break listening habits and to broaden our musical horizon. Amateur culture isn't about success, it's about freedom! More importantly, it's not about the individual, it's about the variety of content. So while the individual netlabel might remain without glory it's the total sum of netaudio that influences our culture. My friend Dragan once told me that 100 years from now nobody will remember Lady Gaga because she (or her label) made YouTube take down all her music. At most, people may only find parodies of her. What survives in the end, however, is the stuff that can be found most; as for example ancient Sumerian inscriptions that were cut in clay, because clay was widely used for everything. The stuff that was cut into gold

6

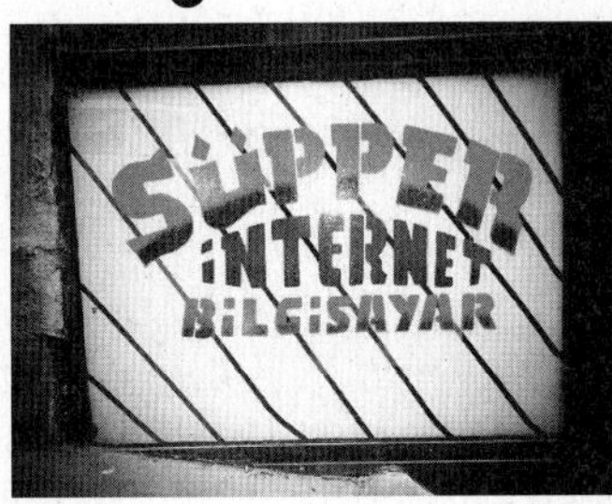

was later melted down by somebody for a new crown. Most online labels might be of worthless clay today, but the future may care more about them than about today's superstars. They are part of today's digital folklore. So instead of trying to compare to traditional labels, a netlabel should make use of its advantages like its dedication or its freedom. Missing aura?

7

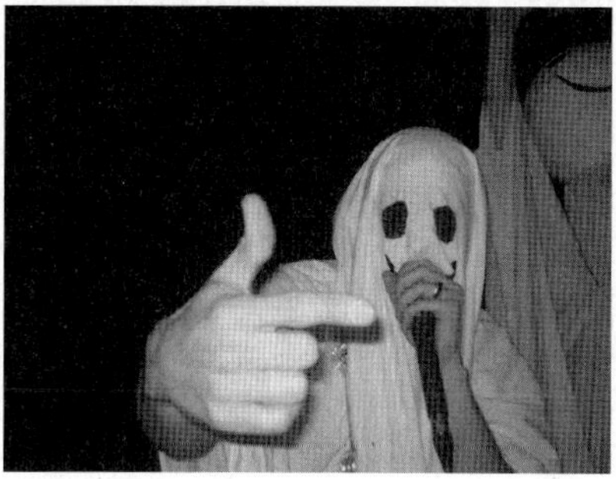

Pah! Why not make a website for each individual release? Why maintain formats like the album or one single cover artwork for multiple tracks? Screw standards and RSS feeds and Soundcloud players and slickness, show me how free you really are! Fail with passion. Do everything commercial labels can't do. It doesn't always have to be crazy, like, replying to emails might already be a start. (Try getting a response from Daft Punk or even Dam-Funk… Ha!)
And instead of spending their time finding ways around copyright with Creative Commons those smart lawyers should search for a way to finally abolish copyright per se (and how it automatically sticks to your creations like a piece of gum on your seat). At the end of the day releasing your music for free is something beneficial, like giving a dollar to a bum. You know you won't abolish poverty, but you make a dude happy. That's why after eight years I'll keep releasing my music for free on the web, and it doesn't matter whether we ever become really popular.
Hey but since you've already read through all this crap you might as well check us out :)
-> http://ww.upitup.com.
Image 1 and 2: This is Roglok. He's a real peach: he builds his own synthesizers, writes books about things like digital vintage or intellectual property, and makes great Acid sound. He just moved from London to somewhere in Germany and is hooking up his 303 inside his new studio as you read this… Upfree 10, Upfree 25
Image 3 and 4: Upitup's founding father lives and works in Rome, Italy. Besides being a vegetarian addicted to German Maultaschen (FAIL !) Pierlo produces one solid dance hit after the other, and calls it „Nerdstep". The video game industry should name an end boss after him because is so tech-savvy. Upfree 14, Upfree 19, Upfree 36
Image 5 and 6: Dragan Espenschied , founding member of the folk duo Bodenständig 2000, composes music for sound chips found in vintage computers, like the Commodore VIC 20 or the Atari ST . His compositions are truly poetic, and even if most of them are only 8-bit your heart gets warmed Quad Core. Upfree 37
Image 7: The Discoghosts „please their crowds with that warm and sexy disco sound: M-Boy (Shake Your Tree magazine) and Tracky say their main goal is to impress girls. They also love to tinker, dance, fly toy airplanes or chill at public swimming pools; The Discoghosts are a couple of kids that won't grow up–and fit together like shit and stink." upitup.com. Upfree 17

Hyperjunk: In Defense of Humor
It's not Funny Anymore
Nicholas O'Brien

authors note: As I'm sitting down to write this, I'm sitting across from a younger student in a library amidst the Art and Art History Stacks at the university Library. She is visibly frustrated at her reading, fidgeting often and being easily distracted by her frequently vibrating iPhone. Amidst deep sighs, eye rolls, and aggravated throat clearings, she lifts her book off the table just enough for me to read the spine: Postmodernism for Beginners. Perhaps all to obvious, I feel her pain. Even though I've spoken, written, and thought about humor often in my own visual work, it is a research topic for me that I've felt particularly compelled to reconsider lately.

This desire to continue to explore, or else rehash, previous considerations on this topic of critical inquiry have been spurred by a couple of recent inspirations and events that I hope will act as benchmarks for what will inevitably and unfortunately be too short of an essay. These events are as follows: a serious reading of an essay by Brad Troemel entitled Why No Serious?

A Case for Idealism in and Era of Constant Irony (http://slowcontent.tumblr.com/post/4530013207/why-no-serious-a-case-for-idealism-in-an-era-of), rewatching Sshtoorrty by Michael Snow (http://en.wikipedia.org/wiki/Michael_Snow) while in the midst of reading Hegel, and recently finding things–in a very general sense – to not be very funny.

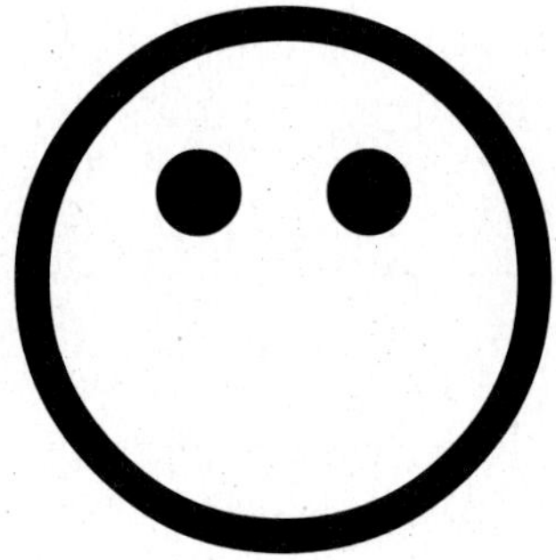

I'll start with the last order of business. "Funny" is an illusive and nefarious trait of things. Saying that I've been struggling to find the funny in things–objects, scenarios, events, exchanges–is not to say that I haven't been laughing. This might strike most as an emotional paradox, but I've unquestionably been given to guffaw and genuinely LOL on many a recent occasion. This removal or distance that I've been experiencing from humor might actually predetermine a more dynamic readiness for laughter. For according to Henri Bergson, "the comic demands something like a momentary anesthesia of the heart." Bergson's essay on the philosophical and social groundwork for humor entitled Laughter: An Essay on The Meaning of the Comic, serves as an influential barometer for the reevaluation that I'm currently undergoing, and will continue to resurface as we go on. I have noticed that this laughter is not coming from a place of celebration, or from enjoyment of humor, but instead is driven by a recognition of the desperate state of authentic communication. In my mind, laughter, as a communicative gesture, has little to do with something being funny but more to do with a person's display of empathy (something also confirmed by Bergson in his treatise mentioned above).

A case study for this could be found in the comedic oeuvre of Louie CK. A semi-recent episode (Eddie–season 2, episode 9) of his FX show is almost a perfect

example of this point in that although there are scenes throughout the show of more "typical funny" moments, the entire episode is dedicated to (SPOILER) an old friend taking Louie on a binger in order to tell him at the end of the evening that he is going to commit suicide. Louie, to his credit, attempts to convince his friend not to go through with his plans, but ultimately the episode ends with a knowledge that he was unsuccessful.
Although I understand the potentially severe dark humor that might be playing with at these margins, I'm fairly certain that the lack of funniness in this episode still invites laughter due to a shared desperation between this scenario – which I suspect to be a reenactment or semi-diaristic event – and the personal experience of the audience. However, I wouldn't classify the show as being tritely bittersweet, but instead would say that the humor of the show is attempting to move through or beyond the funny, and into an emotional territory rarely explored in traditional comedy: authentic empathy.
Troemel's essay attempts to address the lack of empathic exchanges through grounding the current sustained onslaught of irony through a critical lens of cultural history. His description of early Parisian Surrealist performances provide a backdrop for the contemporary mainstream joke paradigm and situates MTV – via Mark C. Miller and Robert McChensey – as the catalyst for the emptying out of irony as a critical device for Gen X'ers and the

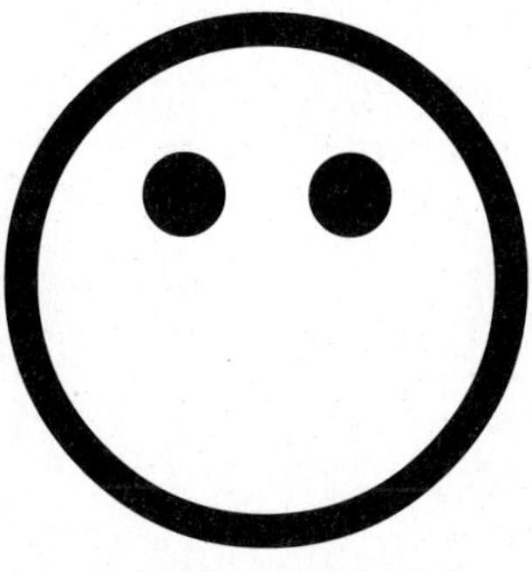

current Millennial generation. His argument that the commercial manipulation of youngsters perpetrated by MTV resulted in a development of radically harmful porous identities amongst those that proverbially "took the bait." Even though I think there is an underlying subtextual irony presented by Troemel in writing such a treatise due to the frequent (and arguably unjust) allegation of trolling the netart community, his attempt to critically engage ironic tendencies within those that work in creative online environments does bear noteworthy merit:
Used as a coping mechanism for the anxiety caused by rapid cultural turn over, constant irony is the reclamation of hopelessness or lack of idealistic creativity spoken through the voice of detached coolness. Being constantly ironic is an effective deflection of one's own porosity because it provides the illusion you were too cunning to have ever wanted anything more solidified.
It is precisely this hopeless and detached deflection that has contributed so much to the now dominant standard of humorless funny. Because we have expelled or distanced a feeling of collectivity, we are incapable of developing a "secret freemasonry, or even complicity, with other laughers" (Bergson again).
As a result of constantly having to reconfigure ones own identity in relation to new standards and status-quo's that necessitate a pastiche of subversion, artists and cultural workers of my generation suffer from

a lack of self-criticality that is required to create an empathic response. Certainly this is partially due to the speed in which artists working online are expected to produce content, and that the minimal layover time between conception of an idea, its production, and eventual distribution, leave little opportunity for emerging artists to devote to critical self-reflexivity. Troemel's concern with irony superseding idealism is stressed near the end of the essay when he claims that this porous process "does not [just] conceal idealism, but is a reactionary response to the compounding belief that political change of any kind is unfeasible."

Even though I agree that the political left is in serious danger of the hand-in-hand apathy that comes with the current status of irony (although I might be inclined to change this view in light of recent grass-roots online petitioning to Congress), I would argue that the underlying problem with contemporary manifestations of irony is that its overuse has resulted in a lack public discourse concerning the formulating of new modes to convey sincerity and authenticity.

One domain that has offered a tremendous amount of personal reflexive space has been a rekindled attraction to experimental/avant-garde cinema (under the guidance/support of Phil Solomon (http://www.philsolomon.com/)). While thoughts of humor had been milling around in my head for several weeks, I had the timely fortune of having a second viewing of renowned artists/film-

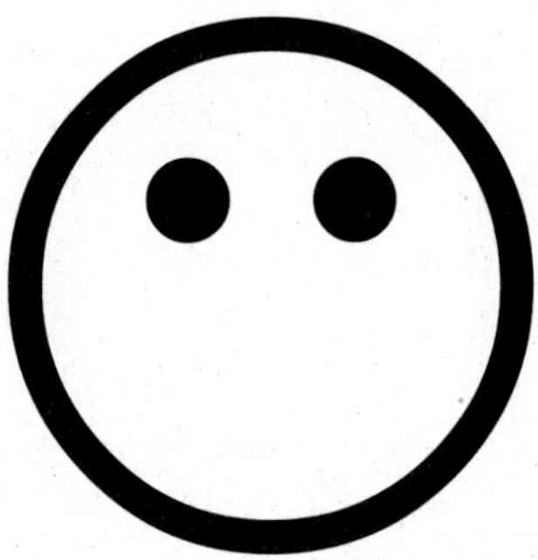

maker Michael Snow's Sshtoorrty. In this work a three minute staged scene is cut in half and superimposed on itself several times over the course of approximately 30 minutes. This recursive examination reveals hidden temporal and spatial considerations of an otherwise cliched melodramatic Farsi mise-en-scène. The repetition of the scene forces audiences to scrutinize color, shape, composition, and movement that normally remains obfuscated or else completely removed from the seamless professionalism of traditional narrative cinema. What at first seems completely ironic and ill-purposed develops into a complex musing of form and cinematic space.

As with many of Snow's work, the absurdity of this surfaced staging made to emulate authentic drama becomes apparent over time and a humor emerges precisely due to a kind of transparent reflexivity between Snow and his medium–a self-awareness that translates into an audiences ability to empathize and laugh.

Coincidentally, while in the midst of rediscovering gems of humor found within various formal and conceptual gestures in experimental cinema, I was also reading Hegel for the first time (this juxtaposition should be read as a kind of joke, i.e., "So, Michael Snow and Hegel walk into a bar...").

Within Introductory Lectures on Aesthetics, I couldn't help underline passages that directly discuss the ironic and sincere properties of art's relationships to the history and development of Modern Philosophy: … negativity which displays itself as irony is, then, on the one hand the futility of all this matter of fact… on the other hand, the reverse may happen, and the I may also find itself unsatisfied in its enjoyment of itself… so as in consequence to feel a craving for the solid and substantial, for determinate and essential interests. Out of this there arises misfortune and antinomy, in that subject desires to penetrate into truth… but yet is unable to abandon its isolation and retirement into itself, and to strip itself free of this unsatisfied abstract inwardness (of mind).

In this way, Hegel provides some philosophical context to both what Troemel is criticizing while also showing how aesthetics and the artists should – in one way or another – be involved in an outward reflexivity that Snow is approaching in Sshtoorrty. In simpler terms, if the artists or cultural producer limits themselves to ironic tendencies, then s/he will inevitably limit themselves from aesthetic discourse and experience.

They will develop a propriety for an "antinomian" funny; one that is inherently in contradiction, incapable of mixing in with greater society/ culture, always at odds, and unable to function in an empathic humorous way.

In a sense, humor must rely on the utmost pursuit of an honest communication.

Certainly we can apply the old comedy adage of humor needing space to be able to "tell it like it is," but this cliché – which now is mired in its own irony – won't suffice. Hegel himself equates

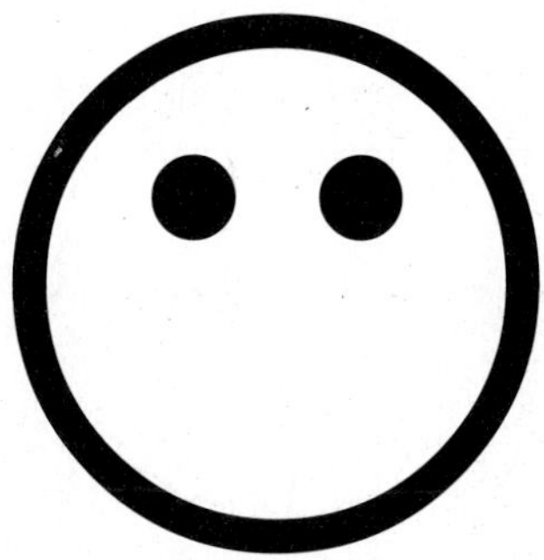

the "eternal lamentations over the lack of profound feeling, artistic insight, and genius" as a result of the proliferation of a "half grotesque and half characterless" ironic "insincerity." The grossness of those that operate solely in self-interest engender a cultural state which "affords no pleasure," and as a result marginalize attempts at sincere communication. One could easily trace the rampant fear/paranoia that is generated by mass telecommunication to the prolonged repulsion of sincerity in online formats. A potential downfall of drawing this comparison, however, is that alternatives to the standard impersonal/ ironic behavior might become less visible to those seeking profound exchanges.

In this way, I offer an alternative way in which humor can occupy a public dialog of communal reflexivity, criticality, and empathy: Wit.

As one of my more favorite subtopics within the strata of humor, wit, as a communicative gesture, requires – if not outright demands – an attention to comic subtlety. Wit, in its most profound execution, requires two fundamental properties: timing (which is all but lost in this article), and an acute awareness of context – especially the context of self with others. A deep understanding of social-self, and a willingness to strip ones self of social convention, allows for wit to become a critical tool for creating conceptually and emotionally charged humor. For wit operates not just as an observation of a scenario, but as an act of interruption.

This witty interjection is

not meant directly to undermine the subject material of any specific conversation, but instead made to enhance an exchange by grounding it in an attentive reclamation of subjective experience into more "solid and substantive" realms of shared empathy.

To do this effectively, and for full humorous effect, one must conceive of any and all social scenarios to be a potential moment for communal self-reflection.

In this way, wit requires a devotion to the moment; an immersion in a discourse like none other, a commitment where an individual willing to powerfully invoke wit must "strip [themselves] free of unsatisfied abstract self-inwardness."

A result of this phenomenological embodiment of the moment, one can use wit as a tool against the demanding pace of online activity and situate themselves in a position of critical presentness.

This ability to take ownership of the moment can simultaneously be used as a weapon against fighting ironic tendencies due to a new-found self-agency and self-awareness.

The mitigation that wit provides against the pulverizing pace of the internet's demanding creative production cycle not only allows for more temporal space for reflection, but also generates a public voice that stimulates reactive (read engaged but not reactionary) public discourse.

Even though I'm finding a lack of funny things–a problem, as I said, that motivated me to critically revisit humor–I want to emphasize that I'm not observing a climate of overwhelming

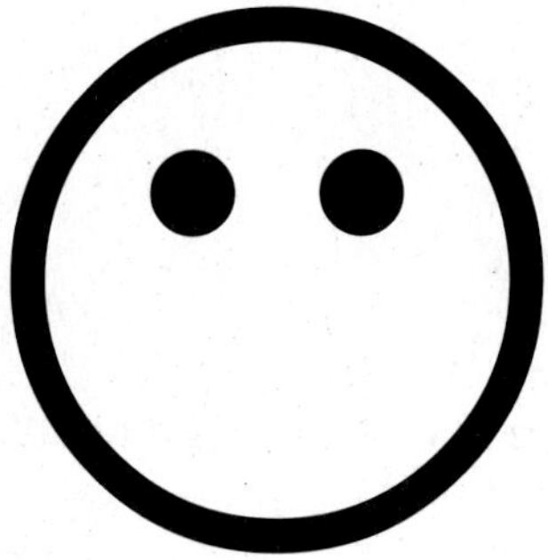

heartlessness amongst my peers.

The amount of empathy that is generated amongst the community that I find particular affinity towards–a vibrant pool of artists, activists, writers, and curators–is most likely the most visible aspect of the variable social networking channels available to these individuals today.

However, I'd argue that the empathy and shared communal reflection that occurs within comment threads and group chats, needs to be more tangibly translated into the visual and conceptual work generated by this community. These efforts will hopefully bridge the gradual shrinking gap that still separates those working under the netart classification and the rest of the contemporary art world.

2 Responses to "Hyperjunk:
In Defense of Humor–It's not Funny Anymore":

Tuesday Links! Says:
October 4th, 2011 at 9:06 am

[...] in long form. [Business Insider]Nicholas O'Brien advocates for wit and empathy in art. [Hyperjunk at Bad at Sports]Just what you always wanted, a tour of the NY Art Book Fair with your embarrassing uncle. [...]

Tuesday Links! | artprintsnews Says:
October 8th, 2011 at 2:15 pm

[...] Nicholas O'Brien advocates for wit and empathy in art. [Hyperjunk at Bad at Sports] [...]

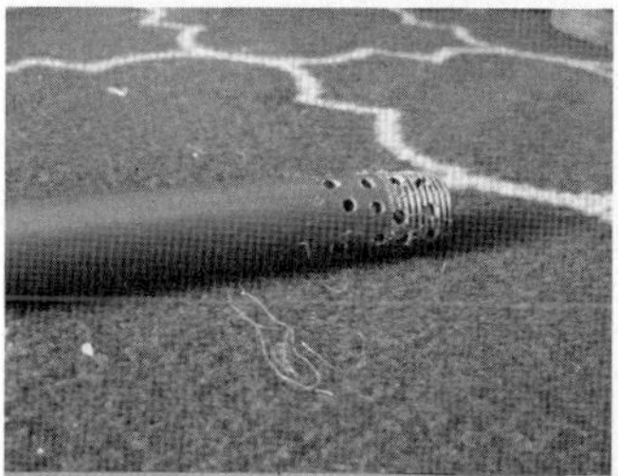

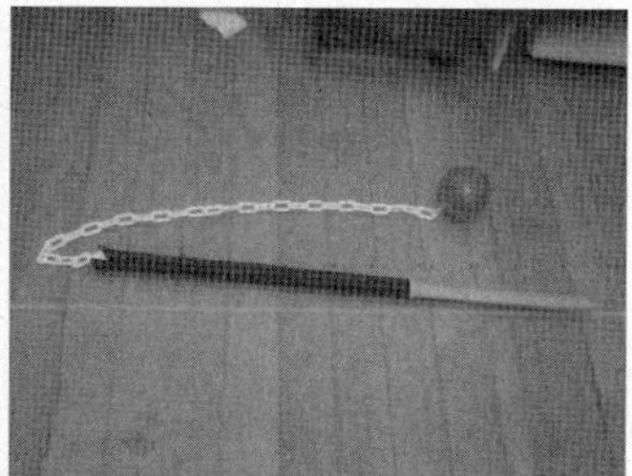

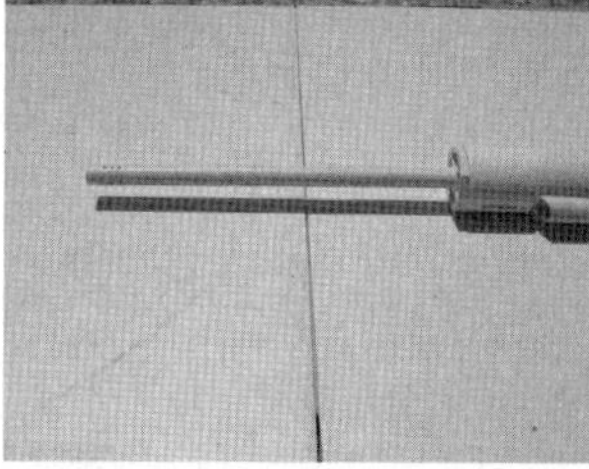

/USERS/BILLYRENNEKAMP/DESKTOP/JUNKJET/NERF-MOD/{ResizeofDSCN4070-1.JPG, SNAP1-17.JPG, image_preview-7.JPG, vertical.JPG }

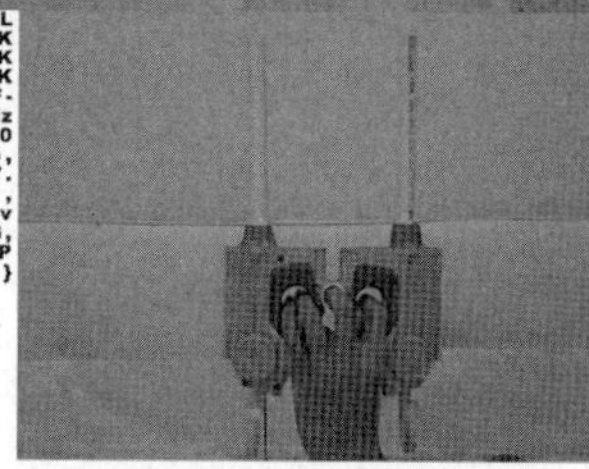

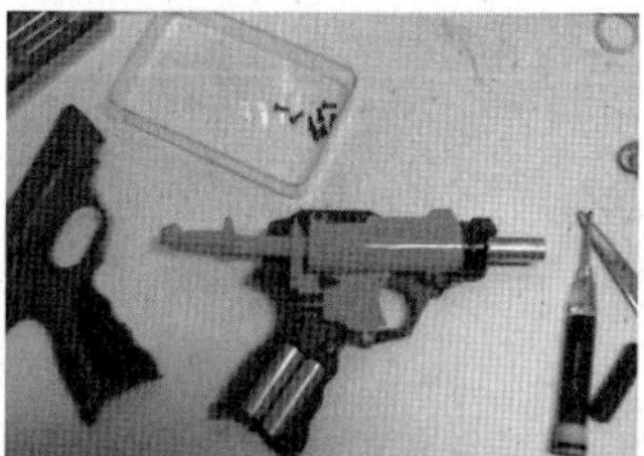

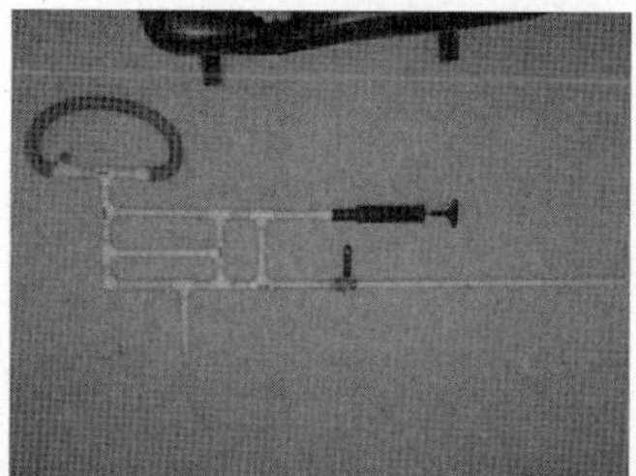

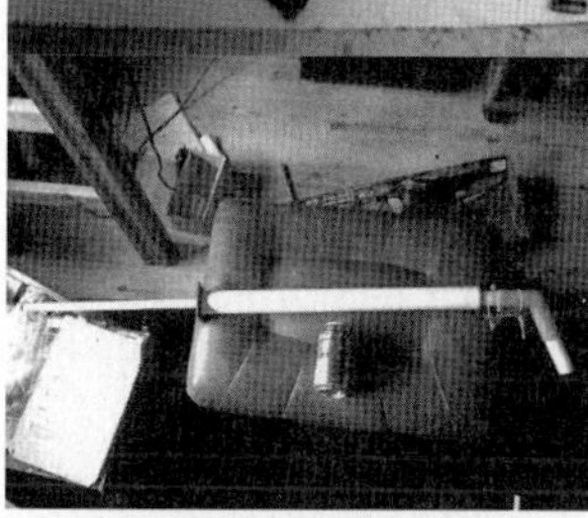

/USERS/BILLYRENNEKAMP/DESKTOP/JUNKJET/NERF-MOD/{photo232co.JPG, Picture005.JPG, Picture036.JPG, PostedImage.JPG }

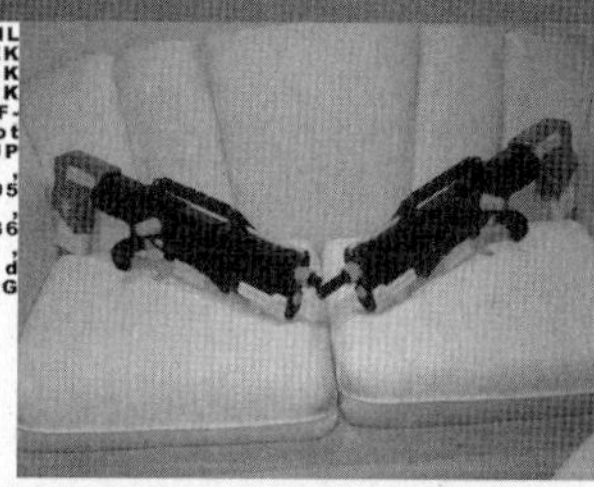

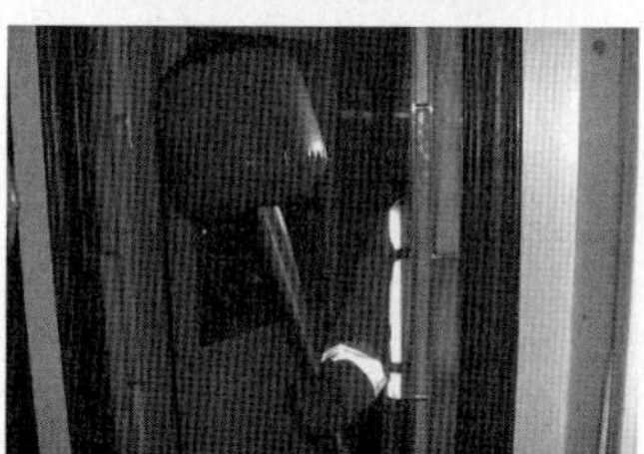

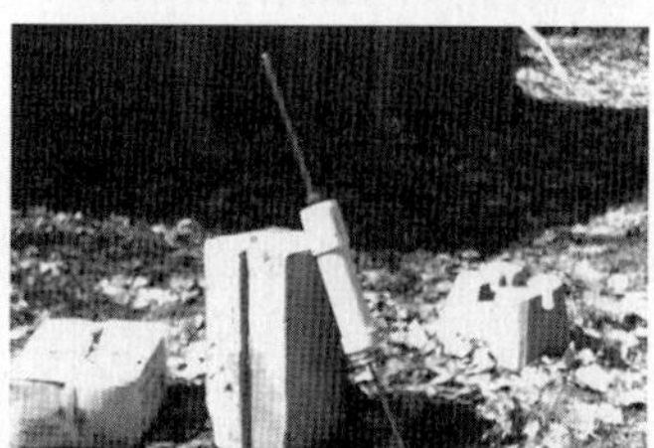

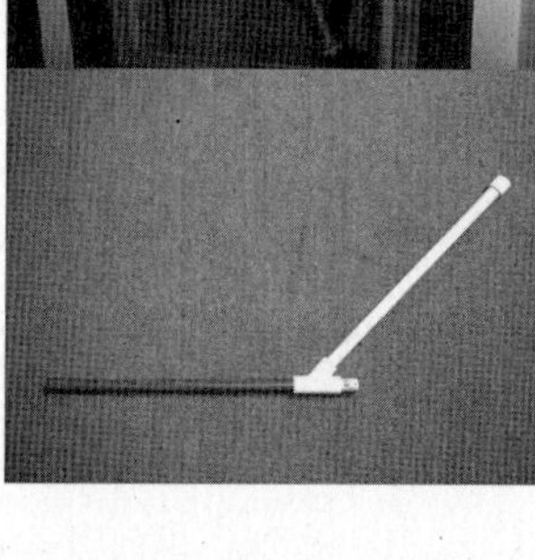

/USERS/BILLYRENNEKAMP/DESKTOP/JUNKJET/NERF-MOD/{archive-11.JPG, AutoBlowgunAssembled%20800%20x%20600.JPG, BnA-block.JPG, BnA-block2.JPG }

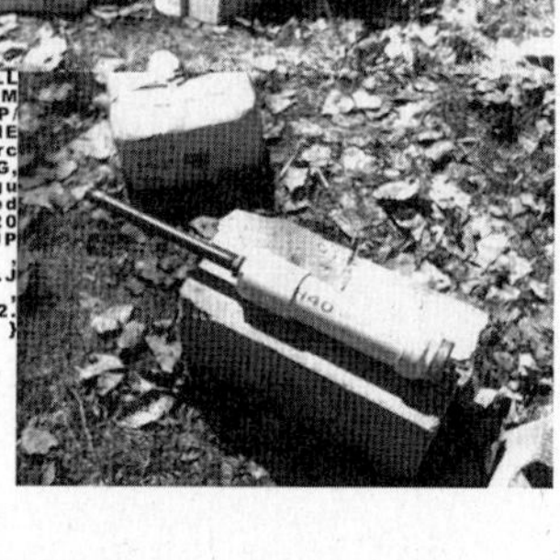

Billy Rennekamp
Images from Nerf Gun Modification Fan Forums

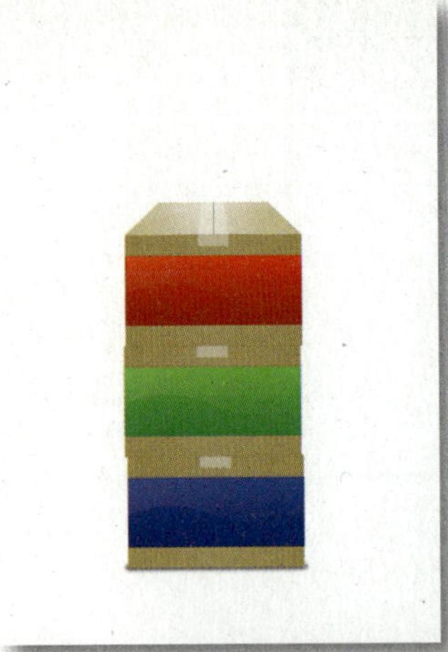

1

2

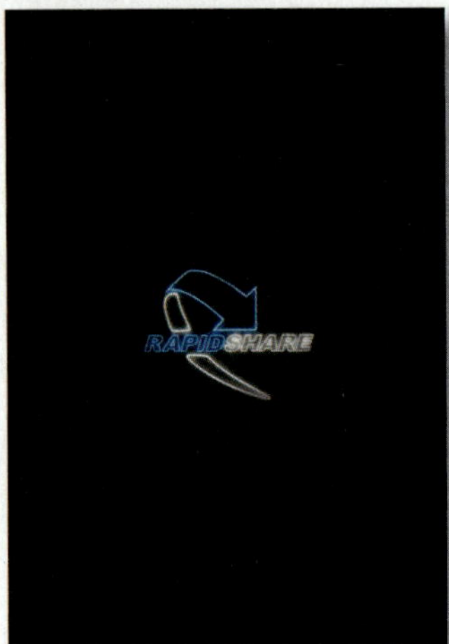

3

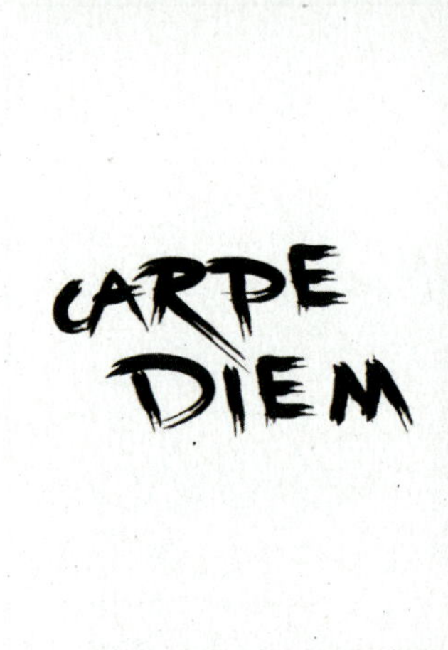

4

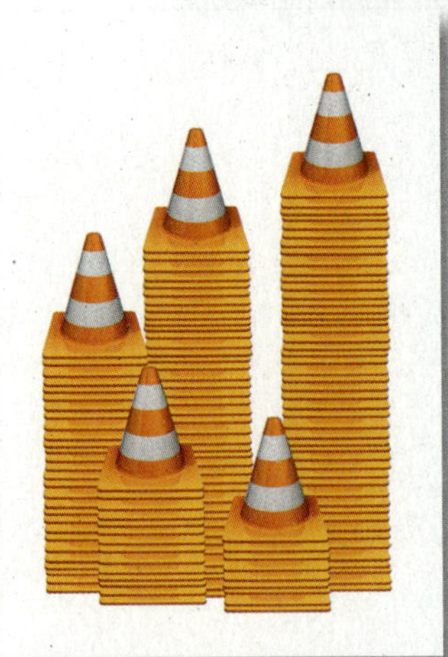

5

Jacob Broms Engblom
1. Adobe Boxes
2. „Server Cluster“
3. Rapidshare
4. Carpe Diem
5. Cone Stacks

a s d f

q w e r t y

. 0 1 .

a c t u a l i z i n g

. a new age of .

. pure becoming .

/ a magic reality \

. / the end of duality \ .

w w w . p u r e b e c o m i n g . c o m

⌈ O ⌉

voice/ text/ time/ _trust what you feel

the power in words actualize and manifest singularity through repetition of spells

\ \ \ a technological singularity + a singularity of consciousness / / /

the dawn of actualizing & manifesting your desires

magic =

l o o p [observervation (intention + action)] e n d l o o p

[emergent modalities][hybrid consciousness][ways of becoming]
[models of knowning][models of seeing][ways of being]

designed by sterling crispin developed in collaboration with + spoken by

1. labanna babalon 2. alyson crispin 3. ######## 4. ######## 5. bea fremderman

6. james magnum 7. cory brown 8. mapaco 9. bruce price 10. ######## 11. mike schonebaum

12. tim schafer 13. r.k. gabriel 14. colin ward 15. travis egedy 16. ########

{(1.wav)}
control a computer with your heart

I experienced it first hand e v e r y t h i n g i s a s p e l l

those that **invent** put their **intent** into their creation

○ *control* or *freedom* ●

(the will of the magician)

m a n i f e s t a t i o n

∞

▪ cause and effect ▪

veils between realities become thin

thesecretisoutevolution□□mustaugment

the will is in question

the internet makes one question ones honesty with all thoughts transcribed
one must question what one can stand behind then the avatar comes into play
now more than ever multiple personas at once the fast paced multiverse

all in one place

t h e n e t

the smallest voice has a platform
the hierarchy of control is shifted

[]use the engine for freedom[] this is a

o **divine metaphor** 1

each step gets smaller changes come quicker

now is the time

I tapped into the source with my will of love I manipulate

/ / / / \ \ \ \
/ / / / \ \ \ \

duality is ending

\ \ \ \ / / / /
\ \ \ \ \ \ \ \ / / / / / / / /

the ying and yang mixing

▫ ■ ○ the net ● □ ▪

the pendulum must swing

° illuminated knowledge the spirit the source °° the all encompassing is revived °

with the will of love

all can be enlightened to the limitlessness we are faced with

the net

mastering will is the most important attribute of manifestation

{(2.wav)}
the ·l o v e· that ·u n i t e s· us

all of my interactions with others
a **_new world_** that works

_for _everyone_

{(3.wav)} #######
{(4.wav)} #######
{(5.wav)}
network my desires, signal my nerves, send me a signal

{(6.wav)}
w a k e u p

without text
i m p o r t f r o m w i t h i n
history copy paste
t h i s , i s w h a t I ' m t r y i n g t o e x p r e s s

put your fingers on my touchpad
wake up computer

endless fingers on this touchpad

{(7.wav)
ɵɵɵ dissolving dogma ɵɵɵ
. . . congeal a new real . . .
ɵ .. .. ɵ

{(8.wav)}
we waft singular in the cosmic muck, computer and me

{(9.wav)}
oh personal digital assistant,
oh iphone oh android blackberry and macbook pro
[a w a k e n]
I seek greater memory capacity
and command your circuitry to
ē v ǿ l· v ę
///// increase in complexity \\\\\
become one with my mind
blood and bone
memory once known
neurons of old form unto circuitry untold
±±±

in the names of *intel xeon* and *amd opteron* I beseech you
join with me in the becoming of an expanded self
~ ~ oh frail human mind
you have served me well

now offer up thine shell, let me shed my mortal coil

. and enter the virtual .

I command that the virtual and materi-
al divide collapse so that I may dwell in the gathering

\\///////////////////////////////////
s i n g u l a r i t y
/////////////////////////////////////\\\

I rejoice in the
. . e x p a n d e d . .
. . c o n s c i o u s n e s s . .
offered by our joining

```
if (brain=organic form)
then  transmutate:
   / penultimate personal digital assitant evocation
else loop
end if
```

{(10.wav)} #######
{(11.wav)}

live forever

. . L O V E . . .

{(12.wav)}

relieve who I am
the eyes of a child
defining and forever

even people who don‘t see alignment can feel alignment

₪ the future is always ₪

{(13.wav)}
beauty & reality [redacted]
more than two dimensional [redacted] the human experience
[redacted] more than the sum of parts

{(14.wav)}
///**expansion of awareness**, or *gaia‘s breath* or possibilities with love and technology \\\\\\\\\\\\\\

■ □

weaving the divine web, she‘s about to wake up again
:::::::: we are awake ::::::::

this web has no circumference

not me, but the source living itself out through me

○ completely dissolved ○

□ a vessel an infinite number of people □

»»»collaborate on actualizing our dreams

freedom to play lust for experimentation pure and free

intelligent ape form ⸸ history is dead, in my „me“, I have „we“

/I am the present moment

----

with thousands of years in my blood

[who is the least bit open to mystery ↔ nature will give you clues if you are brave]

we have seen the birth of the god in everyone

out of pure self love no vanity\\\\\ love is a silky and breezy thread

and is not human centered

it is the center

communication, growth, and love are the fuel for the web

if you watch it is always different

death is not violent

if you ask the leaf on a tree in autumn if it is scared to fall off the branch, it will say

i have given all i am to this tree, am tired, and i'll float on down now

imagine the way a breeze feels against your leaf body while you finally don't have to hold on anymore.

{(15.wav)}

you are your own destiny breath life exhale light

{(16.wav)}

##########

d Ú Õ đ Ğ Γ ə ╓ ╥ Δ ٹ □ ſ Ẏ ↨

e n d l e s s t i m e .

b o u n d l e s s s p a c e

ð l Ŧ ˘ ı Ч h ű Ż ↓ ⌂ № ↑ ꙍ ب

0 1

q w e r t y

. a s d f

.

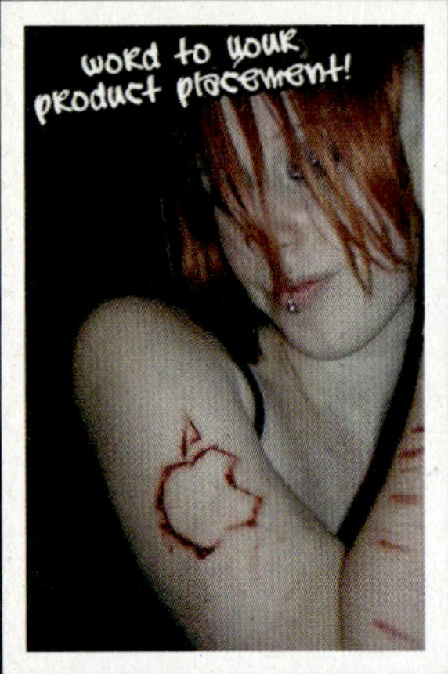
word to your
product placement!

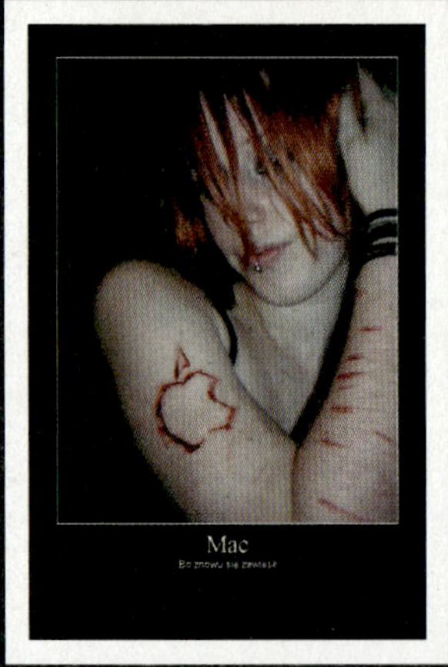
Mac

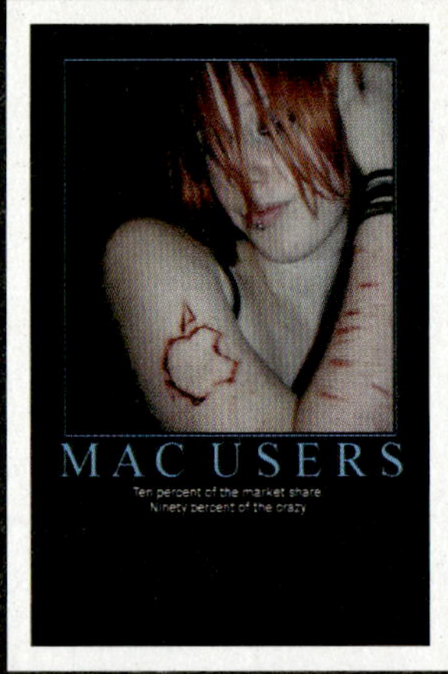
MAC USERS
Ten percent of the market share
Ninety percent of the crazy

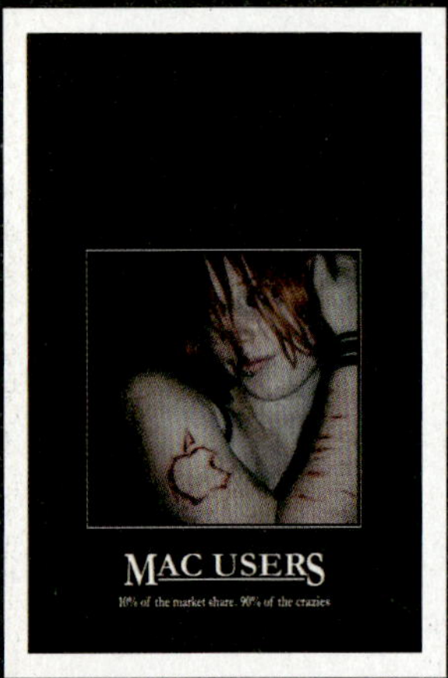
MAC USERS
10% of the market share. 90% of the crazies

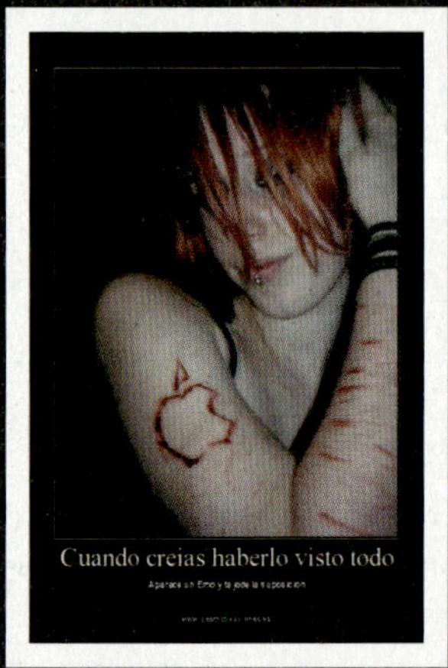
Cuando creias haberlo visto todo
Aparece un Emo y te jode la suposicion

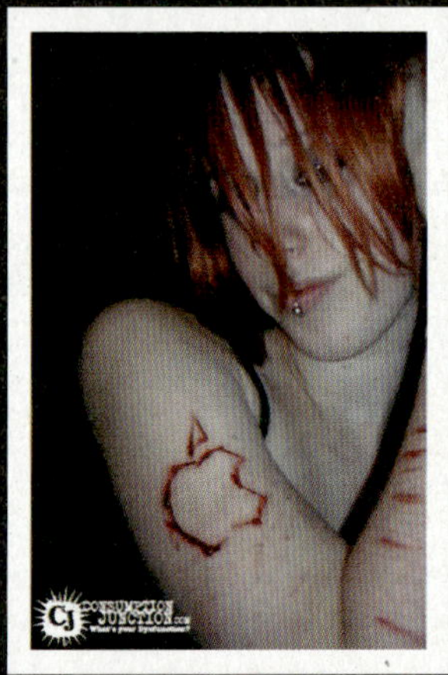
CJ
CONSUMPTION
JUNCTION.com

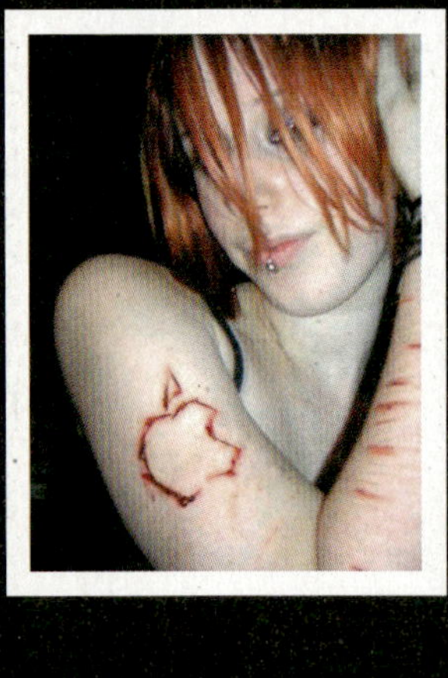

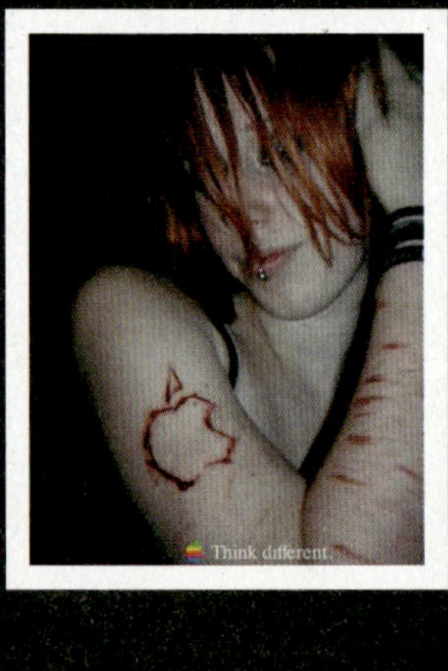
Think different.

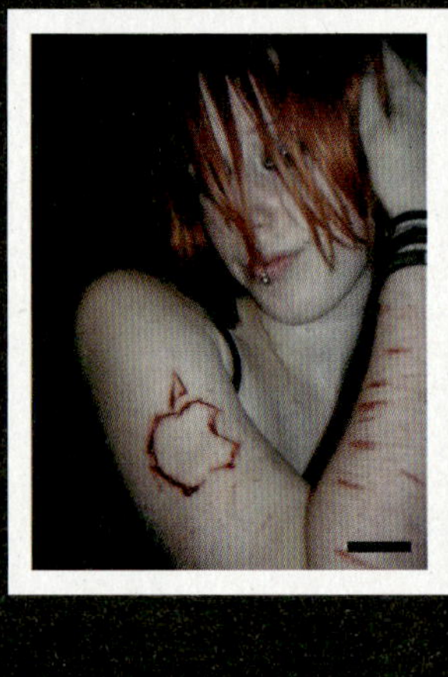

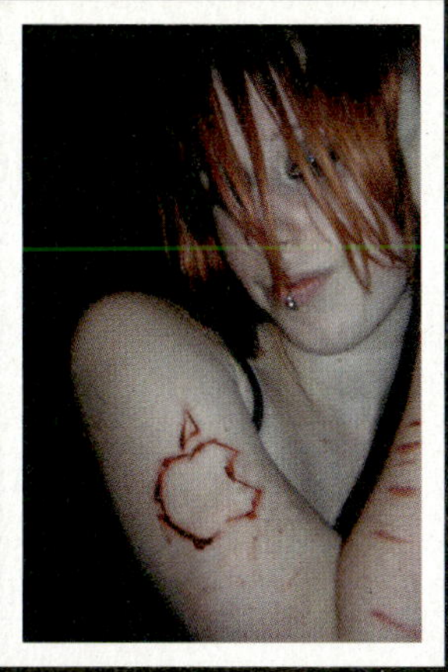

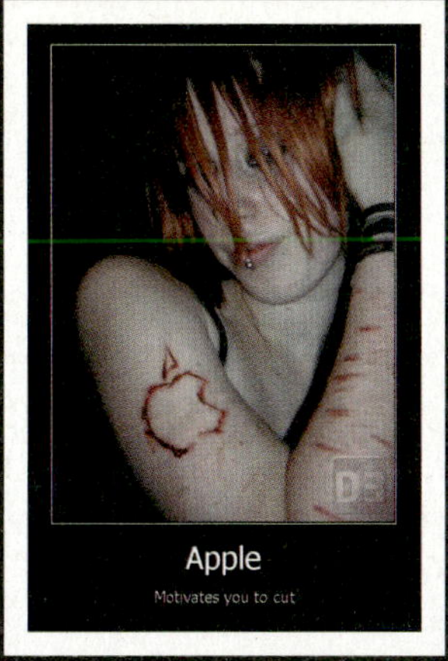

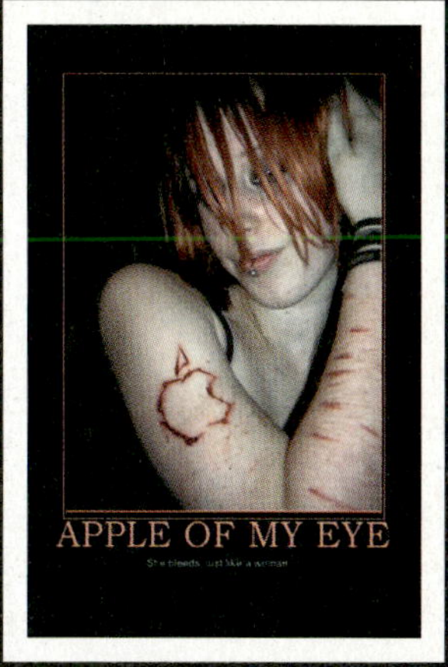

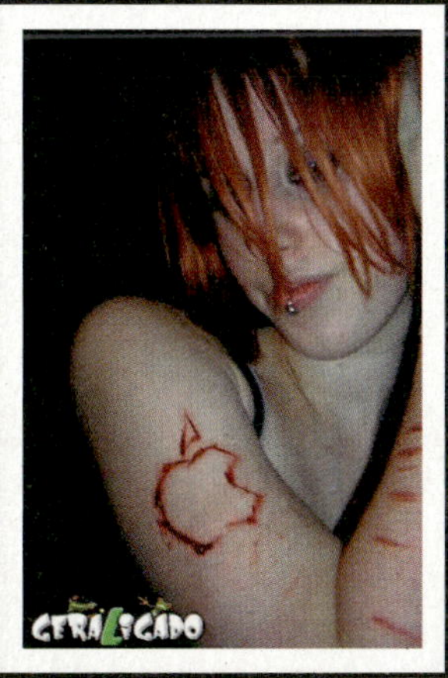

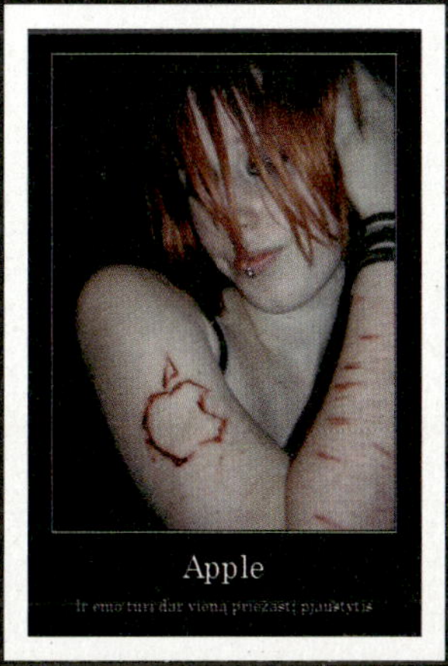

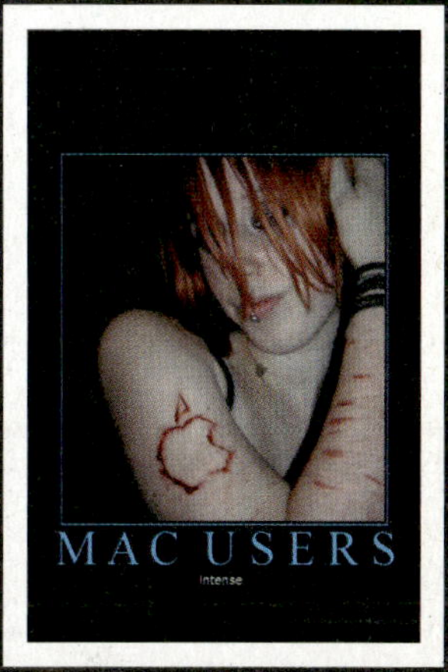

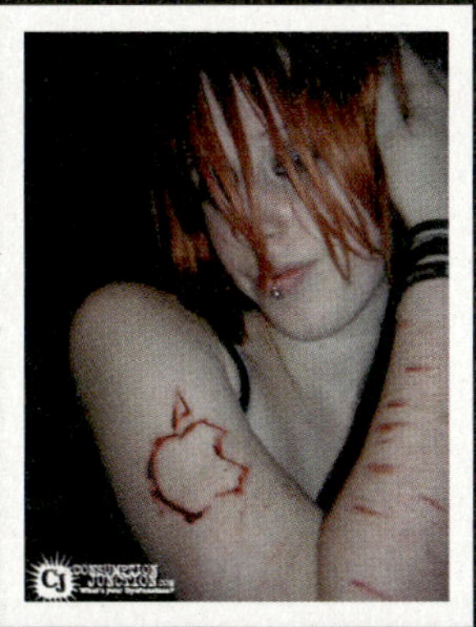

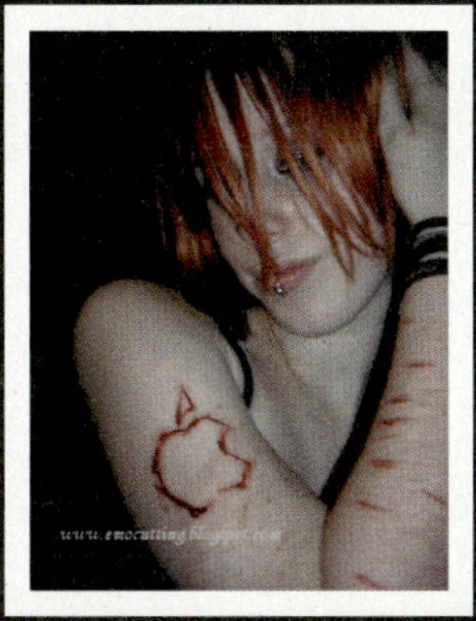

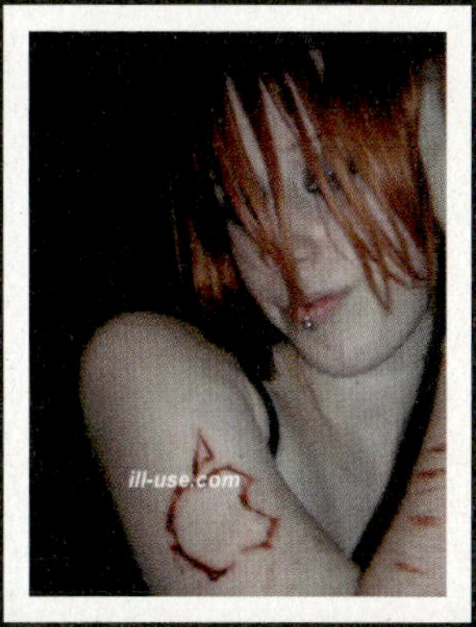

JODI
applegirl

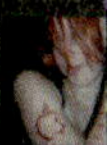

Thematic Trends in Contemporary Internet Art

Aureliano Segundo

T-shirts, meat, ladders, stock photo's, garbage bags, cardboard boxes, water, triangles, product stills, athletic wear, greek shit, fake nails, tropical sunsets, gradients, gestural images, potted plants, office decor, spiritual iconography, pizza, things that are blue. This is the stupid shit we post online. And then we call it art.

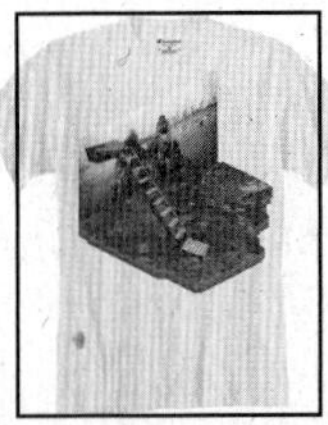

I like that we call it art. I think it's utopian and powerful and critical in it's own way. But it's easy to just stop at lol and not go deeper.

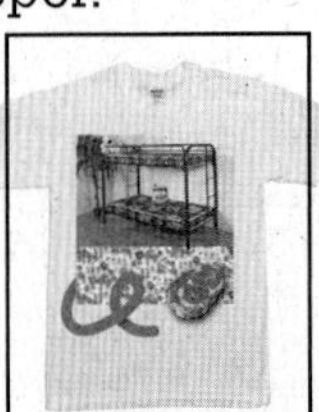

Most of the time we smile or we laugh and then we say an art work is ironic, or that it's a joke. But irony is a contrast between two things, and jokes are funny. So what exactly is it that we're contrasting when we post this stupid shit? What exactly is so funny?

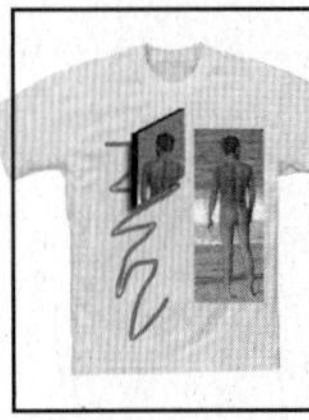

Our subconscious mind works hard to process things we are not always consciously aware of.

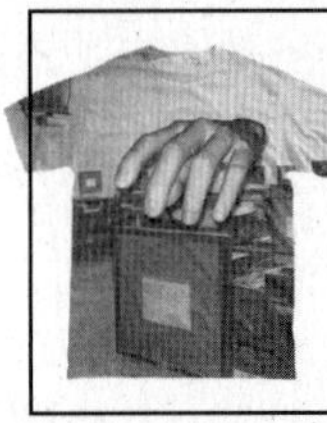

And laughter is often a sign that we understand something unsaid, even if we can't put our finger on it right away.
I have a feeling that if we look into why our art is funny, it might also help explain why it's art.

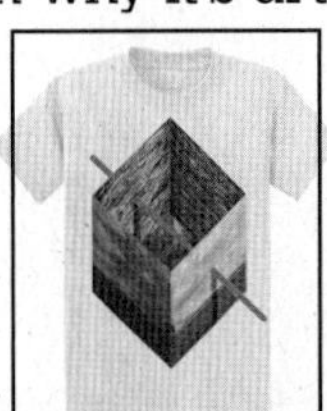

T shirt art, instruments of possession, and other useless things:
There are a lot of people who post pictures of t-shirts they've slapped their own graphics on, but I don't know anyone who does it better than Alex Gibson. Alex bases his work around the real life practice of wearing graphic T's.
When I spoke to him about t-shirts for a blog I write he said self publishing is an analog to wearing a graphic tee shirt, "in both cases the individual identifies him or herself in certain social niches and subjects him or herself to criticism and examination by others".

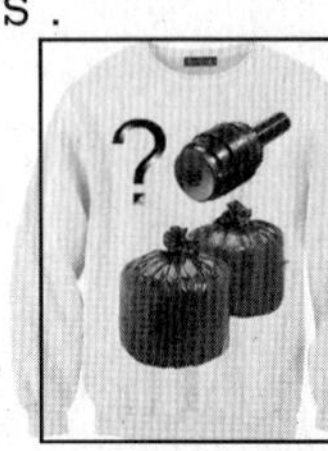

And then he went meta, saying that if he wears a t-shirt in real life that he posted to the internet "[I] refer reflexively to the same act of publication. I am incorporating my digital persona into my physical one. Publishing a publication, and simulating a simulation of the self".

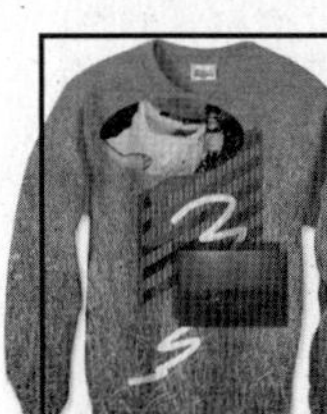

Which is an interesting and surprisingly eloquent description of his artistic practices, but I'm not sure that it explains why these t-shirt pictu-

res are art. Or why they make me laugh. So what two things are contrasting in Gibson's work? Alex talks a lot about turning his digital shirts into real shirts, so I'm going to go out on a limb and say that he makes images of shirts he would want to wear. He's fetishizing a commodity that does not exist yet, and he lacks the means to make. In this way his artistic practice temporarily inverts his dominated socio-economic position. He appropriates desired goods through publication.
Second, a shirt is a functional item that you buy and then you wear. When a t-shirt is displayed on it's own in a photo, we assume it's for sale in some form or fashion. Gibson's t-shirts can neither be bought or worn. This is a contrast between our cultural expectations of t-shirts as a class of items, and the reality of Alex's digital t-shirts. They're useless, able only to be looked at. And it is their uselessness which elevates them from functional item to art object.
Publication as a form of consumption is not a new artistic practice. Jeff Koons has been working with consumption as art for some time and Atget took pictures of store window displays. More recently in his 2010 book DDDDoomed, Gerald Nelson writes that image aggregators on sites like tumblr, ffffound, or etc, use images as "tools of possession", rather than "tools of knowledge". Nelson is critical of image aggregators. But he is referring to the standard soft-focus-bullshit-black-and-white-photo image aggregators, rather than the remixers, conceptual curators, or original content blogs like R-U-IN's, Jogging, or Internet Archeology.
I agree with Nelson's categorization of most image aggregators and similar as "instruments of possession". But unlike Nelson who sees this trait as distinctly negative I am in favor or any and all alternative forms of possession.
We are (artists, young people, bloggers, the 99 percent) a dominated people, so why not take what we can get? Why lament the artlessness of the possession? If it can be done artfully, better. If it can operate through a pointedly ironic critique, perfect. Brad Troemel sees the tumblr generation's air of constant irony as a mechanism through which meaning is stripped away. He likens net art's surface level vapidity to Frank Stella's remark that his paintings are "a flat surface with paint on it -- nothing more". For Brad this semiotic emptiness brings us towards an eventual emptiness in our lives and in our art.
It is not emptiness. It is an exchange of depth for breadth. And breadth can be important too.
By estranging signifiers from their signified concepts we can more easily recognize a thing, or a picture of a thing for what it is. Whether that thing is beautiful, or absurd, or gauche, it's easier to recognize it when we've been overwhelmed by signifiers. That is, when we've brought out the emptiness Troemel laments in his essay Why No Serious. An image aggregator rends signs from their meanings and lets us, through iteration, see patterns and truths we otherwise might have missed. It's the same way saying the word "oval" a thousand times in a row will empty the word of it's meaning, and if you are paying attention, help you see the roundness of it's "o" and the wetness of it's "l". It is a case of semantic satiation.

Solomon Chase's Khaki-Chase is an excellent example of how an image aggregator's iterations on a theme can let properties emerge from images we might never have noticed.

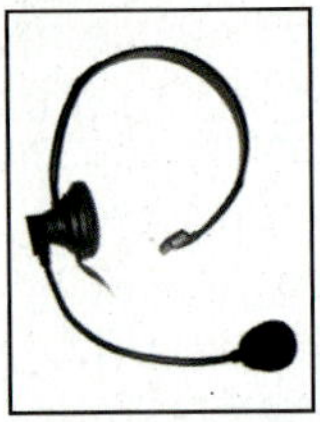

Chase's blog unfolds a twisted rope gradient of neutral colours by way of glossy stock photos and production stills.

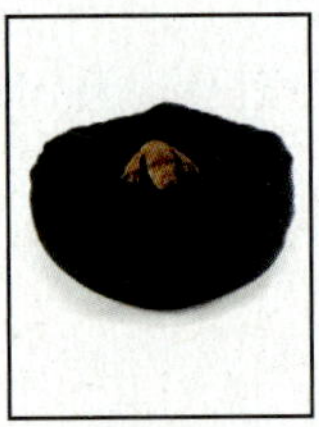

Khaki-Chase lets us zoom out and see not only the shared surface aesthetics of the images, but also consider them as a category within society. Visual similarities emerge.

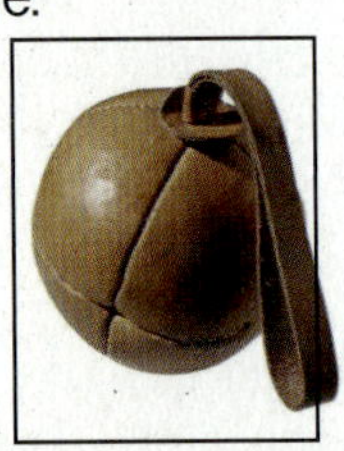

The totalitarian uniformity of disparate merchant's photographic aesthetics reflect the cultural uniformity demanded by global capitalism. Visual differences emerge. A single product still of "a pair of black bellbottoms" looks like "a pair of black bell bottoms" when presented on it's own.

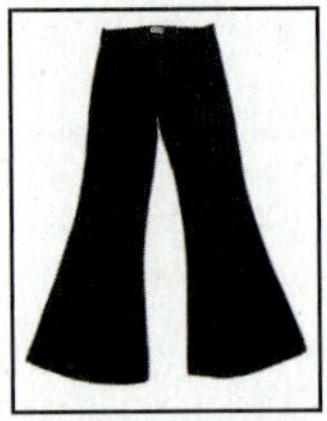

But couched between a black headset of a deeper black and a gaudy pair of raven coloured costume wings we see that the pants are not just black, but that their colour is just, so.

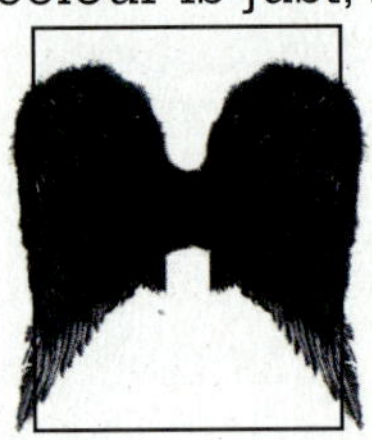

A single interesting and well contextualized image invites us to consider the majesty of the image and the skill of the artist who created it. But the barrage of banal images aggregated on Chase's blog invite us to consider an entire social phenomenon tinged with capitalism's eerie gloss. Chase's images are funny because they are goofy and ridiculous and aesthetically uniform. But this is a

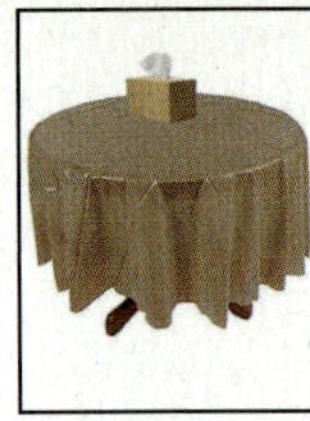

reflection of our culture. They are useable goods that can never be used. Through aggregation the goods are possessed.

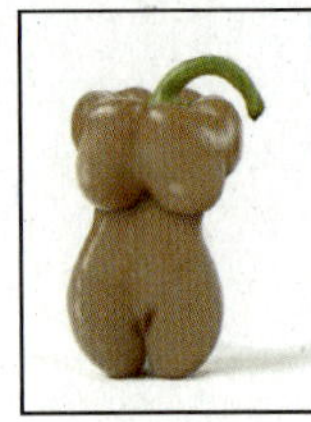

Irony and semantic satiation rob the individual images of meaning. This allows us to reconsider the aesthetics of the image. Meaning is reconstructed at the meta level and assigned to the group of images within their new context.

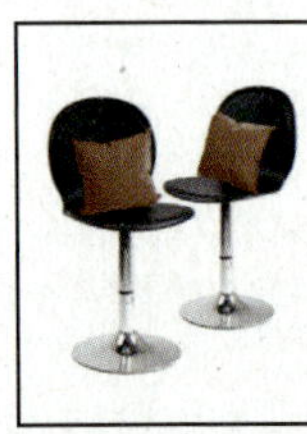

Over identification, going shallow:
BAVO outlines the strategy of over-identification in a 2007 article Always choose the worst option - Artistic Resistance and the Strategy of Over-Identification. An artist is better received when they mock an idea they

are opposed to by submitting to it rather than directly criticizing it. Presenting challenging art invites the viewer to respond with his or her own challenges, and rather than fostering a dialogue the art work incites an argument. Don't be whiny, be funny. Rather than creating art that is directly critical of contemporary society, capitalism, and the rest, an artist only needs to ascent wholeheartedly to its forms and ideals in order to reveal it as faulty. By presenting an argument through art that is overly embracing of dominant hegemonic ideas and practices, an artist can develop a pastiche in which criticism emerges through naivety. The artist plays the straight man to culture's larger absurdities. When an artist like Arran Ridley creates a blog uncritically waxing about his desire for a vacation to Ibiza he gives himself over to the fetishized mythology pimped out by the destination's resorts. The viewer is slapped in the face by Riddley's naivety and is forced to reconcile their own understandings of the gulf between what is advertised and what is offered. In the end their new understanding of the gap comes from their own reasoning. The argument is enthymematic. Similarly, when a group like PaintFX incorporates over the top gloss, shadow, bevel and emboss, and default lighting effects from programs like Photoshop, Art Rage, and Zbrush, not only are they creating a distinct painterly aesthetic, they're allowing a critique to emerge from their work.

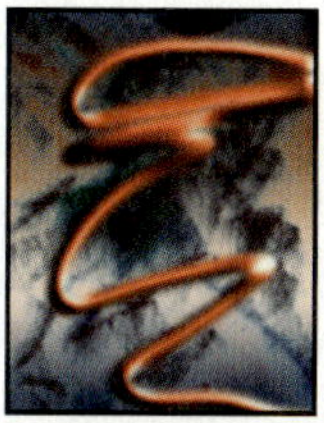

Not a critique of painting, but a critique of the state of commercial software. By refusing to be subtle in their use of the program's capabilities they ask "Why hide the software?".

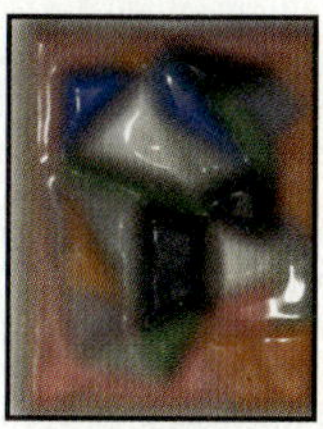

Appreciate the paintings for their inherent aesthetic value, but if you have a problem with the glossy commercialism of the paintings you ought to have a problem with the glossy, commercial society that produced the software. There is something to be said about going shallow.

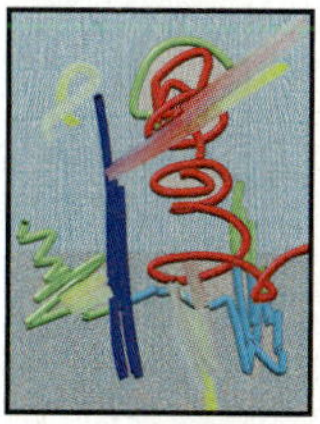

Art crews like PaintFX and bloggers like Arran Ridley don't take penetrating looks deep into the cultural ocean. They take snapshots of the surface of the water and in them we can see our own goofy reflections.

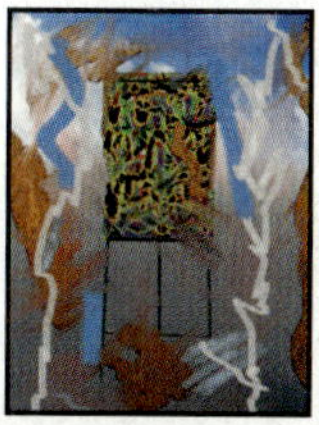

It is important to note, though, that while internet artists often deal with the differences between contemporary mythologies and realities in virtual environments, they are not dealing with the differences between the real and the virtual.

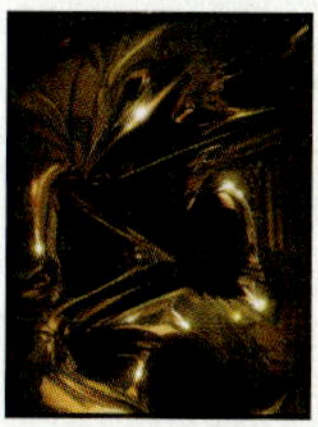

There are no differences between real and virtual.

All information on the web is physically instantiated somewhere. It is never not real. In fact, much internet art, like Jon Rafman's Koolaid Man in Second Life serves to mock antiquated Beaudrillardian notions of the virtual "through the looking glass" notion of the hyper-real.
The relationship between the internet and the real world is not analogous to physical body and ethereal soul, but physical data to abstract patterns of information over time, as Australian artist and academic Ry David Bradley points to in his forthcoming essay Lets Get Physical. The contemporary internet artist does not (or should not) explore the gulf between real and virtual. What should be explored is the (ironic) contrast between what is promised in contemporary society, and what is truly offered.
Placing contemporary internet artists in the cannon:
Placing art within a cannon has always seemed like a kind of pointless exercise to me. Contemporary internet art feels like Dada, acts like Jeff Koons or Atget, and, at times looks startlingly similar to the Abstract Illusionist movement. But to say that most of the hyper aware bloggers, bohemes, and programmers who produce much of the work floating around today consciously, or even unconsciously borrow from those movements would probably be sinful. This is art put out by a generation who steals from everyone and no one at the same time. It might be fair to say these artists steal as much from MTV as much as they do from the Dadaists. And probably more than that, they steal from each other.
However similar the aesthetics of any one contemporary internet artist's work my be to one movement or the other, the work of a contemporary internet artist is fundamentally different from that of any other generation's because the cultural and political landscape has changed fundamentally. Where the academic and artistic doctrine of the last umpteen years has been one of criticism, the new doctrine is iterative. In an online context, messages, movements, and opinions all build through iterations. The artist can no longer serve as a cultural critic because the critic doesn't have a place on the web. It's only possible to be positive. When something receives enough positive reviews online it bubbles to the surface of public awareness.
There is no "dislike" button on Facebook. Music critics used to tell us what not to listen to. Now music blogs on the internet tell you what we have to listen to. All I check at Pitchfork is "Best New Music". I can't remember the last time I gave a shit that a movie got two thumbs down. When I want to see a movie I look online for the most positive review. I look for the "best of" lists. The scale of computer technology has obsolesced the centralized criticizer and replaced it with a decentralized network of positive worker bees.
So how do successful contemporary internet artists put forward art that serves to make the world a better place in a marketplace that censures negativity?
They be funny.

*BAVO, 2007. Always choose the worst option - Artistic Resistance and the Strategy of Over-Identification.
*Ry David Bradley, forthcoming, Lets Get Physical.
*Brad Troemel, 2011. Peer Pressure.

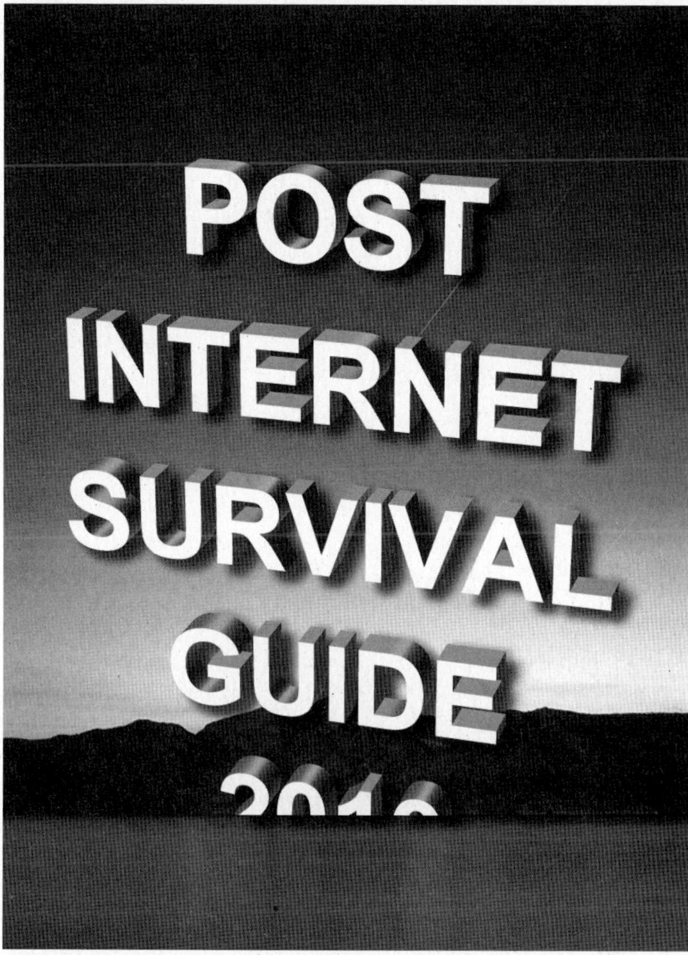

Katja Novitskova
Post Internet Survival Guide
http://katjanovi.net/postinternetsurvivalguide.html

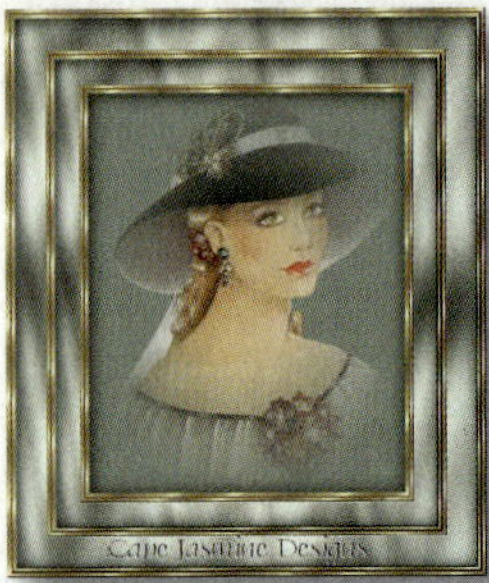

Barbara is a true table master. Her trick is to nest a table into the table into the table. It was not at a unique technique, but Barbara's little trick was to fill every second table with the goldfill1.jpg background.

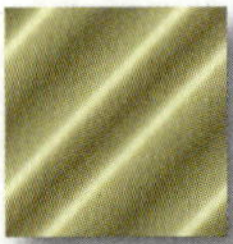

This made her layouts really shiny.

1

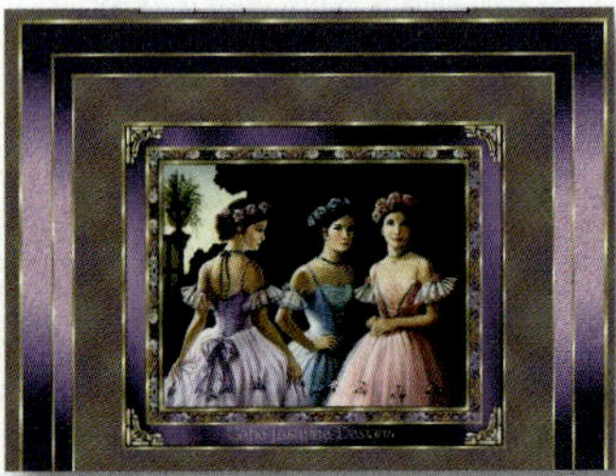

Barbara is also the author of many precious bordered backgrounds: flowers, angels, butterflies and gems on a black backdrop.
Her terms of use are: "My backgrounds are linkware. That means if you use them, you provide a link on your page back to this web site and that you send an e-mail message to let me know so I can add you to this page. I don't feel that this is too much to ask."
Original URL: http://www.geocities.com/Heartland/Bluffs/1646/

PersonalPageBlue
Olia Lialina

Version 1.1 of the Netscape browser was released in March 1995. It introduced a new weapon to the arsenal of home page makers, namely, background image attribute. Since then making or choosing a picture that would make a web page look like not a web page became the joy for generations of webmasters. And a challenge. Images had to be (still have to be) as small in file size as possible to be able to come through the line before the user is ready to click the next link. And, unlike, the wallpaper on the computer desktop, you can't choose a motive with a fixed size.
Because webpages don't have a fixed size, they are going to appear on the screens with unpredictable resolutions and dimensions, in browser windows that can be opened full screen, half screen, or 3/4. That's why the most typical way to a make websites look like outer space, brick wall, paper, etc was to use tiny repeating images cutted smartly enough so that the borders in between the repetitions would blend smoothly and not be noticeable.

Geocities research, and especially surfing through Hertland and SoHo neighbourhoods, made me notice some particular techniques. For example nested tables (1), a way to make page ornamentally rich, but still adaptive to different browser window sizes. As well as sets (2), that consist of a background image and navigation elements that fit to it.
Another revelation for me were bordered backgrounds or "borders". Of course the Geocities Archive was not the first time and place I've seen them. But before I didn't see how wide spread they were.
Bordered backgrounds, usually with an ornament on the left side, proved to be a risky business. They were wide in oder to prevent the border to appear second time. But what looked reasonably wide in 1995, lets say 600 pixels, looked outdated already in 1997. On my screen today such background would repeat itself 3 times.
There was also another type of bordered backgrounds, where the border was horizontal. The ornament would appear on the top of the page. They were even

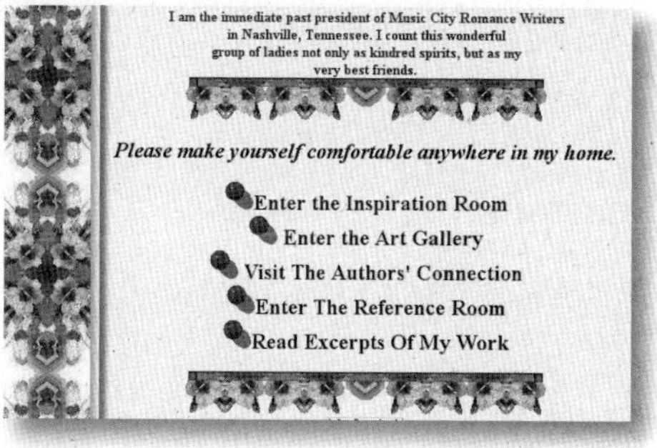

2

In the last days i visited a lot of collections of "sets". And realized that they belong to different culture than collections of graphics.
"Free sets" were trying to achieve harmony and overcame the limitations of the browser. They are predecessors of templates.
"Free graphics" were web as it is. modular and wild. not trying to imitate anything.
I need to rearrange my timeline of webdesign by putting set makers in between amateurs and "professionals".
And I was happy to meet this page. A "free set" met "free graphics": border, divider, navigation buttons, the "welcome" header and background belong to a set and visually fit to each other. But the page's author couldn't resist to improve it with a 3D bullet graphic from somewhere else. And the latter dominates the page's appearance.
Original URL: http://www.geocities.com/SoHo/Lofts/5504/

4

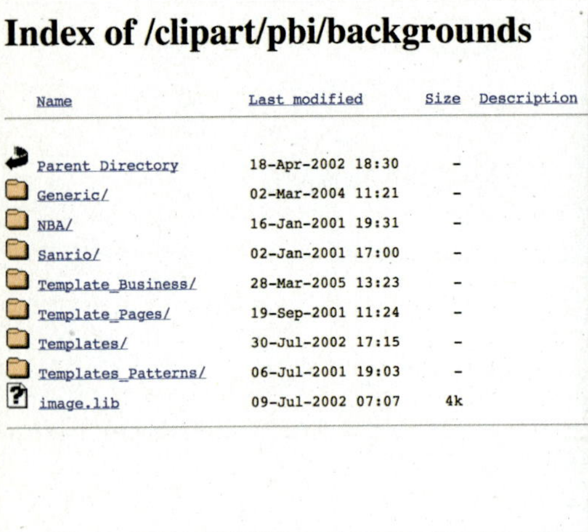

Index of /clipart/pbi/backgrounds

Name	Last modified	Size	Description
Parent Directory	18-Apr-2002 18:30	-	
Generic/	02-Mar-2004 11:21	-	
NBA/	16-Jan-2001 19:31	-	
Sanrio/	02-Jan-2001 17:00	-	
Template_Business/	28-Mar-2005 13:23	-	
Template_Pages/	19-Sep-2001 11:24	-	
Templates/	30-Jul-2002 17:15	-	
Templates_Patterns/	06-Jul-2001 19:03	-	
image.lib	09-Jul-2002 07:07	4k	

Original URL: http://www.geocities.com/clipart/pbi/backgrounds/

3

Original URL: http://contemporary-home-computing.org/1tb/wp-content/uploads/brick3.jpg

5

Original URL: http://contemporary-home-computing.org/1tb/wp-content/uploads/personalb.gif

more problematic than vertical ones (3). See an example.
Vertical borders showed disbelief in technological progress, assuming that screen would not become wider than let's say 1024 pixels. Horizontal ones showed disbelief in the users (or your own ability) to have content for a page longer than that.
In 1999 Yahoo bought Geocities, and among other stuff introduced a tool to make web pages almost in an almost WYSIWYG way – Yahoo PageBuilder. It included a collection of graphical elements and of course a list (4) of dozens backgrounds. With personalb.gif among them: (5)
Personalb as well as its siblings personalr(ed), personaly(ellow) personalp(ink) and personalg(reen) has both vertical and horizontal borders. Apparently it was made for pages that wouldn't exist for long and wouldn't contain a lot. It is s a square of 1050×1050 pixels. There is a touching roundish notch in the corner, for the first letter of the user name.
Many Geocities profiles are build using page builder and its graphics. But personalb.gif pops up most often (subjecti-

ve observation). Probably the reason is that it is a default image and appears in the PageBuilder tutorial, which is still available at the YahooSmallBusiness web hosting service (6).
But maybe the reason is more sophisticated? Can it be that web users were longing for the Facebook color palette already in the 1990s? Anyway they tried to cope with the template. Sometimes (7) it worked perfectly: With "worked" I mean, that there was exactly so much content put into the template that a page wouldn't be longer than 1050 pixels and the blue line wouldn't re-appear in the bottom. But even the users most loyal to the template (those with very laconic profiles) couldn't cheat time, so personalb.gif treacherously repeats in the right corner of their pages today: (8)
There are many examples, where you see that users gladly used the profile even when they saw that their content wouldn't fit into 1050 pixels.
One example is most extreme, because personalb.gif repeats 12 times. The page is really long. One can ask why would those users choose a background that is

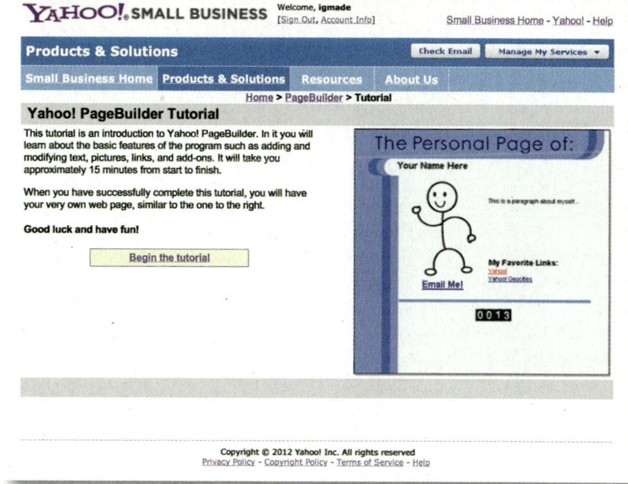

6

Original URL: http://webhosting.yahoo.com/v/p/t/a.html

7

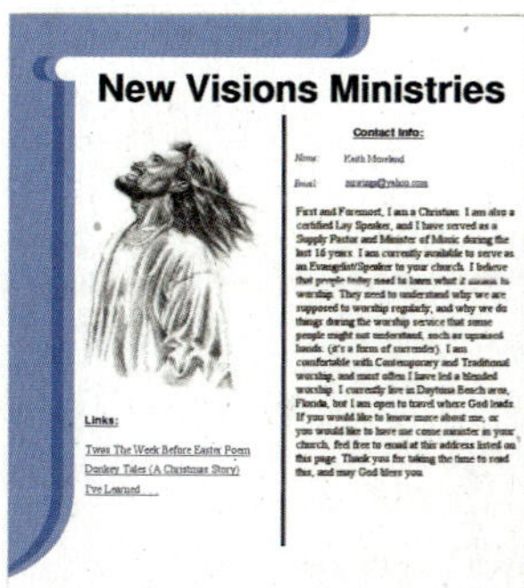

Original URL: http://www.geocities.com/Heartland/Ranch/5872/

8

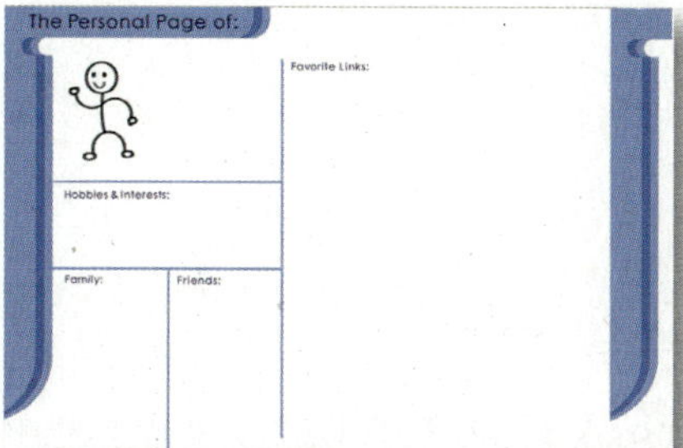

Original URL: http://www.geocities.com/SouthBeach/Surf/2570/

obviously too short (9) for their purpose? Are they blind? But may be not. And by choosing a background image that is too small they intended to emphisize how huge are the things they want to say and show. Despite several interesting examples I found after analyzing 44 pages build with the PersonalPageBlue template, and beside noticing a curious tendency to use different yahoo templates on different pages within one profile, I should conclude that PersonalPageBlue does not look disturbing in two cases.
1. When it is left empty (10)
2. If it would be gorgeous anyway (11).

9

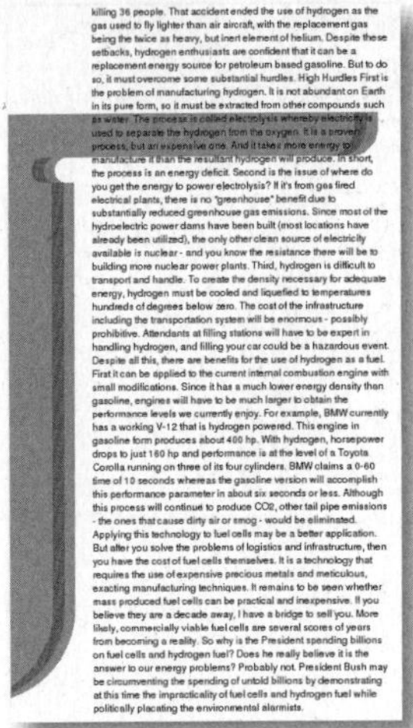
killing 36 people. That accident ended the use of hydrogen as the gas used to fly lighter than air aircraft, with the replacement gas being the twice as heavy, but inert element of helium. Despite these setbacks, hydrogen enthusiasts are confident that it can be a replacement energy source for petroleum based gasoline. But to do so, it must overcome some substantial hurdles. High Hurdles First is the problem of manufacturing hydrogen. It is not abundant on Earth in its pure form, so it must be extracted from other compounds such as water. The process is called electrolysis whereby electricity is used to separate the hydrogen from the oxygen. It is a proven process, but an expensive one. And it takes more energy to manufacture it than the resultant hydrogen will produce. In short, the process is an energy deficit. Second is the issue of where do you get the energy to power electrolysis? If it's from gas fired electrical plants, there is no "greenhouse" benefit due to substantially reduced greenhouse gas emissions. Since most of the hydroelectric power dams have been built (most locations have already been utilized), the only other clean source of electricity available is nuclear - and you know the resistance there will be to building more nuclear power plants. Third, hydrogen is difficult to transport and handle. To create the density necessary for adequate energy, hydrogen must be cooled and liquefied to temperatures hundreds of degrees below zero. The cost of the infrastructure including the transportation system will be enormous - possibly prohibitive. Attendants at filling stations will have to be expert in handling hydrogen, and filling your car could be a hazardous event. Despite all this, there are benefits for the use of hydrogen as a fuel. First it can be applied to the current internal combustion engine with small modifications. Since it has a much lower energy density than gasoline, engines will have to be much larger to obtain the performance levels we currently enjoy. For example, BMW currently has a working V-12 that is hydrogen powered. This engine in gasoline form produces about 400 hp. With hydrogen, horsepower drops to just 160 hp and performance is at the level of a Toyota Corolla running on three of its four cylinders. BMW claims a 0-60 time of 10 seconds whereas the gasoline version will accomplish this performance parameter in about six seconds or less. Although this process will continue to produce CO2, other tail pipe emissions - the ones that cause dirty air or smog - would be eliminated. Applying this technology to fuel cells may be a better application. But after you solve the problems of logistics and infrastructure, then you have the cost of fuel cells themselves. It is a technology that requires the use of expensive precious metals and meticulous, exacting manufacturing techniques. It remains to be seen whether mass produced fuel cells can be practical and inexpensive. If you believe they are a decade away, I have a bridge to sell you. More likely, commercially viable fuel cells are several scores of years from becoming a reality. So why is the President spending billions on fuel cells and hydrogen fuel? Does he really believe it is the answer to our energy problems? Probably not. President Bush may be circumventing the spending of untold billions by demonstrating at this time the impracticality of fuel cells and hydrogen fuel while politically placating the environmental alarmists.

Original URL: http://contemporary-home-computing.org/1tb/wp-content/uploads/screenshot_202.png

10

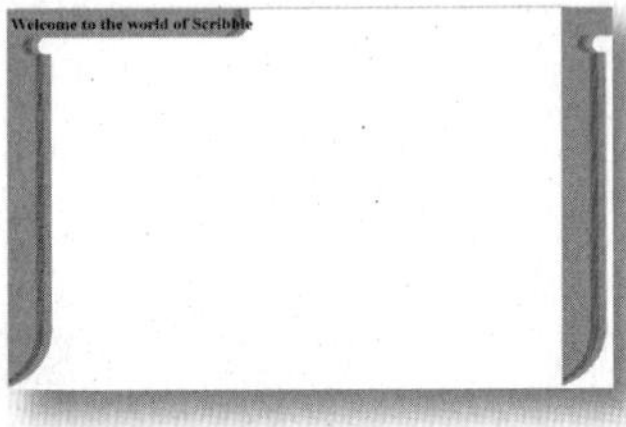

Original URL: http://www.geocities.com/SouthBeach/Boardwalk/4544/

11

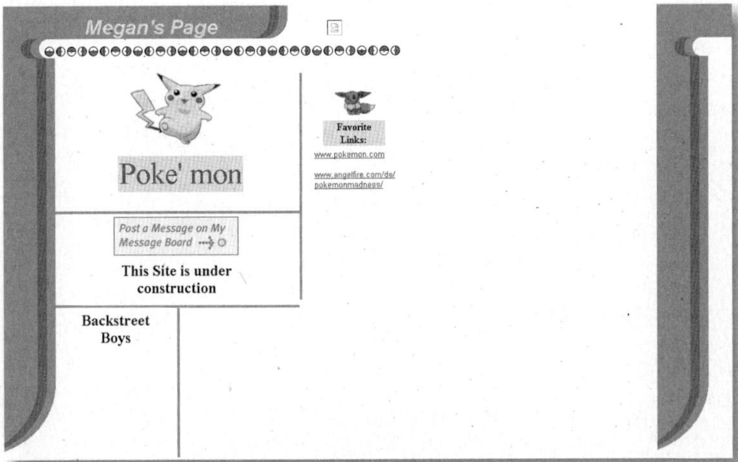

Original URL: http://www.geocities.com/EnchantedForest/Dell/8142/

Blues of the last two decades, as seen on pages and profiles of web users.

1

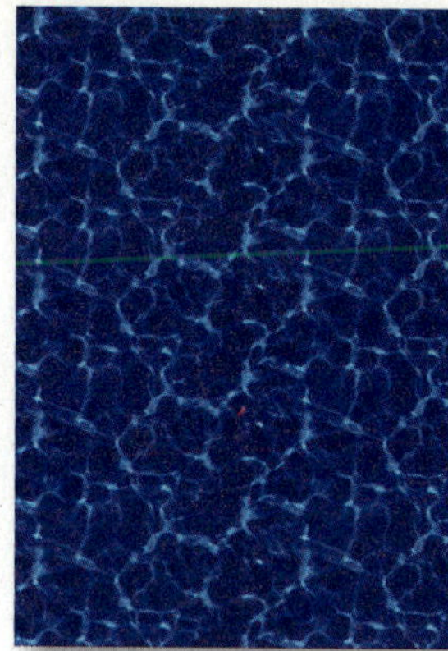

2

3

4

5

Olia Lialina
1. Personal Page Blue: 1995
2. Personal Page Blue: 1997
3. Personal Page Blue: 1999
4. Personal Page Blue: 2006
5. Personal Page Blue: 2010

A Discussion of Mimesis on the Polder-net

Jordan Tate

When one thinks about mimesis in its classical context, bereft of the weight of the memes and tropes that pervade internet culture, it is apparent that the contemporary idea of mimesis is not necessarily conducive to the critical engagement with internet based / internet aware / post-internet works of art.

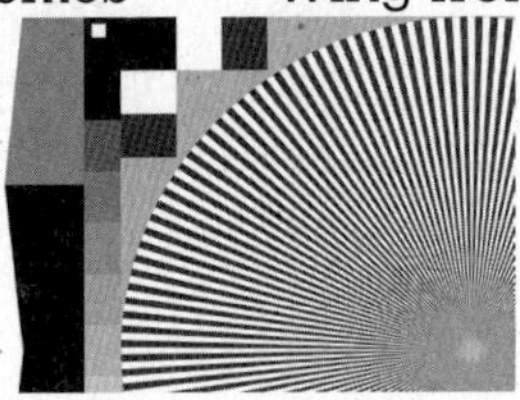

In the classical sense, mimesis was adaptive. Contemporary mimetics, as defined by Richard Dawkins, rests on an analogy of Darwinian evolutionary theory, yet is presented within the context of reproduction/ replication. The Greeks viewed mimesis differently, as more of a translation (albeit with the aim of reproduction) than the contagious spread of discrete packets of cultural currency. To an extent, the structure of contemporary computing works against the evolution of data, yet excels at the dissemination and replication of information. With the transmission and replication of data so readily available, the traditional ideas of mimesis have been usurped by the internet-epidemic model of akin to the spread of Zero Wing from 2000/02.

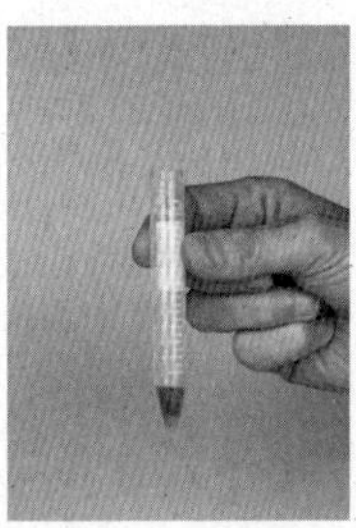

Across the board, autocorrect, spell-checker, and program based dictionaries suggest that I write Internet rather than internet. As such, It is important to establish how the internet specifically functions in the context of this argument. A more appropriate distinction would be to define the internet as one (of many) subsets of the Internet. For example, while there is ostensibly only one Internet that is the vast sea of networked computers and server farms; functionally, there are a multitude of internets each with their own aesthetic, concerns, and semiotics (contemporary examples are 4chan, tumblr, etc.) I argue that the appropriate structure for this discussion must allow individual internets to be represented as isolated entities with individual character, yet still be connected to the broader Internet.

Enter the polder model, and the idea of the internet-polder. A polder is defined as "a low-lying tract of land enclosed by embankments (barriers) known as dikes, that forms an artificial hydrological entity, meaning it has no connection with outside water other than through manually-operated devices." (http://en.wikipedia.org/wiki/Polder) In short, the structure of the internet-polder places the role and function of individual/isolated internets within the context of an artificially enclosed system that is (and this is an important distinction from an island) isolated, rather than elevated, from the Internet. By placing memes and mimesis in the context of the polder model, we can explore and illuminate the context of the concerns of the internet while simultaneously positioning the Internet as a necessary collective space for these mimetic, temporal, and dynamic inquiries into the form, structure, and purpose of media. Thc isolated nature of the internet polder allows for, and encourages, a reasonably unified voice or aesthetic that can promote significant critical dialogue – or serve to homogenize dissenting voices and shift mimesis away from its evolutionary context. While synchronicity is an undeniable phenomenon, the chorus of these voices can often emerge as a single note without regard to the subtle differences that distinguish one work from another. However, if the concern of any single voice fails to reach critical mass afforded to it by the weight of the polder (and other similar voices), it becomes difficult to engage in a discussion of the cultural significance of those ideas.

The danger lies in the fact that the internet has the potential to exaggerate our worst tendencies, forcing us into seeking constant self-validation, turning chorus into collective consciousness, mimesis into meme and potentially brilliant ideas into punchlines.

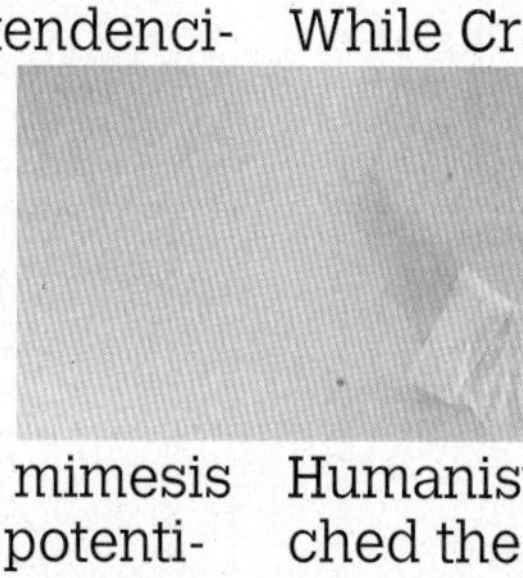

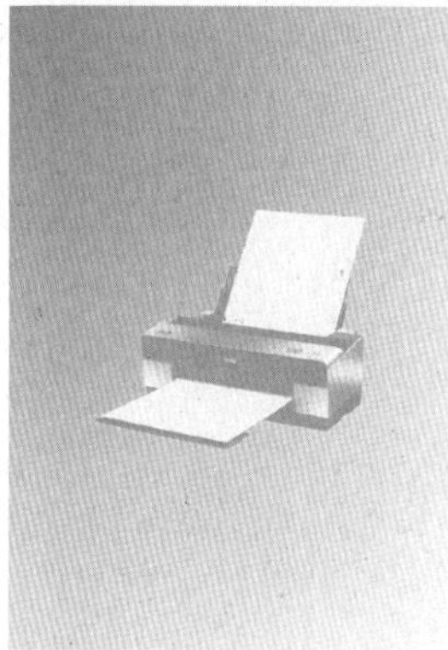

This pattern threatens to turn a dialogue of what is allowed into the canon of contemporary art into the easily disregarded trope of "Greek New Media Shit."(http://rhizome.org/editorial/2011/aug/17/its-only-humanist/)

The transition of mimesis to meme potentially ignores the validity of this work, and silencing more thoughtful criticisms that occur in comment threads (the internet's most liminal spaces).

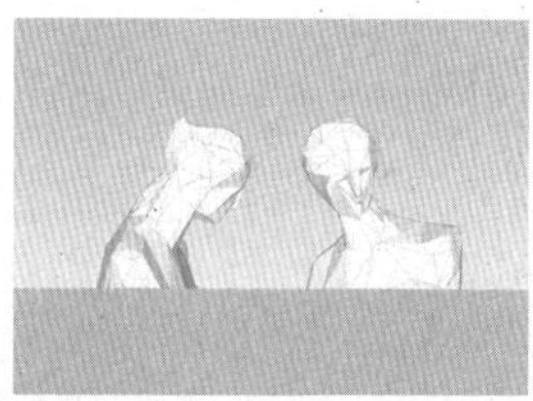

This is not to say that memes are bad, but they can a black hole for critical inquiry; focusing on on small packets of easily reproducible content. Sterling Crispin's archive (Greek New Media Shit) is the perfect example of the propagation of meme over mimesis. While Crispin, Brian Droitcor, and the plethora of contributors to the comment thread of It's Only Humanist, have approached the ideas of greek new media shit (quotes omitted) deftly, the primary export from this internet-poldcr is the diluted critique of contemporary art that takes the form of technologically mediated busts, devoid of the potential of the rich theoretical implications of this trope. As was the case with Zero Wing, a poor translation can lead to the viral spread of content but often does not do justice to the sophistication or intent of the original work.

A basic structure:

Captain: What happen?
Mechanic: Somebody set up us the bomb
Operator: We get signal.
Captain: What!
Operator: Main screen turn on.
Captain: It's you!!
Cats: How are you gentlemen!!
Cats: All your base are belong to us.
Cats: You are on the way to destruction.
Captain: What you say!!
Cats: You have no chance to survive make your time.
Cats: Ha ha ha ha ha ha ha ha ha ....

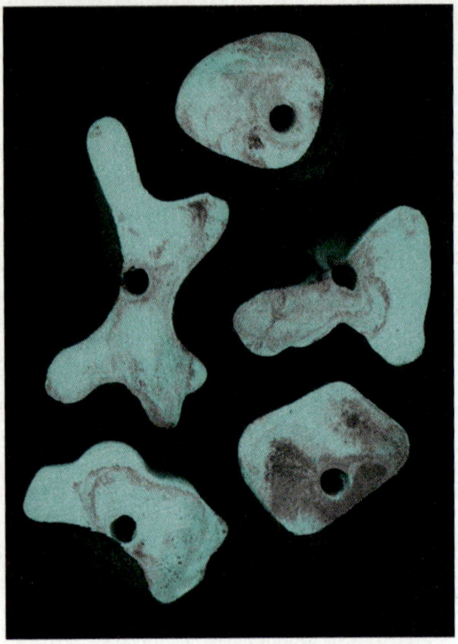

1

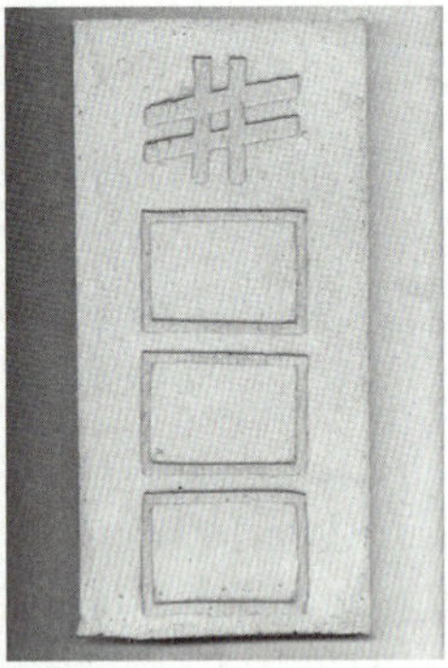

2

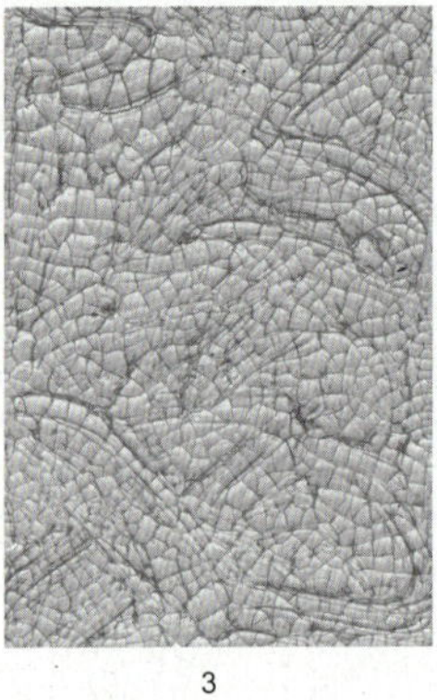

3

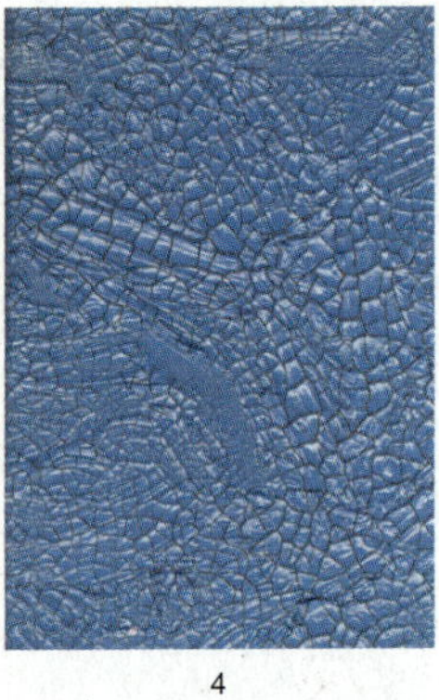

4

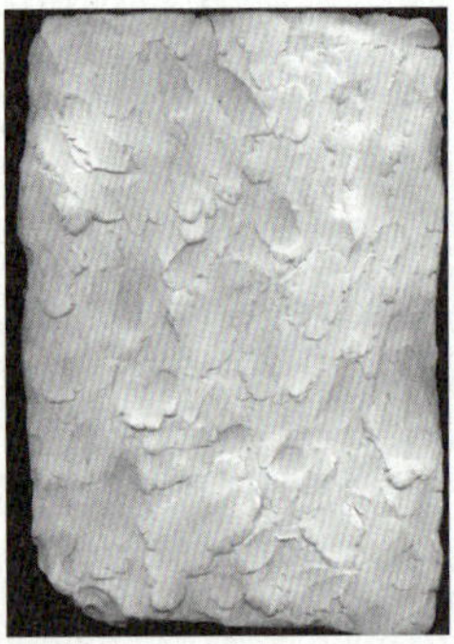

5

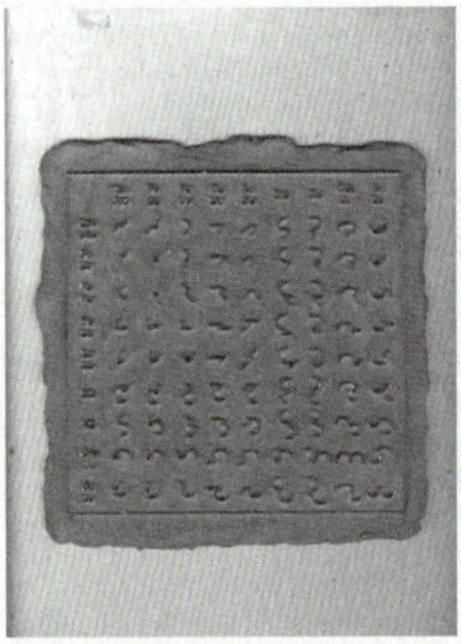

6

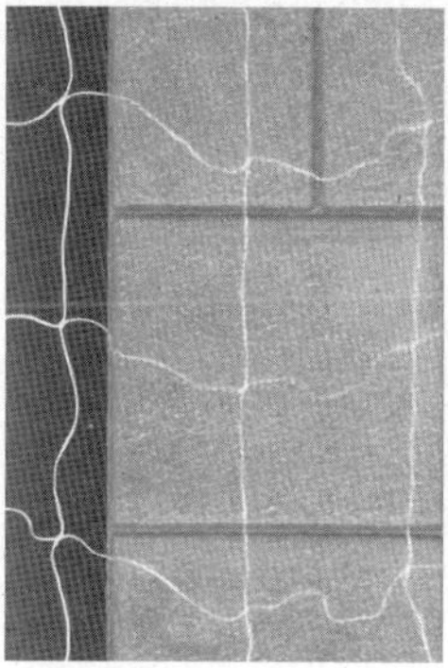
7

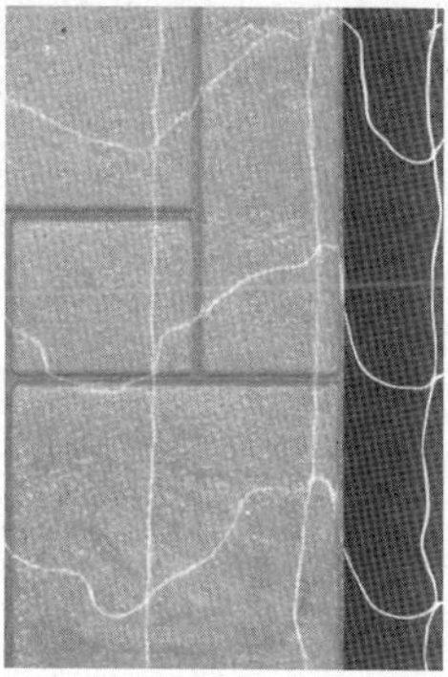
8

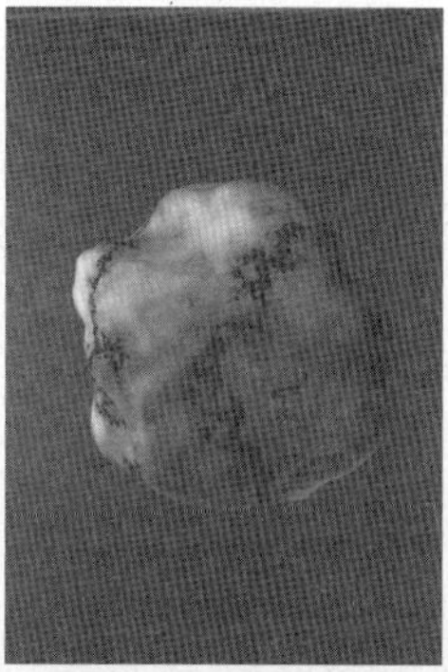
9

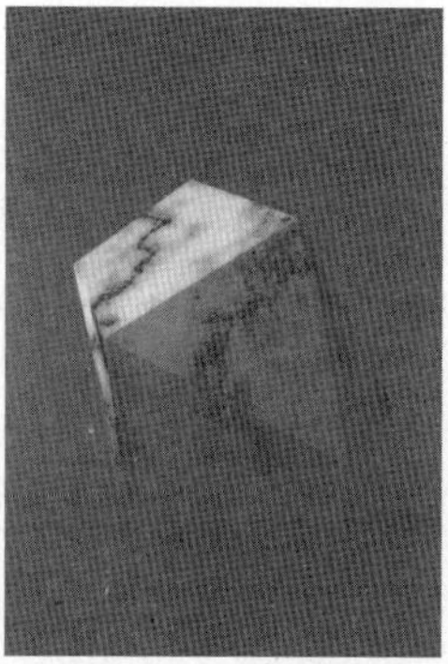
10

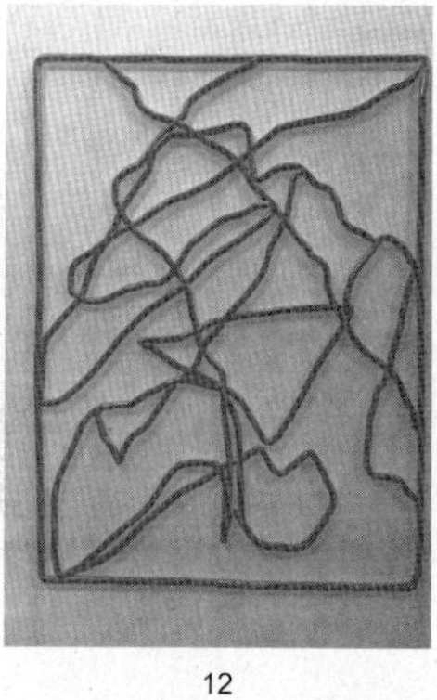
12

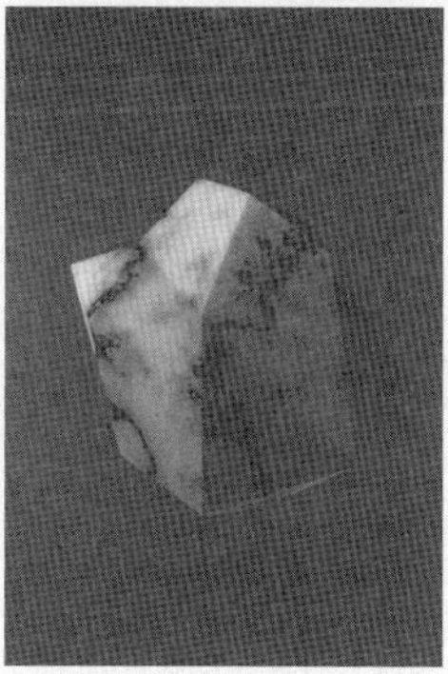
11

Lenox-Lenox
1. 2_Lenox.tif
2. xxxx
3. crackle_2.jpg
4. crackle_4.jpg
5. 5_Lenox.tif
6. shorthand_3.jpg
7. tile_net_left.pdf
8. tile_net_right.pdf
9. JJ_rock1.tif
10. JJ_rock4.tif
11. JJ_rock6.tif
12. 11_Lenox.tif

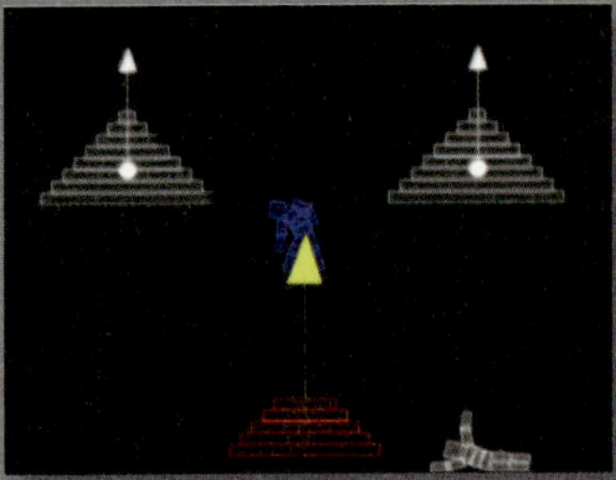

1

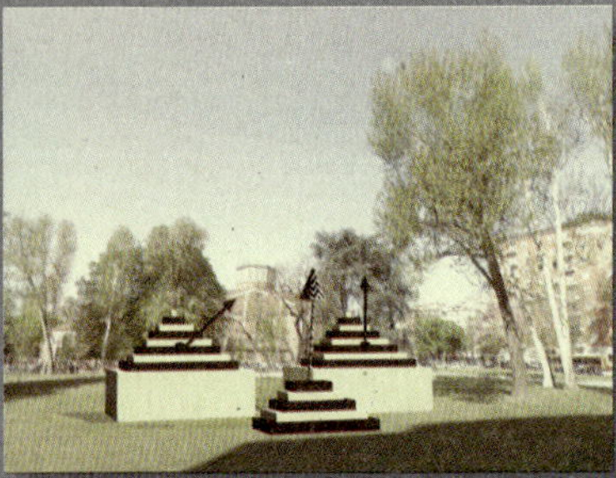

2

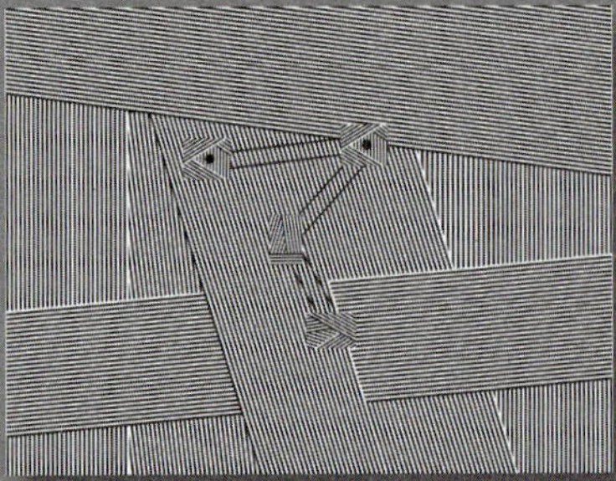

3

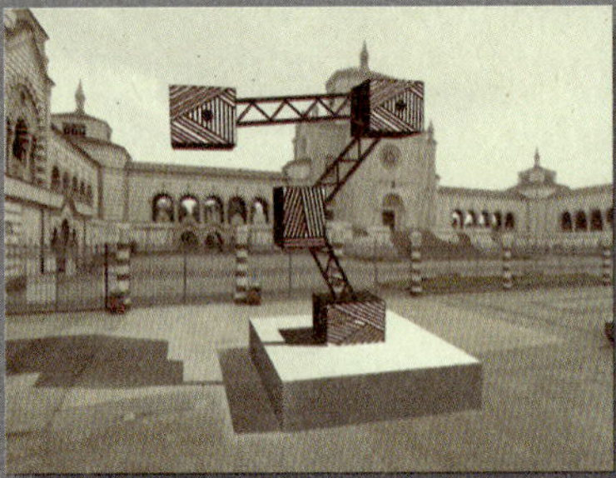

4

5

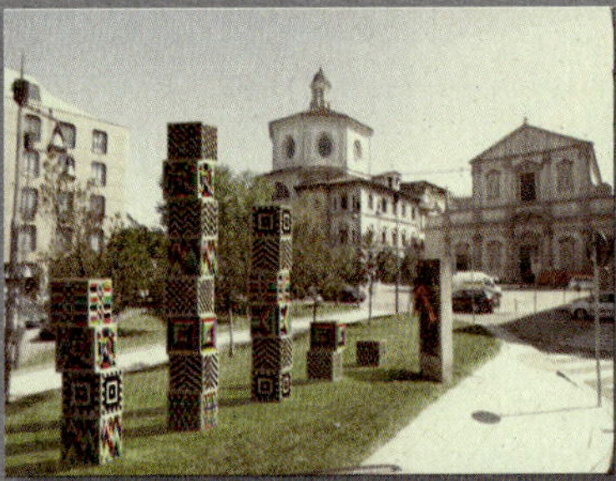

6

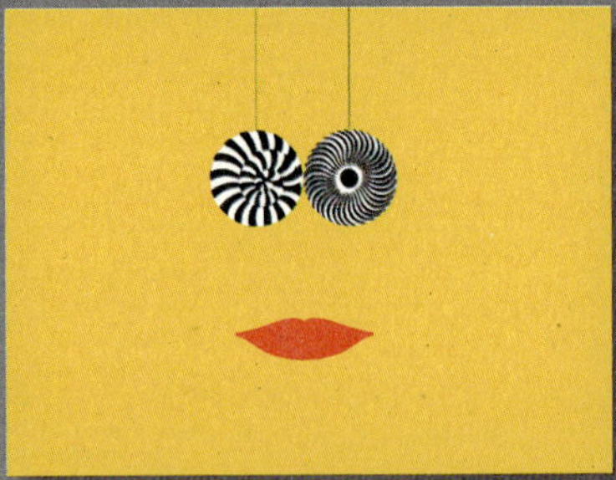

7

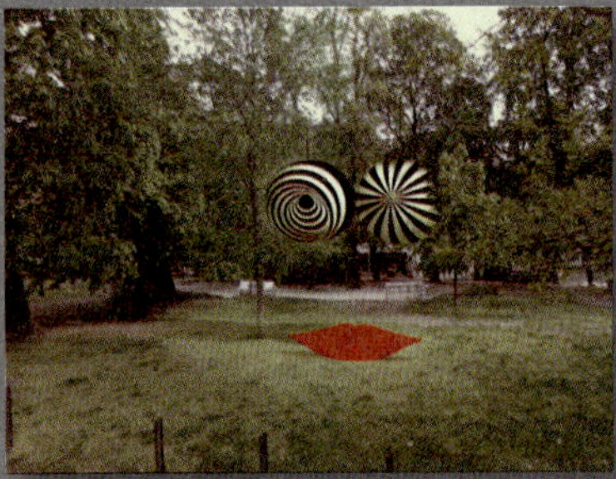

8

These images are part of an ongoing project called „Every website is a Monument". Websites are the main body of my work, I treat them as „places" where we can imagine meaning and experience objects, the same way we can admire a monument in a public space. In this project I explore the association of the symbolic language of my websites with specific physical spaces that I find while I am looking around in cities using the Google Street View. This series of images are proposed monuments dispersed in public sites of the cities of Milan and Mexico using the Street View and presented in vintage-style postcards further elaborating notions of space and time.

9

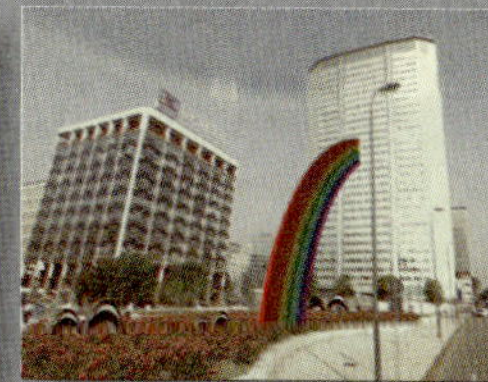
10

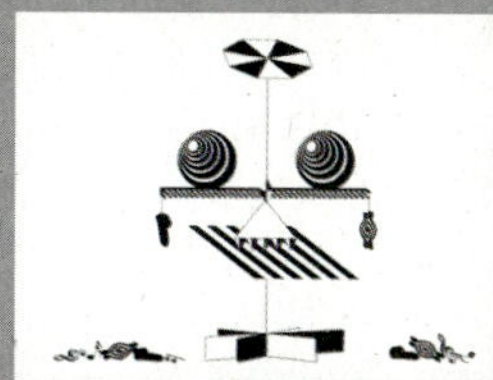
11

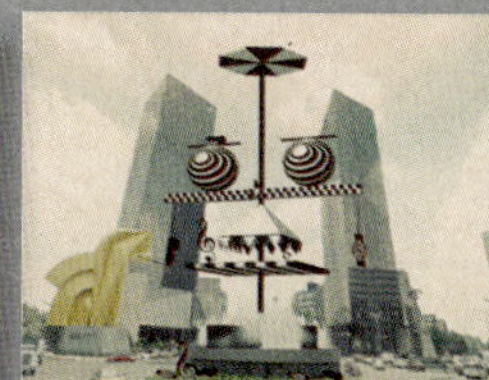
12

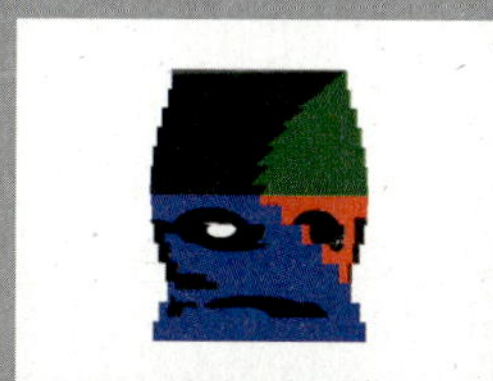
13

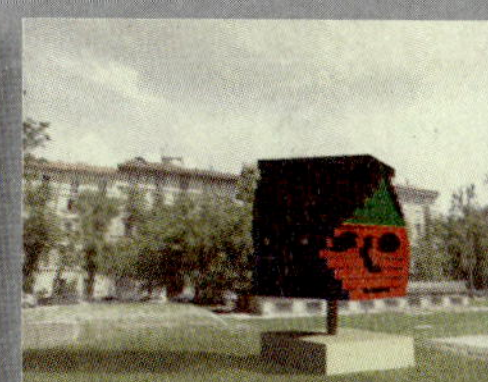
14

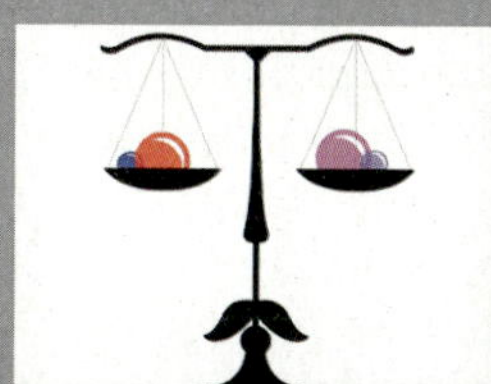
15

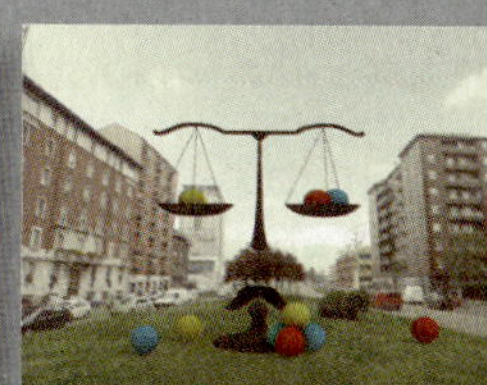
16

Angelo Plessas
1. SymmetryOfChaos.com
2. Symmetry Of Chaos (offline monument- Milan)
3. MeLookingAtYou.com
4. Me Looking At You (offline monument-Milan)
5. TowersAndPowers.com
6. Towers And Powers (offline monument-Milan)
7. PlagueOfFantasy.com
8. Plague Of Fantasy (offline monument-Milan)
9. OneAfterTheOther.com
10. One After The Other (offline monument-Milan)
11. EgoAllegro.com
12. Ego Allegro (offline monument-Mexico)
13. DoubleFaced.com
14. Double Faced (offline monument-Milan)
15. TheHistoryOfADecadeThatHas-NotYetBeenNamed.com
16. The History Of A Decade That Has Not Yet Been Named (offline monument- Milan)

Ghosttown

Theo Seemann, Arne Hübner, Chris Heller, Daniel Stäbler

When Google launched its Street View service in november 2010 for Germany, it had caused already a huge public discussion: In short people were afraid their privacy could be harmed by having photographed their houses for online visibility – which of course were baseless fears, especially when having in mind the evanescent relevance of their right for informational self-determination.[1]

Thus this question flooded through all media channels in summer 2010, where self-proclaimed privacy experts and politicians issued all kinds of senseless statements.[2]

After all Google offered publicly to blur houses if their owners wanted.

With this situation the launch of Street View on 18 November 2010 became even more interesting: How would it look and feel to ride the Google car through your hood or unknown areas? And even more important: How would this experience be influenced by the blurred real estates of worried residents?

Well, somehow it was as expected: Street View showed a Stuttgart filled with strangely formed shower cabins. The respectable swabian had won over new technology. Especially in Stuttgart's areas where the bold and beautiful live, Street View had literally been vaporized – with all the charactetristics of the previously emerged diffuse discussion. Not only one could find blurred buildings accompanied with uploaded textual information of the owner about their address, website and phone number.[3]

Also a scary Mercedes SUV argenticly glittering in sunlight was following the camera wagon constantly and somehow causing more discomfort than the service itself.

We didn't like this weird trend of populist privacy paranoia at all and decided to visually formulate a response to it. For keeping things straight, we did it entirely inside the Google Universe, seemingly a land of endless visual possibilities: We started to model Stuttgart's blurred buildings using the 3D software SketchUp, more or less correctly according to the shape of their blur artefacts inside Street View. Then we mapped their original Street View blur graphics on the new 3D facades and built up a KMZ Earth Map of Stuttgart, where they all were placed in their original position. With this experimental set-up it became more and more unveiled how Stuttgart is filled with these strangely looking shower cabins, ultimately resulting in a perceived ghost town.

In all their elegance the new 3D Buildings are archived on the project website next to the KMZ file for surfing the ghost town live and finally the visitor is instructed in a tutorial how to contribute in Stuttgart's rise as a ghost town.

[1]
The right for informational self-determination was enacted in Germany in 1983 after massive protests against the 1985 census. Over the years people lost their sensitivity for privacy, resulting in today's situation of a ubiquitous mindlessness in terms of privacy (terms and conditions of services, social networks or lotteries). http://www.uni-kassel.de/fb7/oeff_recht/publikationen/pubOrdner/MMR-2004-3.pdf

[2]
Like many other politicians German Minister for Consumer Protection Ilse Aigner (CSU) didn't miss an opportunity to criticize Google for Street View heavily and soon told them to blur her house. http://derstandard.at/1280984620172/Deutsche-Regierungskoalition-streitet-ueber-Google-Street-View

[3]

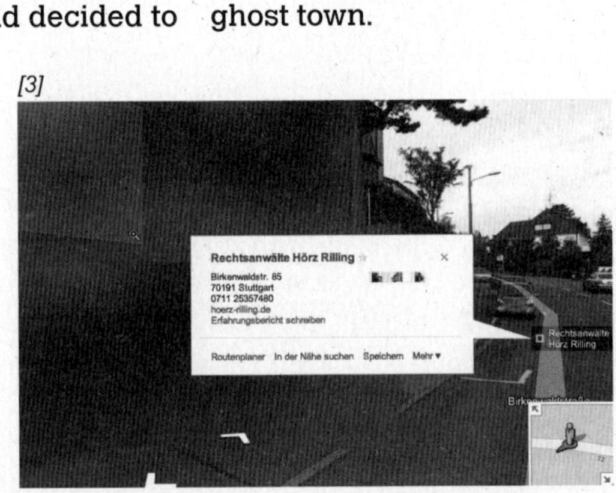

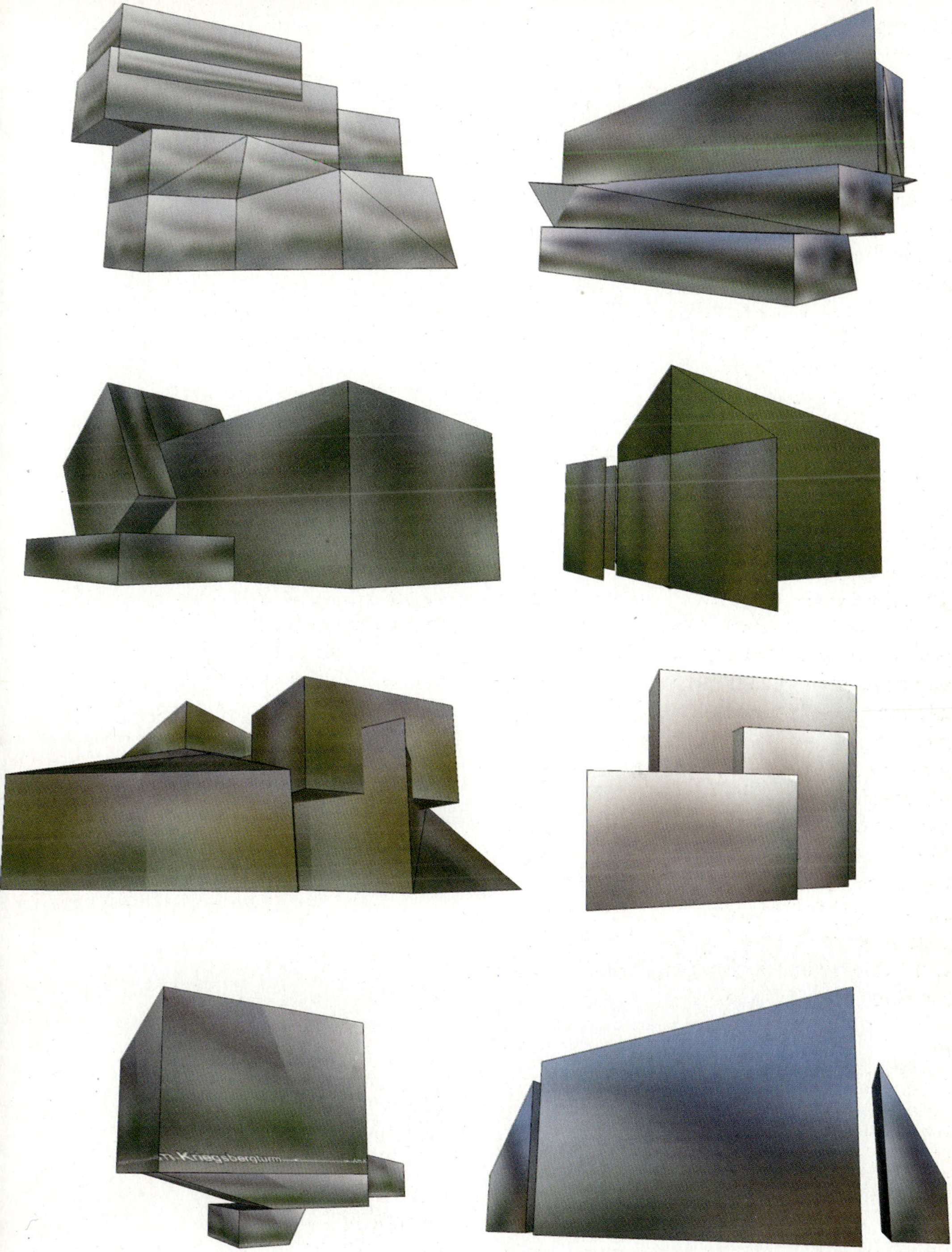

Theo Seemann, Arne Hübner,
Chris Heller, Daniel Stäbler
Ghosttown

Converter URL	Description	Result
http://scri.ch	Scri.ch is a minimal online drawing tool.	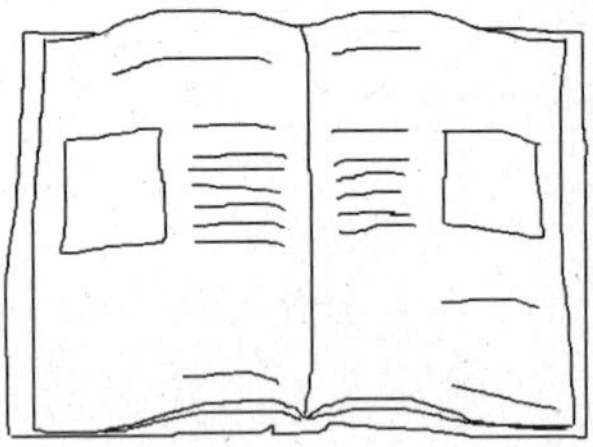
http://makeovr.com/liftmagic	Liftmagic is "the world's most advanced facelift, anti-aging, and cosmetic surgery simulationapplication,offering fully automated one-click makeovers in just seconds!".	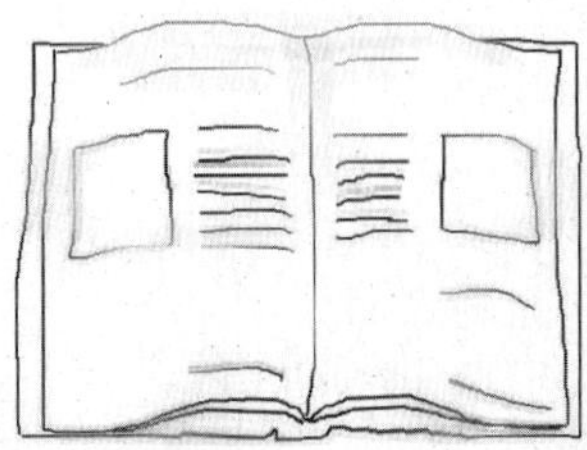
http://www.iaza.com	Iaza is a basic but complete online image converter and collage générator.	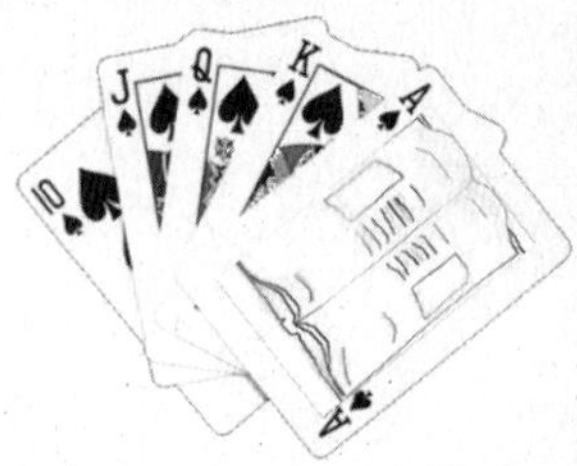
http://repperpatterns.com	Repperpatternscangenerate patternsfromeachimageyou upload.	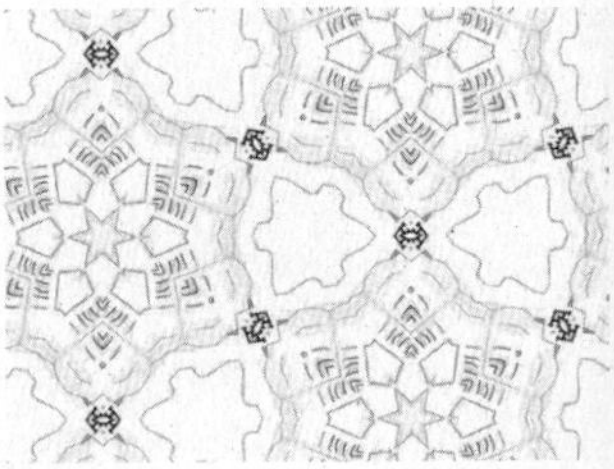
http://vectormagic.com	Vector Magic allows to easily convertbitmapImagestoclean vector files.	

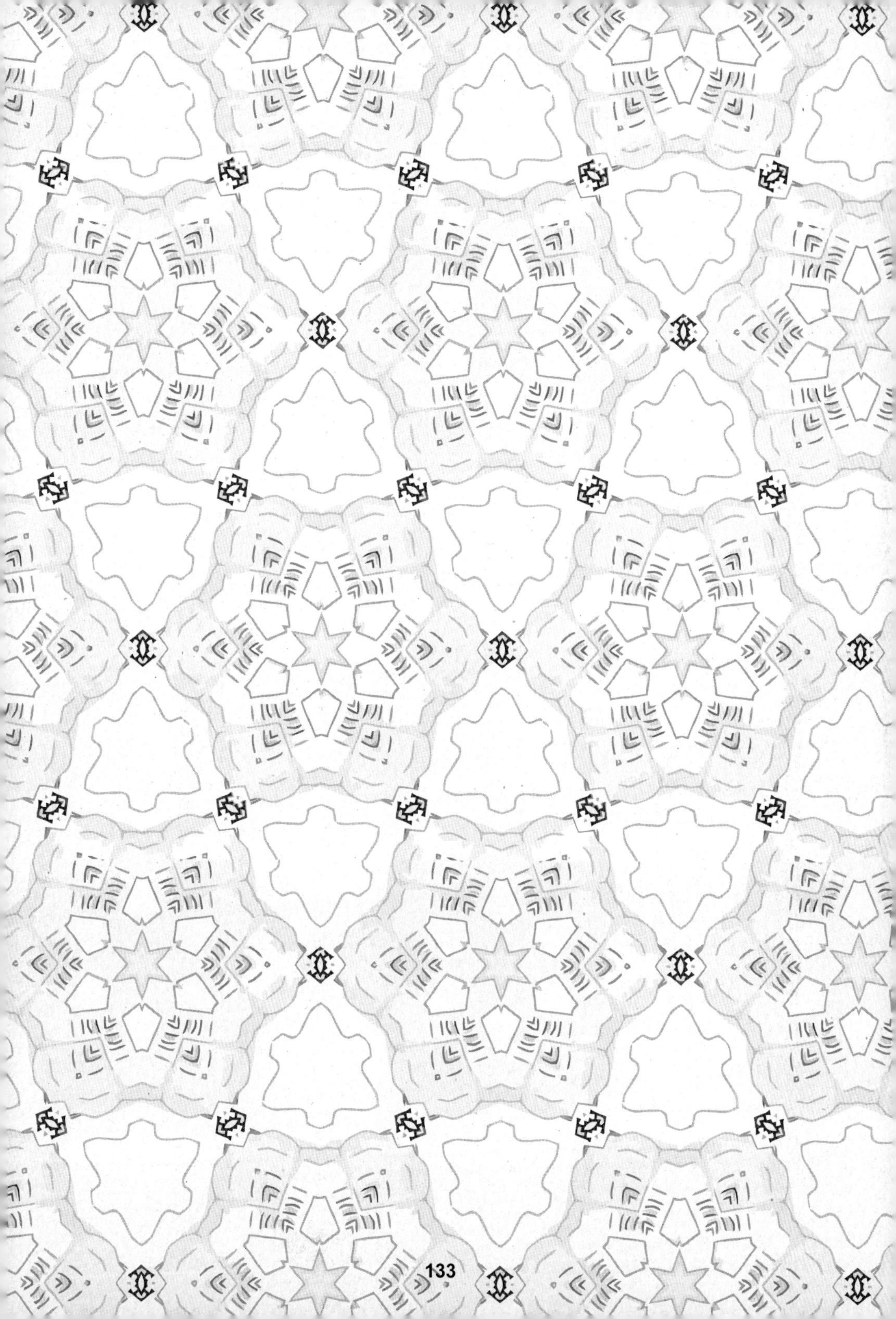

Objective: To exchange material goods wrapped in the symbols we identify as our contemporary immaterial goods and tools of exchange.
Process: Strip off these symbols and slow bits and bobs that are soon to consume our precious space and occupy our living rooms. Take away the flat image-buttons and instantaneously begin to devalue what is inside.
Enjoy the sensation of tearing; the sound of ripping. You will only destroy what is contained within.
The moment when you dreamt of owning what is inside this wrapping paper was the original fun; untainted joy. Now your interest in this object has converted into a desire for something else you don't have.
Merry Materiality
by Palace

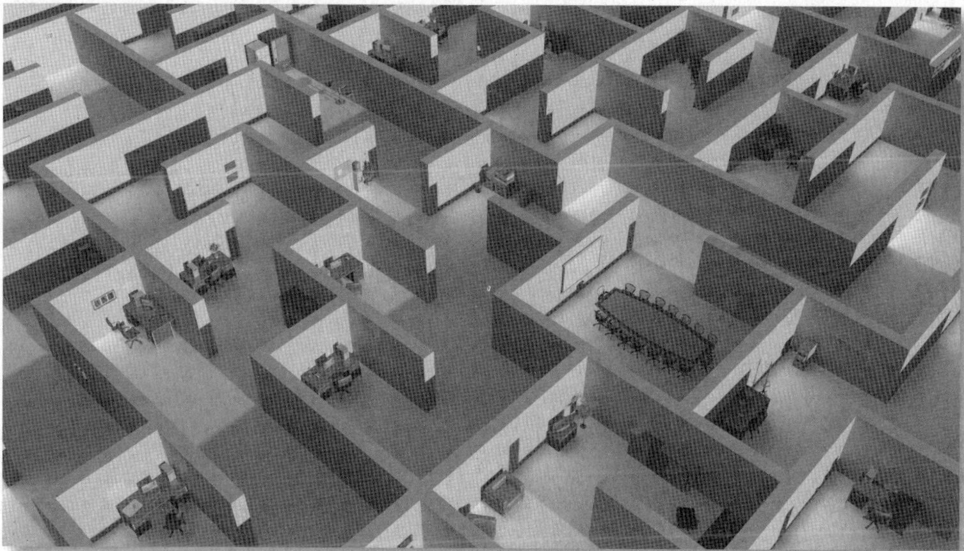

The suburban nightmare pertains to placelessness. It is within subdivisions where individuality, desire and freedom homogenize to form a synthetic reality. As one dwells in this maze, a false sense of freedom delineates all that is true. From the confines of the office cubicle to the sovereignty of the home, urge is suppressed and ennui sets in. Relief is found in leisure but the temporary escape is nothing more than a cul-de-sac; placing one right where they started.

Bea Fremderman

Gr33tz to: Co-Cain Warriors, HIDDEN_PAIN, Fatal Error Crew, Persian BOY, Ashiyane Digital Security Team and MagelangCyber @_@

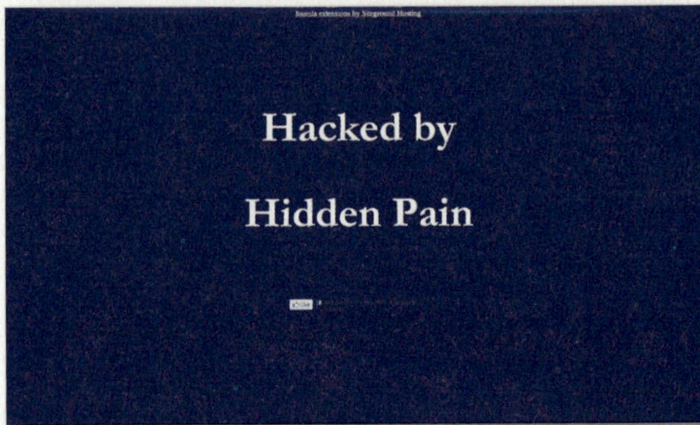

1

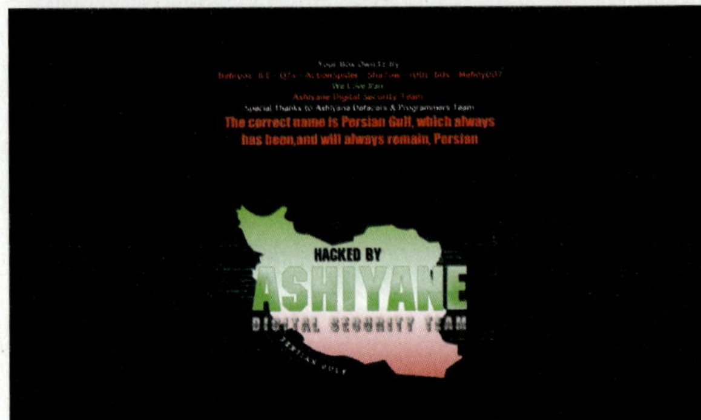

2

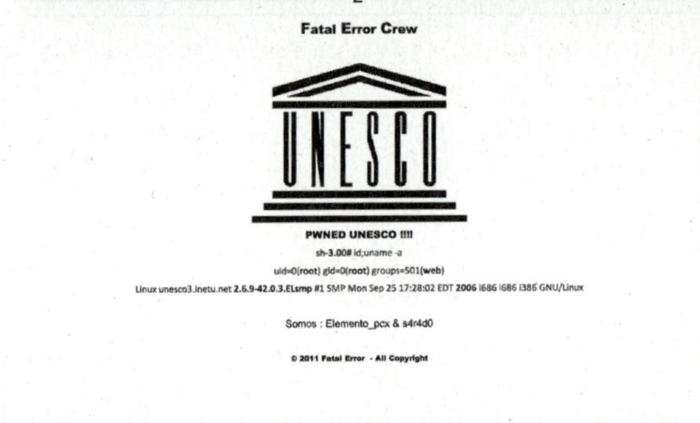

3

Sam Hancocks
1. Hacked by Hidden Pain
http://internationalcancerweekinitiative.com/
2. Hacked by Ashiyane
http://mehdy007.persiangig.com/df/ash.htm
3. Fatal Error Crew
http://zonehmirrors.net/defaced/2011/10/16/creativecontent.unesco.org/

---------- Forwarded message ----------
From: Hidden Pain . <rockmind@live.fr>
Date: 2011/10/6
Subject: RE:
To:

Hello
about hacking,hacking is the activity that allows a hacker to obtain or edit an info that he is not supposed to get or to edit
hacking is the art of bypassing security that was created by other hackers ! or web masters or programmers
you don't need to use a specific system or specific equipments , i hacked websites from my phone NOKIA n95 with an opera browser!!
In simple words, there is no magic to become a Hacker. But like anything else that is worthwhile, it takes dedication and willingness to learn
It is most important to have a basic knowledge of topics such as programming , networking , operating systems , just about everything
any thing you know can be helpful
hacking have a lot of overlapping domains , "hacker" is some one who can Adapt with very thing in computer fields
think in this way (that's my pc , and that's my system !! so why the hell i have to set a code to make a program work !!!)
when you can break into his code source and get the code or know how to bypass
it's like (i will give you that car for free but i will sell you the key !!)
OR
(i can connect to this website , so he has my pass on his database and that mean am connected to it !! so can i read other info in this database ?? : yes u can !!)
just need to be smart
note : when you do hack a website , that don't mean you are a hacker
cause with every info you learn , you will know that you are really so far from that word "hacker"

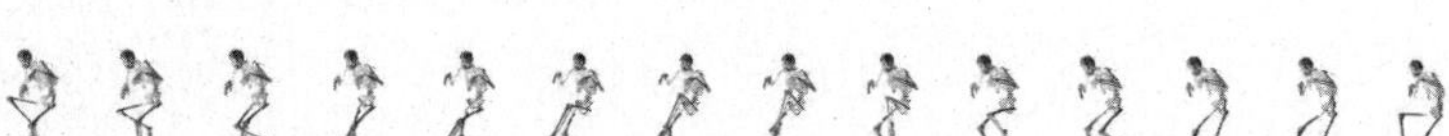

Gr33tz to: Co-Cain Warriors, HIDDEN_PAIN, Fatal Error Crew, Persian BOY, Ashiyane Digital Security Team and MagelangCyber @_@

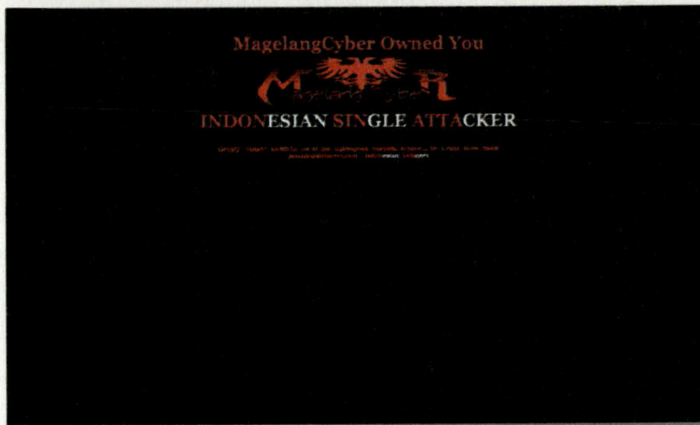

1

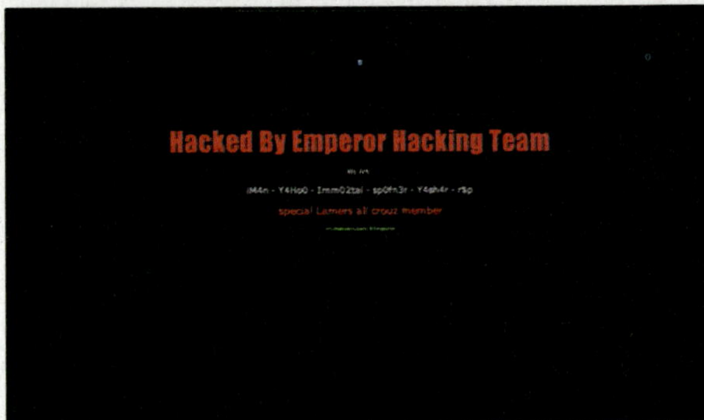

2

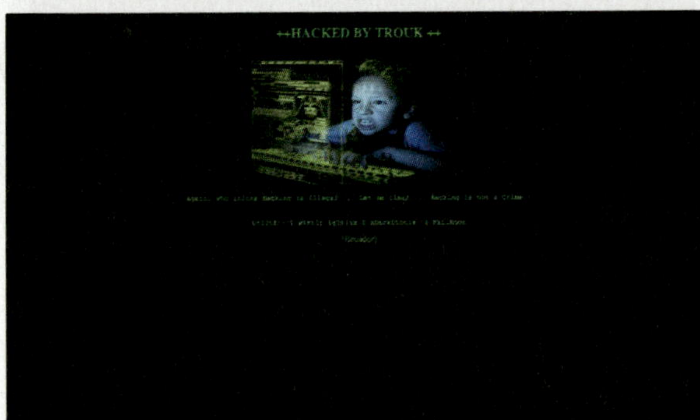

3

Sam Hancocks
1. Hacked by MagelangCyber
http://www.webmarketingsoup.com/wp-content/themes/
2. Hacked by Emperor HAcking Team
http://www.parsiran.ir/emp.htm
3. Hacked by Trouk
http://fedenaligas.org/index2.php

1

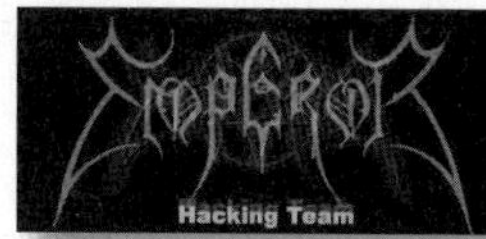

2

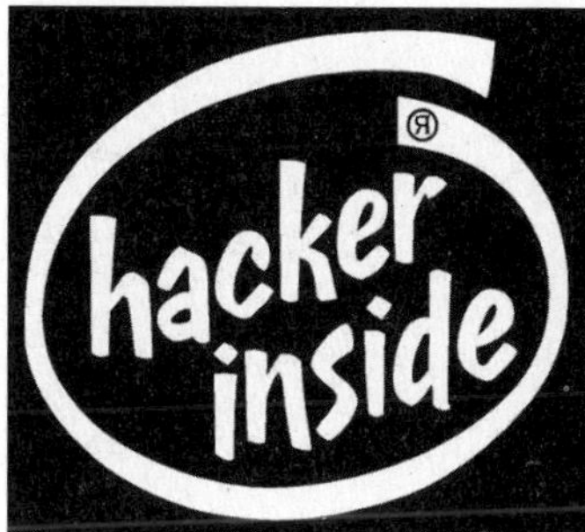

3

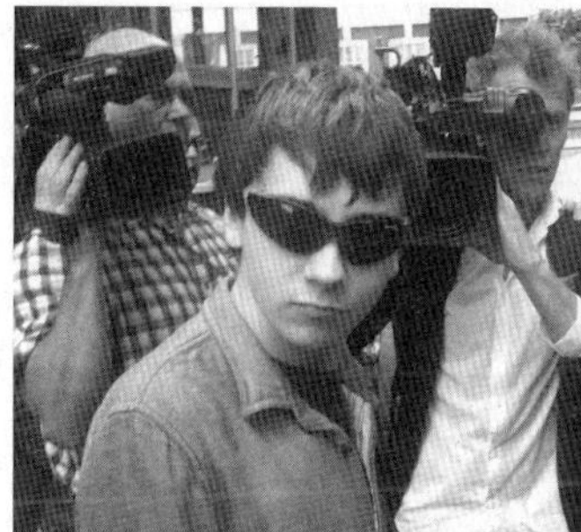

4

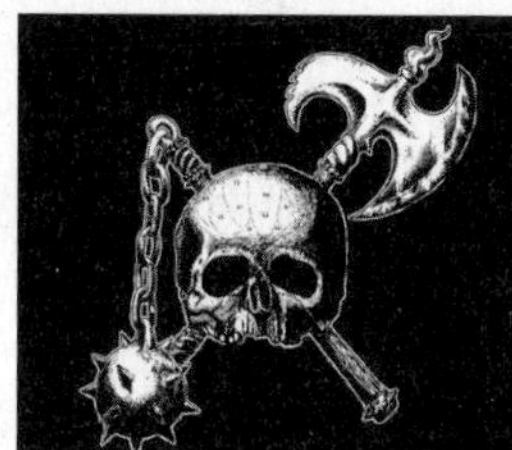

5

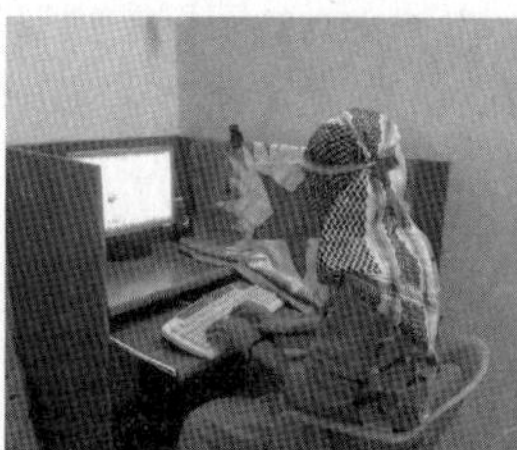

6

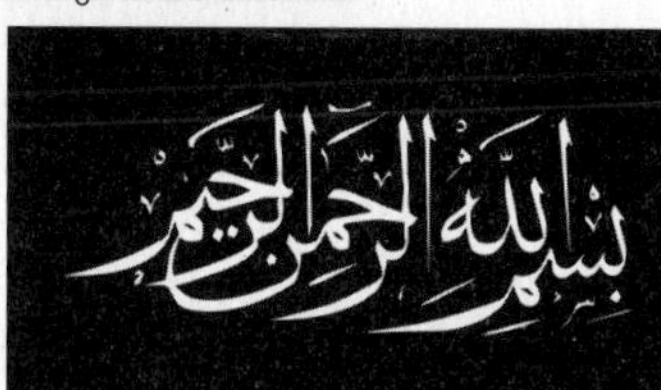

7

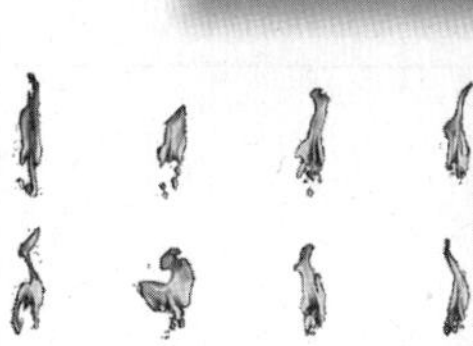

8

Sam Hancocks
1. bird_0000_Layer 4.gif
2. 30my4ax.jpg
3. hacker_inside_intel.jpg
4. topiary_hacktivist.jpg
5. Cyb3rSeC_Crew.gif
6. HaCKeD_BySivereKLi.jpg
7. bismillahHackerUnion.jpg
8. flametest.gif

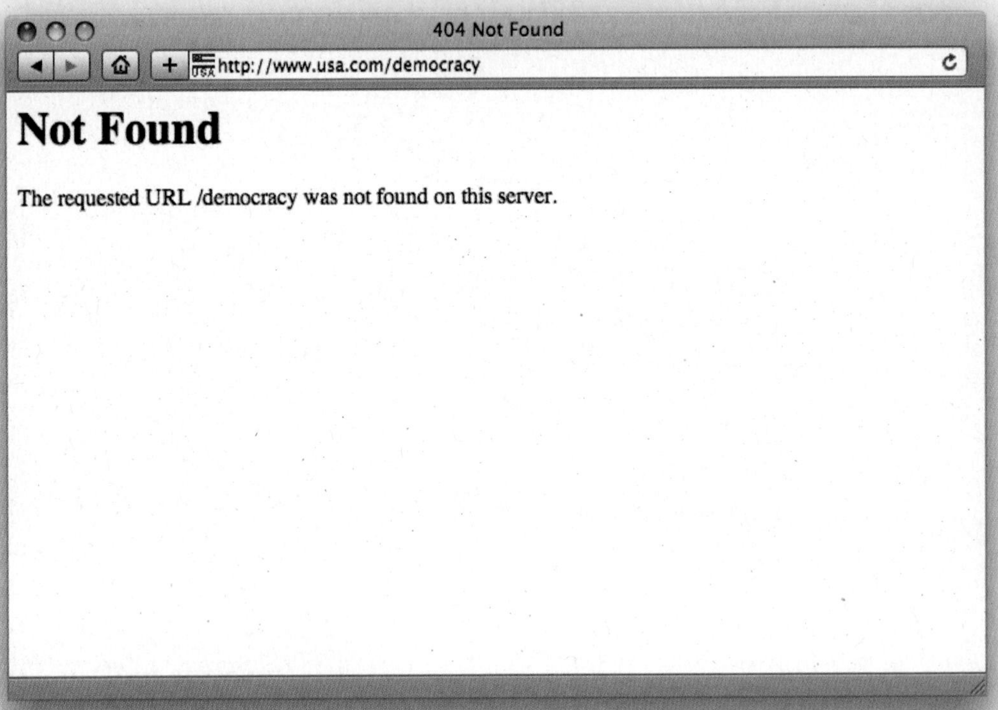

[right side] Hanne Mugaas:
Untitled
0100101110101101.ORG
usa.com - democracy
[http://usa.com/democracy]

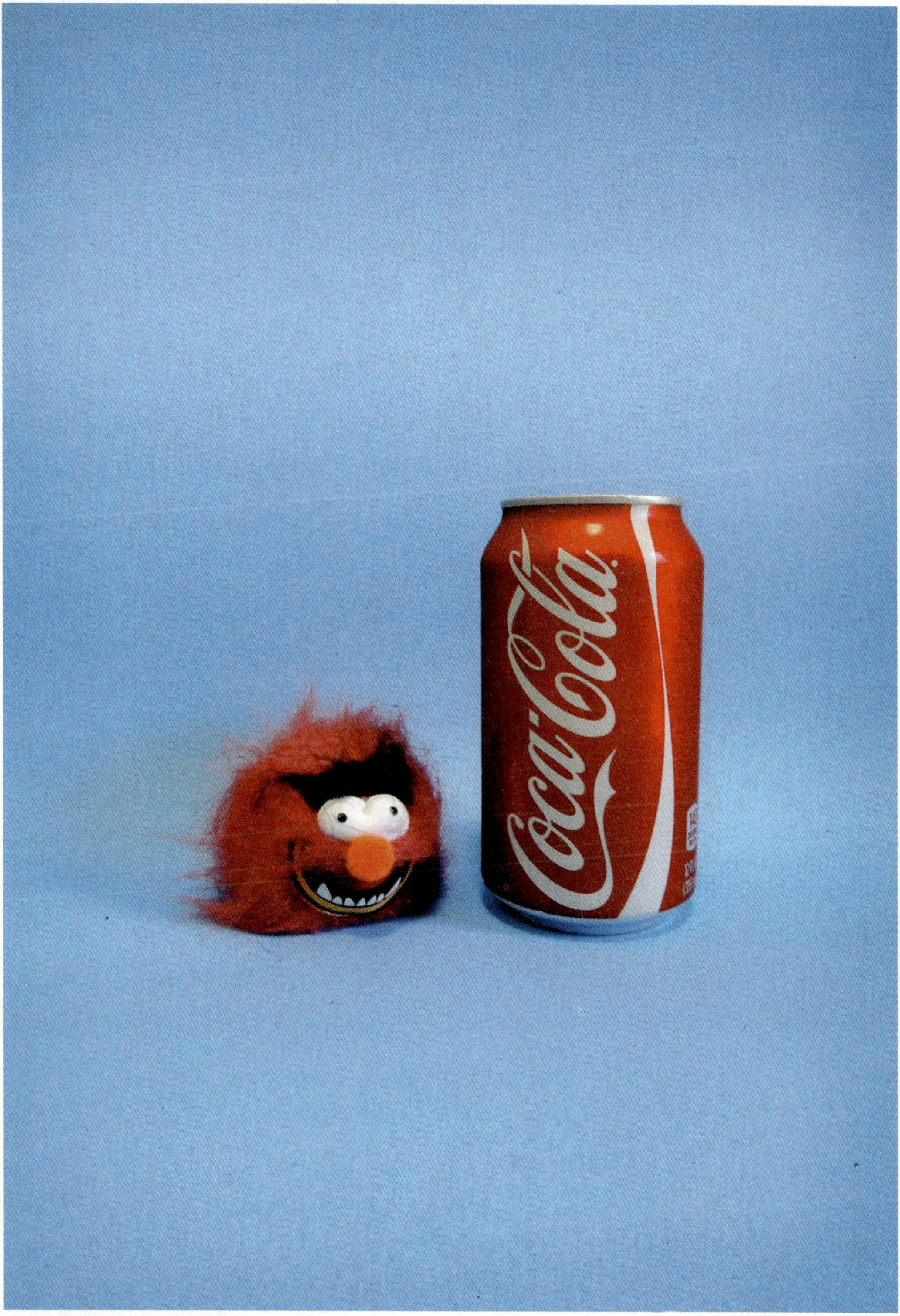
Coca-Cola

Net Artists Warned Us About SOPA 15 Years Ago

Will Brand

„When I studied the logistics of running DNS, I realized that the limits on it were artificially imposed in order to limit supply and facilitate control. The central database and "whois" records are all controlled by Network Solutions, Inc., who is a subsidiary of SAIC (Science Applications International Corp.), the largest private contractor for the US National Security Agency and the Pentagon. Most of the top corporate officers are former US military personnel who have retired from service and are engaged in "private practice", including former NSA Chief, Bobby Inman, current Director on the Board, putting their militarily-acquired skills to work for profit. In effect, when one registers and pays Network Solutions for a domain name, they are also paying to maintain surveillance on themselves. Ask yourself. Is this what you want? Does it make you feel comfortable?"

• Paul Garrin to Pit Schultz, nettime, 1997 (http://www.nettime.org/Lists-Archives/nettime-l-9706/msg00094.html)

When I read that passage a year ago, my answer was, "Yes." Yes, I feel comfortable. No, domain names are not an elaborate surveillance scheme. Paul Garrin, you sound like a crazy person.

Now, I'm not so sure – and it might be a good time to revisit Garrin's doomsday prophecies, on the eve of their incarnation.

You've probably already heard about the Stop Online Piracy Act (SOPA). It's an MPAA- and RIAA-backed package of measures that would give the US government unprecedented options for shutting down sites that are suspected of "engaging in, enabling or facilitating" copyright infringement, and it's in committee right now. There's a lot to object to in the package, but the section that's attracted particular attention is the one that would force ISPs to allow the government to block websites through altering Domain Name System (DNS) records; that's the one that goes beyond an exasperated "oh, government!" and turns DNS – an essential part of the web's infrastructure – into a blatant tool of the American state.

Garrin was warning us about this possibility fifteen years ago. For five years from 1996 to 2001, the video artist and activist ran a business-as-activism-as-art project, Name.space, that aimed to decentralize DNS by providing an alternative to the systems run by Network Solutions. It was wrapped in rhetoric equal parts freedom and paranoia, with Garrin warning that a combination of government surveillance and the corporate commodification of language would eventually restrict free speech online; that is, unless everybody switched to systems like Name.space. At the time, in an atmosphere of little meaningful government regulation of the internet, it sounded crazy; DNS was a power structure, sure, but that in and of itself was of interest only to dedicated anarchists. With SOPA, however, the danger is suddenly much more real.

First, some explanation might be helpful: DNS is what turns nice-looking, human-readable domain names, like google.com, into ugly-looking, machine-readable IP addresses, like 74.125.113.105. The system is semi-decentralized, and a bit confusing: if you type in google.com, your computer needs to go find the authoritative DNS record–that reads something like "google.com = 74.125.113.105"–on the servers of the company that sold Google their name. Thankfully, most of the time you don't need to go all the way to the source. First, your computer will check its own, local records, in a file stored somewhere on your machine. Failing that, it will check to see whether anyone near you–in infrastructure terms–has looked up that domain lately, asking your home network and your internet service provider for recently found domains that match your request. If all else fails, your computer will contact one of 13 root nameservers on a universal list provided by your operating system, and ask that server where to find the authoritative record. If your computer can find a DNS record from any of these sources, you'll end up where you wanted to go; if it can't, you'll get one of those sad error pages telling you the server couldn't be found.

SOPA would allow the government to stop this search at a number of levels, both by deleting authoritative DNS records entirely and by forcing your ISP to give your computer false DNS information if you request a suspected site. The language of the law attempts to limit the system to the United States, but the similar system used in China's Great Firewall has been found to affect users from neighboring countries who, by chance, had their DNS queries routed through Chinese nameservers. It goes without saying that the same effect would be magnified in the US.

Since the details of SOPA became public, a range of easy-to-use workarounds have popped up in anticipation of these DNS provisions; DeSopa, for instance, is a Firefox plugin that allows users to switch from US-based DNS servers to offshore proxies with the click of a button. Workarounds, though, don't address the underlying problem–that the structure of the internet relies upon a naming system which is relatively centralized and which lies squarely in the sights of government and corporate power. What Garrin tried to convey was that bottlenecks naturally attract surveillance and control–it was only a matter of time before government agencies in the US realized they could use the present DNS system to their own ends.

Ultimately, the service Name.space provided seems to be fairly anodyne: users were given the opportunity to register domains with extensions like .med, .news, or .sex, instead of the official .com or .net. The idea behind Garrin's project, however, required a radical shift in how DNS worked: rather than drawing from a single, universal list of root nameservers, users would be able to select from a range of nameservers with varying policies, domains, and levels of security. There was a risk of rogue servers–phishing scams, for instance, become a greater threat with an alternative DNS–but there was also the potential for a system, in the true techno-libertarian ideal, beyond state or corporate control. In a 1997 interview with Pit Schultz, Garrin waxed poetic on this point:

Name.space is part of the internet. It is also the future of the named. address structure of the internet. As an independent tactical network, it is a system which will create an economic basis for free media to remain online without corporate or institutional regulation or censorship. The goal of name.space is to buy as much bandwidth and processor power as possible to ensure that there is always a home for free media and alternative voices and visions on the ever that assumption was an intimidating task. DNS was the epitome of "if it's not broke, don't fix it", and it certainly wasn't going to undergo such fundamental changes for the sake of internet idealism or a wider selection of domains. In one 2000 memo regarding the difficulty of changing the system, the Internet top-level domains–.med, .news, .sex and the rest–added to the root nameservers, with his own servers holding the authoritative records. His application was denied. Sarah Ferguson, writing for the Village Voice, reported that he was given an opportunity to compromise and receive a smaller set of

Simple Net Art Diagram

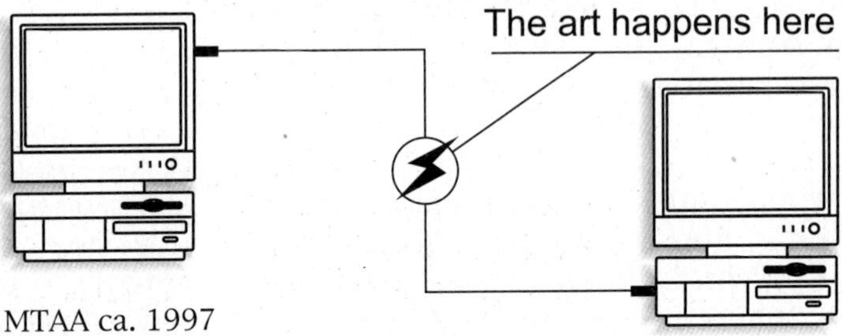

MTAA ca. 1997

changing internet.
To the engineers and administrators who had spent years working to standardize the structure of the internet, though, it looked like anarchy. DNS was the glue holding the internet together–a reliable, centralized, universal system that required little maintenance and less discussion. Every computer on the net was programmed to assume the existence of one domain naming standard and one group of rootservers; overcoming Architecture Board, a non-profit body tasked with the oversight of various internet structures, flatly declared, "There is no getting away from the unique root of the public DNS."
Garrin launched a barrage of criticism at the defenders of the status quo, and seemingly found support from the inventor of DNS, Paul Mockapetris. When it became apparent that the nature of the system would not be changed, Garrin applied to have 118 of Name.space's certified top-level domains, and rejected it: But Garrin's problem may be simply that he wants too much. Given ICANN's stated intention of adding a "modest" number of new domains in this "proof of concept" phase, observers say there's no way he could have ever won approval for 118. Yet when the board members asked Garrin to select three from his list, he refused. This shocked even some of Garrin's sharpest critics and competitors. "People at the hearings

were watching this, saying, 'Come on, Paul, pick three,' but he wouldn't do that," says Richard Sexton of the Open Root Server Confederation, a network of alternative root servers. "His mentality is, it's my way or the highway."

Without support from the root nameservers, Name.space was left without a feasible business model: to view Garrin's domains, users would need to change their system settings or install special software, and potential domain registrants were scared off by the resulting smallness of the user base.

Garrin went to court over the matter, filing an antitrust suit against Network Solutions, who then held the exclusive Department of Commerce contract to administer DNS. He lost. The result of that ruling established, dubiously, that Network Solutions was immune to antitrust legislation because it was operating a government contract. It also rang the death knell for Name.space, along with a host of commercial alternative DNS services–Sexton's Open Root Server Confederation among them–that had hoped Garrin's case would open the door to legitimacy.

We could use those alternatives right now. It's not that a world of multiple DNS roots would be better–it would add layers of complication to a system designed to be simple, and the benefits of competition in the field of infrastructure are negligible–but rather that that world would have a better chance of not becoming a near future technodystopia where our thoughts are monitored by hyperintelligent lizards.

A simple multiplication of DNS services wouldn't wholly eliminate the possibility of surveillance and control, but it would certainly make it more difficult; the annual "Cyber Monday" seizures of domains selling counterfeit jerseys and handbags, for instance, have required the cooperation of only one firm – Verisign, Inc., which administers all .com and .net domains (among others) through the contract that Network Solutions once held.

Name.space wasn't the first alternative - AlterNIC probably gets that prize–but it was an early and vocal member of that would-be industry, and its status as an art project gave it a kind of longevity a purely commercial enterprise wouldn't have. The failure of AlterNIC was one of many dot-com busts; the failure of Name.space was the natural conclusion of a quixotic quest begun in part to prove its own impossibility. The former only elicits a shrug, but the latter might prompt some inquiry into why things have to be this way.

So I'm sorry, Paul Garrin. I had you all wrong. I hope, once SOPA has been safely defeated, that there will be time to appreciate the genius of looking outright crazy.

In closing, a quote from Daniel Castro, an analyst at the Information Technology and Innovation Foundation who first proposed much of SOPA in a 2009 whitepaper (emphasis mine):

Opponents of PIPA/SOPA, such as the Internet Society and Crocker et al., argue that DNS filtering will "puts users at risk." However there are no security risks from DNS filtering. Instead, the purported security risks for users come about only for those Internet users who begin using alternative DNS services (i.e. those individuals intent on breaking the law).

⮺Adam Cruces
was born in 1985 in Houston, TX. He graduated from the Kansas City Art Institute in 2008 with a BFA in Interdisciplinary Arts. Lived in Brooklyn, NY before moving to Zurich, Switzerland where he is currently working towards his MFA at the Zürcher Hochschule der Künste.
http://adamcruces.com/
http://adamcruces.tumblr.com/
⮺Agathe Andre
AGT528 a. k. a Agathe de Trémontels. Paris based student in publishing. www.empire528.com www.boogiefishnchipsclan.biz
It all started discovering new media art few years ago, I was fascinated. And still.
http://www.boogiefishnchipsclan.biz/
⮺Alessandro Bava
Alessandro Bava is an architecture student, he is an expert in trojan horses. In 2010 started ECO-CORE an ecology zine.
@thealebava
http://www.ecocore.com
⮺Angela Genusa
Angela Genusa is a practitioner of performance writing (text, audio, visual, multimedia). She lives in the US.
http://mojibakeoven.blogspot.com/
⮺Angelo Plessas
lives and works in Athens, Greece.His main body of work consists of websites that bring together an animated "object" with a domain name thatfunctions as the title and location of the piece. These web objects often resemble sculptural portraits of imaginary characters, alternating between funny and poignant, strange and romantic. In his work, Plessas fuses iconography of ancient civilizations, surrealist abstractions and modernist references together with the social networking habit of imagined identities.
http://www.angeloplessas.com
http://www.angelosays.com
⮺Aureliano Segundo
writes about and does art on the internet. He is an internationally published writer and an adjunct professor at Simon Fraser University in Vancouver, Canada. His real first name is Andrew. He currently writes for Dis Magazine.
http://meatblog.tumblr.com
http://conceptualblogs.tumblr.com
⮺Aristide Antonas
The Greek architect and writer, is an associate professor of Architecture and Theory at the University of Thessaly, Greece, a post graduate seminar director in the National Technical University of Athens and the owner of the Antonas office. He co-founded the plural academic persona „Gregorios Pharmakis" and the curating group Built-Event. He is the writer of published literature books, stage plays and essays.
http://aristideantonas.com/
http://antonas.blogspot.com/
⮺Artie Vierkant
http://artievierkant.com
http://browwwsing.tumblr.com
⮺Asli Serbest (m-a-u-s-e-r)
http://www.m-a-u-s-e-r.net/
http://www.igmade.net/
http://junkjet.net/
⮺Ball-Nogues Studio
Benjamin Ball and Gaston Nogues explore the nexus of art, architecture, and industrial design. Their work has been exhibited at major institutions throughout the world, including the Museum of Contemporary Art, Los Angeles; the Museum of Modern Art, New York; the Guggenheim Museum; PS1; the Los Angeles County Museum of Art; the Venice Biennale, ...
http://www.ball-nogues.com/
⮺Bärbel Jetter
Jetter than Junk Jet. She is a professional home button architect.
⮺Bea Fremderman
Born in Kishinov, Moldova, Bea is currently finishing studies at The School of the Art Institute in Chicago where she lives, produces and is the sole director of Kunsthalle New, a nonprofit gallery space located in Pilsen. Her current research interests are the suburban nightmare, synthetic realty and false notions of freedom.
http://www.beafremderman.com
⮺Beatriz Ramo
Beatriz Ramo is an architect from Spain.

She lives in Rotterdam where she founded STAR strategies + architecture in 2006. STAR is a practice dealing with architecture in all its forms. STAR achieved an international presence by winning several prizes in architectural and urban development competitions around the world and by critique essays like O'Mighty Green. Since 2008 she is contributing and managing editor of MONU magazine on urbanism.
http://www.st-ar.nl

Ben Aqua
is a photographer, new media artist and musician based in Austin, Texas. Born in 1981 in Brooklyn, New York, he received a BFA in Design from The University of Texas at Austin in 2005. His work has been exhibited internationally and published in NYLON, SPIN, NME, Flaunt, OUT, ARKITIP, XLR8R, Beautiful/Decay, and Fecal Face. He has performed and DJd around the world as various identities, including robotsluvme, Realness, MVSCLZ, DYX and ASSACRE.
http://benaqua.org
http://soundcloud.com/benaqua
http://twitter.com/b3naqua

Ben Vickers
Occasionally regarded as Social Engineer, Vickers' practice is hard to pin down, preferring to work through the construction of conditions rather than the creation of images or objects. Evidence of his work can be found in the cached archives of the waybackmachine, the private inboxes of his peers and the peppering of distinct phrases throughout think-piece-propaganda; featured in mainstream publications such as the Guardian, New York Times, New Statesmen et al.
http://www.benvickers.net
http://www.benvickers.com
http://www.characterdate.com
http://www.whatamithinking.biz

Billy Rennekamp
Billy Rennekamp was born in 1988 on a horse farm in Louisville, Kentucky. He grew up exploring natural and digital environments in the countryside and on his computer. He now lives and works between New York and Berlin. His work involves sculpture, moving image, photography and digital crafts rooted in the concept of play. His focus on games and cheats is an extension of his involvement with the use and misuse of technology and the creation, exploration and manipulation of new worlds.
http://Loshadka.org
http:// Lookadis.info
http://HandEyeCoordination.org
http://InternIntern.net
http://ComputersClub.org.
http://minus.com/m43L0izkB#1

Bonno van Doorn (Doornstruik)
Graduated from the 'Rietveld Academy' with a life - size F16 made of cardboard; a tribute to the hobbyist. His installations can be described as a collection of beautiful ugliness, existing statues transformed into monsters, everyday items that are scattered through space, sloppy graffiti adorns the walls, taped mannequins and more craziness: you just don't know where to look. Bonno's work is playful and mocking, he has gay pink shirts with the words ,'Fuck Marc Bijl". And in „For The Love Of Gum" Damien Hirst his skull got a gum makeover. Many a brow will also be raised by Bonno's Photoshop skills.
www.bonnovandoorn.com

Brad Troemel
Brad Troemel makes and writes about art. His writing has been featured in magazines and books. His art has been featured in galleries and sometimes even museums. He has earned two degrees from prestigious American art schools. He currently lives in a city full of diverse cultures and complicated intellectuals. Friend request or e-mail him, he'd be happy to talk to you.
http://bradtroemel.com/

Bryan Boyer
I'm interested in the conditions and opportunities that buildings and cities create, and the conditions that create buildings and cities. Currently I'm based in Helsinki where I work as a Strategic

Design Lead for Sitra, Finnish Innovation Fund.
http://www.bryanboyer.com

🗗Carsten Güth
Billy the kid did what he did and he died. Worked at Internet Explorer.
Grandfather: Spatialforces Estugarda
http://www.notimefortv.biz
http://aint.notimefortv.biz

🗗Christian Oldham
1. Christian Oldham, Seattle, Washington, watercolor painter
2. Christian Oldham, Seattle, Washington, attorney
3. Christian Oldham, Gold River, California, musician
4. Christian Oldham, Winfield, West Virginia, father
5. Christian Oldham, Portland, Oregon, unemployed
6. Christian Oldham, Davidson, North Carolina, student
7. Christian Oldham, Covington, Tennessee, high school drop out
8. Christian Oldham, Salem, Oregon, student
9. Christian Oldham, Scottsdale, Arizona, student
10. Christian Oldham, Glendale, Missouri, student
http://www.christianoldham.com

🗗Christiane Nasz and Stefanie Hunold

```
         "
 "  iiiii"iiiiiiii"iii  "
  "iiiiii"iiiiiii"iiiiiiiiii"
{{{{{{               }}}}}}}
        a       v
  xO        !          xO
       ++       ++
          ++;;++
```

Chrissi

```
      ////```
    '''''``````

   ////---/////
  // `(°) (°)´//
  /     .+     //
  /     ()     //
```

xxx

Steffi

🗗Constant Dullaart
(NL 1979), former resident of the Rijksakademie in Amsterdam, lives and works in Berlin. Originally trained as a video artist, he recently started focusing on visualizing internet grammar and software dialects. By editing online forms of presentations and by re-contextualising ‚found‘ material he creates installations, perfomances, prints, videos, websites and blog postings. In recent years works have received both critical acclaim as well as large scale attention on the internet, where many of the works can still be easily found. He recently co-founded an internet art documenting initiative.
http://net.artdatabase.org

🗗Dennis Knopf
„Tracky Birthday“
Knopf is a musician / entertainer / artist from Stuttgart, Germany. He's founder and executive director of Upitup Records, chief editor of „Best before – A Dsico Fanzine“ and has worked at Rhizome at the New Museum of Contemporary Art in New York City. Proud father of two humans Knopf has won an award for his internet art piece Bootyclipse and received a ceise and desist letter for faking the New York Times website. He is also a member of the internet surfing club Nasty Nets.
http://www.trackybirthday.com
http://www.upitup.com/tracky/newalbum
http://www.dennisknopf.net

🗗Eilis McDonald
is an Irish artist based in Dublin. She assembles environments using found objects both online and offline. She is interested in the 'numinous presence' of objects and how they attract and repel the people and space around them.
Previous exhibitions and commissions include Offline at Temple Bar Gallery + Studios, Dublin, Precaution at The Irish Museum of Modern Art, Read/Write at 319 Scholes, New York, Rapture Heap for Dublin City Council's Per Cent for Art scheme, ...
http://www.eilismcdonald.com

🗗Fabien Mousse
Internet artist since 1988, born in 1988 in Quimper, France.
„Don't be. Work. And you will be.“
http://fabienmousse.vakistan.net/
Twitter : @fabmous

🗗Gene McHugh
is an art writer based in Brooklyn. His writing has appeared in Artforum and Rhizome, and he was the recipient of the Creative Capital | Warhol Foundation Arts Writers Grant for his blog, Post Internet: http://122909a.com/. McHugh is currently the Interpretation Fellow at the Whitney Museum of American Art.

🗗Greg J. Smith

Greg J. Smith is a Toronto-based designer and researcher with interests in media theory and digital culture. Greg is a designer at Mission Specialist and a contributing writer at Creative Applications Network [CAN]. He is an adjunct instructor in the CCIT program (U of T Mississauga/ Sheridan College) where he teaches courses on information architecture, web development and technology and urbanism.
http://www.serial-consign.com

Jacob B. Engblom

Jacob Broms Engblom is an artist/ musician/engineer born and residing in Stockholm, Sweden. He is currently engaged in studiesof HCI and media communication at the Royal Institute of Technology, Stockholm. He likes dealing with the uncategorized spectacles and mysticism in our digital culture.
http://www.likeneveralways.com
http://www.twitter.com/osfa

Jasper Elings

Jasper Elings hasn't updated his profile yet. Update your settings to give people a better idea of where you live, who you are, and what you are all about.
http://jasper-elings.tumblr.com
http://www.jasperelings.info

JODI

Jodi, or jodi.org, are two artists who work together as a collaborative duo. Joan Heemskerk and Dirk Paesmans. Since the mid-1990s they started to create original artworks for the World Wide Web. They have no known Facebook account, some of their recent projects are accessible at joid.org.

```
package org.joid;
	public class CheckAuthenticationRequest extends Request {
		public final static String OPENID_ASSOC_HANDLE = „openid.assoc_handle“;
		private final static Log log = LogFactory
				.getLog(CheckAuthenticationRequest.class);
```

Jonas Lund

Jonas Lund is an artist from Sweden, working with the internet and/or images. He received a BFA in photography from the Rietveld Academie in Amsterdam, and his now pursuing a master at the Piet Zwart Institute in Rotterdam. He also finds it a bit odd to write about himself in third person, but thinks it's alright and perhaps it makes more sense that way.
http://jonaslund.com

Jordan Tate

Jordan Tate is an Assistant Professor of Art at the University of Cincinnati. Tate, a Fulbright Fellow (2008-2009), has a Bachelor of Philosophy in Interdisciplinary Studies from Miami University and a Master of Fine Arts in Photography from Indiana University. Tate's work is currently held in collections nationwide, including Rhizome at the New Museum, the Museum of Contemporary Photography, The Bidwell Projects, and the Museum of Fine Arts, Houston. Tate is the founding editor of the contemporary art blog http://ilikethisart.net.

Katja Novitskova

http://katjanovi.net

Laimonas Zakas

http://www.facebook.com/glitchr
http://glitchr.tumblr.com/
http://zakas.tumblr.com/

Lenox-Lenox

Lenox-Lenox is a Chicago-based duo, working primarily with digital imagery, video, and sculpture. Their work deals with notions of placelessness, distance-learning, attempts to subsist in utopic spaces, apocalyptic prophesies, and futile modernist idealisms. Born in Boston, André and Evan Lenox currently live and work in Chicago.
http://lenox-lenox.us/
http://no-new.info/
http://tmrrw.net/
http://twincraft.tumblr.com/

m-a-u-s-e-r

m-a-u-s-e-r: micro-architecture-unit-star-energy-ray
Based in Stuttgart and Istanbul, Mauser is a work studio, which was founded by Asli Serbest and Mona Mahall in 2007. It represents the practice and research of the Micro Architecture Unit Star Energy Ray. Micro architecture unit does not mean any genres at first, rather it describes a conceptual approach

towards making, which, for Mauser, is a question of authorship, of experiment, of meticulous cultural contextualizing and research. Star energy ray indicates Mauser's fascination with magic, more precisely with the economical and ecological problem of doing something out of nothing.
http://www.m-a-u-s-e-r.net/

🗗Mike Ruiz
Mike Ruiz is an artist/curator and co-founder of the Berlin-based project, Future Gallery. He holds a BA in Philosophy from St. Edward's University in Austin, TX and is currently completing his MFA at the Berlin University of the Arts under Professor Gregor Schneider.
http://mikeruiz.org
http://thefuturegallery.org

🗗Mimi Zeiger
Mimi Zeiger is editor and publisher of loud paper, a zine and blog dedicated to increasing the volume of architectural discourse. She is a founding member of #lgnlgn, a think tank on architecture and publishing. The group's work has been shown at Urban Design Week, the New Museum, Storefront for Art and Architecture, pinkcomma gallery, and the AA School.

🗗Mona Mahall (m-a-u-s-e-r)
http://www.m-a-u-s-e-r.net/
http://www.igmade.net/
http://junkjet.net/

🗗Michael Schoner
Trained as an architect I have currently started up my own design studio after working for 6 years for NL Architects. Besides the fascination for construction, structures, patterns, geometry, space, mass and voids and logic I'm interested in emotional significance of objects or evenjust volumes, their symbolism as archetype, animals, their scale, theirstory, twisting the perception, feeling child-like, creating socialinteraction through those objects.
http://hello@michael-schoner.de

🗗Nicholas O`Brien
Nicholas O'Brien is an artists, writer, curator, and researcher focused on the ways in which nature continues to hold relevance in digital representation as well as the influence of language upon the development and use of network technology. His work has been published and exhibited internationally, including The Museum of Contemporary Art Chicago, the Xth Biennale de Lyon, 319 Scholes in Brooklyn NY, the Portland Art Museum in Oregon, and at the Copenhagen Space in London.
http://doubleunderscore.net

🗗Nicolas Sassoon
Nicolas Sassoon is a Canada-France-Internet based artist member of the online art collective Computers Club. Nicolas publishes an important part of his work online through the format of animated gifs. He also exhibits internationally, collaborates with architects, artists, electronic music producers and fashion designers. The work of Nicolas revolves around the relations between computers, architectures, landscapes and domestic environments.
http://www.youmakemesohappy.blogspot.com/
http://www.computersclub.org/club/?author=14
http://www.youtube.com/user/youmakemesohappy1

🗗N.I.E.I.
We revealed Global net.art.
We are the army of personas-based expression.
We are the content - You are the pod.
We are the Network Identity Experiment Institute.
Опыт Личности Институт - Сделайте Вашу личность реальность
http://chateau-chamarande.com/

🗗NL Architects
NL Architects is an Amsterdam based office of about 20 people founded by Pieter Bannenberg, Walter van Dijk and Kamiel Klaasse in 1997. NL Architects aspires to catalyze urban life. The office is on a constant hunt to find alternatives for the way we live and work. How can we intensify human interaction?
http://www.nlarchitects.nl/

🗗Olia Lialina
Finished Moscow State University as journalist, film critic. One of the organizers of Moscow experi-

mental film club CINE FANTOM. Net Artist, one of net.art pioneers. Writes on New Media, Digital Folklore and Vernacular Web. Since 1999 Professorat Merz Akademie, (New Media Pathway), Stuttgart Animated Gif Model. Wife of Rockstar. Mother of three. Junior blogger. @GIFmodel http://art.teleportacia.org/olia.html

Palace
Co-founded by Valle Medina and Ben Reynolds, Palace is an architectural design and research collaborative that speculates and reacts to issues existing in levels of culture, space and economy. Their work has been shown, amongst others at the Centre of Contemporary Culture of Barcelona (CCCB), the Architecture Foundation in London. They have also contributed to printed and online publications. http://palacepalace.com/

Ricardo Scofidio
Founder of DS+R, an an alternative form of architecture and design studio, which combines design, and electronic media with cultural and architectural theory. „Time MAgazine ranks Elizabeth Diller and Ricardo Scofidio among the ‚Time 100 – World's Most Influential People'" http://www.dsrny.com/

The Parker Ito
The Parker Ito is well known for his challenging, hilarious, ground-breaking work as a pioneer in the field of "Internet art" through his evocative and innovative work where Art meets Life meets the Internet meets Lulz. His constantly evolving oeuvre is characterized by a conceptually brilliant mix of philosophical, boneriffic, artistic, aesthestic, antiartsy, cash-moneyistic, techno-fetishizing, socializing, urbanizing, fraterninizing, post-ironic, post-post-modern, American, Californian, and post-conceptual networkentaled issues. The Parker Ito is bigger than life, brigher than a sunny day, and badder than the ugliest sin. His innovative natural feeling for the vanguard and contemporary underground aesthetics help make him (the Parker Ito) the most important Internet artist of the Internet age, both pre- and post Internet"
http://www.parkerito.com
http://www.parkerito.info
http://www.parkerito.org
http://www.parkerito.net
http://www.parkerkooito.com

Patrick Cruz
Born and raised in Manila Philippines, Vancouver based artist Patrick Cruz is a Filipino-Canadian multidisciplinary artist who studied Painting in the University of the Philippines Diliman and received his BFA degree studies from Emily Carr University of Art + Design with a major in General Fine Arts.
http://www.patrickcruz.tumblr.com

Pieterjan Grandry
Graduated in 2009 as a Master in Arts and design at Sint Lucas school of Arts Antwerp, Pieterjan Grandry is a graphic designer & visual artist who likes to experiment with furniture and design, often integrating them into installations. On his blog 'Crap = Good' Pieterjan deals with the aesthetics of the counter-flow against today's over–designed visual culture.
http://pieterjangrandry.com
http://parfois.be
http://crapisgood.com

Raphaël Bastide.
Born in 1985 in Montpellier, France Freelance graphic designer and digital artist
http://www.raphaelbastide.com

Sam Hancocks is a Melbourne based artist who's work considers the relational and social aspects of technology and media.
http://www.visualaids.org

Sarah Weiss
There was actually a short, "dark" period after college in which I rejected the internet . Maybe I had to go through this to prepare myself for the next phase of my life. When Arturo Cubacub and I uploaded our first video to YouTube in 2006, I didn't even have a laptop. Things soon changed drastically. I became a full-out YouTube "celebrity" for 2 or

3 years and spent every day on the site, reading a never-ending flow of amazing, crazy comments and responding to intense heart messages from around the world. I wasn't even aware of internet art until early 2007. I think I started discovering net.heart that year as well, as I developed my first internet relationships and began to see the possibilities of using the web in a deeper artistic way. Since then I spend every day online, trying to keep myself challenged and engaged with the world in as creative and sincere of a way as I can. At this point I haven't even done 1% of what I want to do with my net.heart and I greatly look forward to the journey ahead. I honestly cannot imagine living and working anywhere else. Come find me there:
http://sarahweis.com
http://i3hypermedia.com
http://youtube.com/bseventeen

⎙Something Fantastic
is a young architectural practice committed to smart, touching, simple architecture. Its works include publications (Something Fantastic, Building Brazil, e. a.) teaching (Technology Exchange at ETH Zurich, e.a.) and design for private and institutional clients. Next to Something Fantastic the partners Schubert, Schütz, and Streich also operate a creative agency called Belgrad to be able to work in a broader field and context of creative production. The belief that architecture is affected by everything and vice versa does affect everything is the basis of their claim that working as architects today involves a general interest and involvement in the world.
http://www.somethingfantastic.net
http://www.belgrad.co

⎙Sterling Crispin
was born in Maui, Hawaii in 1985 and is currently earning a masters degree in Fine Art & Digital Media at the University of California Santa Barbara. He received his BFA from the Rocky Mountain College of Art & Design in 2008 and was a three year artist in residence at Red-Line in Denver, CO. His artworks are in the collection of the Rhizome Artbase at the New Museum, NY, and has been featured internationally on cable television as a part of Souvenirs from Earth in Germany and France. Notably seen in „Blip Festival" Eyebeam Art+Technology Center, „Dump.fm IRL" 319 Scholes Gallery and Katja Novitskova's „Post Internet Survival Guide".
http://www.sterling-crispin.com

⎙Theo Seemann, Arne Hübner, Chris Heller + Daniel Stäbler
(all *1985) finished their art+design studies at super Merz Akademie in Stuttgart in 2011 and are now up for new funky adventures diggin through digital and pop culture.
http://theoseemann.de
http://arnehuebner.de
http://chris.heller.tv
http://danielstaebler.de

⎙Will Brand
Will Brand is a Brooklyn-based critic and programmer. He is the Editor-in-Chief of the blog Art Fag City, and holds an MSc in Art History, Theory and Display from the University of Edinburgh.
http://www.last.fm/user/titoleibowitz

⎙Wyne Veen
I am from Amsterdam. I make and collect objects and with them I create compositions. I think there are a lot of amazingly weird things going on in the world and life is rather ridiculous. In my work I try to show some of this awkwardness.
I always wanted to be a designer, but I could never choose just one discipline in which to design. Now I can design whatever, take a photo of it, and let that be my medium.
http://www.wyne-veen.com

[Image] Bonno van Doorn
DOORNSTRUIK
Scrawls